Praise for *Effective C++, Third Edition*

"Scott Meyers' book, *Effective C++, Third Edition*, is distilled programming experience — experience that you would otherwise have to learn the hard way. This book is a great resource that I recommend to everybody who writes C++ professionally."
— *Peter Dulimov, ME, Engineer, Ranges and Assessing Unit, NAVSYSCOM, Australia*

"The third edition is still the best book on how to put all of the pieces of C++ together in an efficient, cohesive manner. If you claim to be a C++ programmer, you must read this book."
— *Eric Nagler, Consultant, Instructor, and author of* Learning C++

"The first edition of this book ranks among the small (very small) number of books that I credit with significantly elevating my skills as a 'professional' software developer. Like the others, it was practical and easy to read, but loaded with important advice. *Effective C++, Third Edition*, continues that tradition. C++ is a very powerful programming language. If C gives you enough rope to hang yourself, C++ is a hardware store with lots of helpful people ready to tie knots for you. Mastering the points discussed in this book will definitely increase your ability to effectively use C++ and reduce your stress level."
— *Jack W. Reeves, Chief Executive Officer, Bleading Edge Software Technologies*

"Every new developer joining my team has one assignment — to read this book."
— *Michael Lanzetta, Senior Software Engineer*

"I read the first edition of *Effective C++* about nine years ago, and it immediately became my favorite book on C++. In my opinion, *Effective C++, Third Edition*, remains a must-read today for anyone who wishes to program effectively in C++. We would live in a better world if C++ programmers had to read this book before writing their first line of professional C++ code."
— *Danny Rabbani, Software Development Engineer*

"I encountered the first edition of Scott Meyers' *Effective C++* as a struggling programmer in the trenches, trying to get better at what I was doing. What a lifesaver! I found Meyers' advice was practical, useful, and effective, fulfilling the promise of the title 100 percent. The third edition brings the practical realities of using C++ in serious development projects right up to date, adding chapters on the language's very latest issues and features. I was delighted to still find myself learning something interesting and new from the latest edition of a book I already thought I knew well."
— *Michael Topic, Technical Program Manager*

"From Scott Meyers, the guru of C++, this is the definitive guide for anyone who wants to use C++ safely and effectively, or is transitioning from any other OO language to C++. This book has valuable information presented in a clear, concise, entertaining, and insightful manner."
— *Siddhartha Karan Singh, Software Developer*

D11194385

"This should be the second book on C++ that any developer should read, after a general introductory text. It goes beyond the *how* and *what* of C++ to address the *why* and *wherefore*. It helped me go from knowing the syntax to understanding the philosophy of C++ programming."
— *Timothy Knox, Software Developer*

"This is a fantastic update of a classic C++ text. Meyers covers a lot of new ground in this volume, and every serious C++ programmer should have a copy of this new edition."
— *Jeffrey Somers, Game Programmer*

"*Effective C++, Third Edition*, covers the things you should be doing when writing code and does a terrific job of explaining why those things are important. Think of it as best practices for writing C++."
— *Jeff Scherpelz, Software Development Engineer*

"As C++ embraces change, Scott Meyers' *Effective C++, Third Edition*, soars to remain in perfect lock-step with the language. There are many fine introductory books on C++, but exactly one *second* book stands head and shoulders above the rest, and you're holding it. With Scott guiding the way, prepare to do some soaring of your own!"
— *Leor Zolman, C++ Trainer and Pundit, BD Software*

"This book is a must-have for both C++ veterans and newbies. After you have finished reading it, it will not collect dust on your bookshelf — you will refer to it all the time."
— *Sam Lee, Software Developer*

"Reading this book transforms ordinary C++ programmers into expert C++ programmers, step-by-step, using 55 easy-to-read items, each describing one technique or tip."
— *Jeffrey D. Oldham, Ph.D., Software Engineer, Google*

"Scott Meyers' *Effective C++* books have long been required reading for new and experienced C++ programmers alike. This new edition, incorporating almost a decade's worth of C++ language development, is his most content-packed book yet. He does not merely describe the problems inherent in the language, but instead he provides unambiguous and easy-to-follow advice on how to avoid the pitfalls and write 'effective C++.' I expect every C++ programmer to have read it."
— *Philipp K. Janert, Ph.D., Software Development Manager*

"Each previous edition of *Effective C++* has been the must-have book for developers who have used C++ for a few months or a few years, long enough to stumble into the traps latent in this rich language. In this third edition, Scott Meyers extensively refreshes his sound advice for the modern world of new language and library features and the programming styles that have evolved to use them. Scott's engaging writing style makes it easy to assimilate his guidelines on your way to becoming an effective C++ developer."
— *David Smallberg, Instructor, DevelopMentor; Lecturer, Computer Science, UCLA*

"*Effective C++* has been completely updated for twenty-first-century C++ practice and can continue to claim to be the first *second* book for all C++ practitioners."
— *Matthew Wilson, Ph.D., author of* Imperfect C++

Effective C++
Third Edition

Addison-Wesley Professional Computing Series

Brian W. Kernighan, Consulting Editor

Visit www.awprofessional.com/series/professionalcomputing for more information about these titles.

Effective C++
Third Edition

55 Specific Ways to Improve Your Programs and Designs

Scott Meyers

ADDISON-WESLEY

Upper Saddle River, NJ • Boston • Indianapolis • San Francisco
New York • Toronto • Montreal • London • Munich • Paris • Madrid
Capetown • Sydney • Tokyo • Singapore • Mexico City

Many of the designations used by manufacturers and sellers to distinguish their products are claimed as trademarks. Where those designations appear in this book, and the publisher was aware of a trademark claim, the designations have been printed with initial capital letters or in all capitals.

The author and publisher have taken care in the preparation of this book, but make no expressed or implied warranty of any kind and assume no responsibility for errors or omissions. No liability is assumed for incidental or consequential damages in connection with or arising out of the use of the information or programs contained herein.

The publisher offers excellent discounts on this book when ordered in quantity for bulk purchases or special sales, which may include electronic versions and/or custom covers and content particular to your business, training goals, marketing focus, and branding interests. For more information, please contact:

> U.S. Corporate and Government Sales
> (800) 382-3419
> corpsales@pearsontechgroup.com

For sales outside the U.S., please contact:

> International Sales
> international@pearsoned.com

This Book Is Safari Enabled

 The Safari® Enabled icon on the cover of your favorite technology book means the book is available through Safari Bookshelf. When you buy this book, you get free access to the online edition for 45 days.

Safari Bookshelf is an electronic reference library that lets you easily search thousands of technical books, find code samples, download chapters, and access technical information whenever and wherever you need it.

To gain 45-day Safari Enabled access to this book:

- Go to http://www.awprofessional.com/safarienabled
- Complete the brief registration form
- Enter the coupon code EMEB-FHPF-41A5-R8FU-VS1Q

If you have difficulty registering on Safari Bookshelf or accessing the online edition, please e-mail customer-service@safaribooksonline.com.

Visit us on the Web: www.awprofessional.com

Library of Congress Control Number: 2005924388

Copyright © 2005 Pearson Education, Inc.

All rights reserved. Printed in the United States of America. This publication is protected by copyright, and permission must be obtained from the publisher prior to any prohibited reproduction, storage in a retrieval system, or transmission in any form or by any means, electronic, mechanical, photocopying, recording, or likewise. For information regarding permissions, write to:

> Pearson Education, Inc.
> Rights and Contracts Department
> One Lake Street
> Upper Saddle River, NJ 07458

ISBN 0321334876

Text printed in the United States on recycled paper at Courier Westford in Westford, Massachusetts.

6th Printing   June 2007

For Nancy,
without whom nothing
would be much worth doing

Wisdom and beauty form a very rare combination.

— Petronius Arbiter
Satyricon, XCIV

And in memory of Persephone,
1995–2004

Contents

Preface   **xv**

Acknowledgments   **xvii**

Introduction   **1**

Chapter 1: Accustoming Yourself to C++   **11**

  Item 1: View C++ as a federation of languages.   11
  Item 2: Prefer consts, enums, and inlines to #defines.   13
  Item 3: Use const whenever possible.   17
  Item 4: Make sure that objects are initialized before
              they're used.   26

**Chapter 2: Constructors, Destructors, and
Assignment Operators**   **34**

  Item 5: Know what functions C++ silently writes and calls.   34
  Item 6: Explicitly disallow the use of compiler-generated
              functions you do not want.   37
  Item 7: Declare destructors virtual in polymorphic
              base classes.   40
  Item 8: Prevent exceptions from leaving destructors.   44
  Item 9: Never call virtual functions during construction or
              destruction.   48
  Item 10: Have assignment operators return a reference to *this. 52
  Item 11: Handle assignment to self in operator=.   53
  Item 12: Copy all parts of an object.   57

Chapter 3: Resource Management   **61**

  Item 13: Use objects to manage resources.   61

Item 14: Think carefully about copying behavior in
resource-managing classes.   66

Item 15: Provide access to raw resources in
resource-managing classes.   69

Item 16: Use the same form in corresponding uses of new
and delete.   73

Item 17: Store newed objects in smart pointers in standalone
statements.   75

Chapter 4: Designs and Declarations   78

Item 18: Make interfaces easy to use correctly and hard to
use incorrectly.   78

Item 19: Treat class design as type design.   84

Item 20: Prefer pass-by-reference-to-const to pass-by-value. 86

Item 21: Don't try to return a reference when you must
return an object.   90

Item 22: Declare data members private.   94

Item 23: Prefer non-member non-friend functions to
member functions.   98

Item 24: Declare non-member functions when type
conversions should apply to all parameters.   102

Item 25: Consider support for a non-throwing swap.   106

Chapter 5: Implementations   113

Item 26: Postpone variable definitions as long as possible. 113

Item 27: Minimize casting.   116

Item 28: Avoid returning "handles" to object internals.   123

Item 29: Strive for exception-safe code.   127

Item 30: Understand the ins and outs of inlining.   134

Item 31: Minimize compilation dependencies between files.   140

Chapter 6: Inheritance and Object-Oriented Design 149

Item 32: Make sure public inheritance models "is-a."   150

Item 33: Avoid hiding inherited names.   156

Item 34: Differentiate between inheritance of interface and
inheritance of implementation.   161

Item 35: Consider alternatives to virtual functions.   169

Item 36: Never redefine an inherited non-virtual function.   178

Item 37: Never redefine a function's inherited default
parameter value.   180

Item 38: Model "has-a" or "is-implemented-in-terms-of"
through composition.   184

Item 39: Use private inheritance judiciously.   187

Item 40: Use multiple inheritance judiciously.   192

Chapter 7: Templates and Generic Programming   199

Item 41: Understand implicit interfaces and compile-time
polymorphism.   199

Item 42: Understand the two meanings of typename.   203

Item 43: Know how to access names in templatized
base classes.   207

Item 44: Factor parameter-independent code out of templates.   212

Item 45: Use member function templates to accept
"all compatible types."   218

Item 46: Define non-member functions inside templates
when type conversions are desired.   222

Item 47: Use traits classes for information about types.   226

Item 48: Be aware of template metaprogramming.   233

Chapter 8: Customizing new and delete   239

Item 49: Understand the behavior of the new-handler.   240

Item 50: Understand when it makes sense to replace new
and delete.   247

Item 51: Adhere to convention when writing new and delete.   252

Item 52: Write placement delete if you write placement new.   256

Chapter 9: Miscellany   262

Item 53: Pay attention to compiler warnings.   262

Item 54: Familiarize yourself with the standard library,
including TR1.   263

Item 55: Familiarize yourself with Boost.   269

Appendix A: Beyond *Effective* C++   273

Appendix B: Item Mappings Between Second
and Third Editions   277

Index   280

Preface

I wrote the original edition of *Effective C++* in 1991. When the time came for a second edition in 1997, I updated the material in important ways, but, because I didn't want to confuse readers familiar with the first edition, I did my best to retain the existing structure: 48 of the original 50 Item titles remained essentially unchanged. If the book were a house, the second edition was the equivalent of freshening things up by replacing carpets, paint, and light fixtures.

For the third edition, I tore the place down to the studs. (There were times I wished I'd gone all the way to the foundation.) The world of C++ has undergone enormous change since 1991, and the goal of this book — to identify the most important C++ programming guidelines in a small, readable package — was no longer served by the Items I'd established nearly 15 years earlier. In 1991, it was reasonable to assume that C++ programmers came from a C background. Now, programmers moving to C++ are just as likely to come from Java or C#. In 1991, inheritance and object-oriented programming were new to most programmers. Now they're well-established concepts, and exceptions, templates, and generic programming are the areas where people need more guidance. In 1991, nobody had heard of design patterns. Now it's hard to discuss software systems without referring to them. In 1991, work had just begun on a formal standard for C++. Now that standard is eight years old, and work has begun on the next version.

To address these changes, I wiped the slate as clean as I could and asked myself, "What are the most important pieces of advice for practicing C++ programmers in 2005?" The result is the set of Items in this new edition. The book has new chapters on resource management and on programming with templates. In fact, template concerns are woven throughout the text, because they affect almost everything in C++. The book also includes new material on programming in the presence of exceptions, on applying design patterns, and on using the new TR1 library facilities. (TR1 is described in Item 54.) It acknowledges that techniques and approaches that work well in single-threaded systems may not be appropriate in multithreaded systems. Well over half the material in the book is new. However, most of the fundamental information in the second edition continues to be important, so I found a way to retain it in one form or another. (You'll find a mapping between the second and third edition Items in Appendix B.)

I've worked hard to make this book as good as I can, but I have no illusions that it's perfect. If you feel that some of the Items in this book are inappropriate as general advice; that there is a better way to accomplish a task examined in the book; or that one or more of the technical discussions is unclear, incomplete, or misleading, please tell me. If you find an error of any kind — technical, grammatical, typographical, *whatever* — please tell me that, too. I'll gladly add to the acknowledgments in later printings the name of the first person to bring each problem to my attention.

Even with the number of Items expanded to 55, the set of guidelines in this book is far from exhaustive. But coming up with good rules — ones that apply to almost all applications almost all the time — is harder than it might seem. If you have suggestions for additional guidelines, I would be delighted to hear about them.

I maintain a list of changes to this book since its first printing, including bug fixes, clarifications, and technical updates. The list is available at the *Effective C++ Errata* web page, http://aristeia.com/BookErrata/ ec++3e-errata.html. If you'd like to be notified when I update the list, I encourage you to join my mailing list. I use it to make announcements likely to interest people who follow my professional work. For details, consult http://aristeia.com/MailingList/.

SCOTT DOUGLAS MEYERS   STAFFORD, OREGON
http://aristeia.com/   APRIL 2005

Acknowledgments

Effective C++ has existed for fifteen years, and I started learning C++ about three years before I wrote the book. The "*Effective C++* project" has thus been under development for nearly two decades. During that time, I have benefited from the insights, suggestions, corrections, and, occasionally, dumbfounded stares of hundreds (thousands?) of people. Each has helped improve *Effective C++*. I am grateful to them all.

I've given up trying to keep track of where I learned what, but one general source of information has helped me as long as I can remember: the Usenet C++ newsgroups, especially comp.lang.c++.moderated and comp.std.c++. Many of the Items in this book — perhaps most — have benefited from the vetting of technical ideas at which the participants in these newsgroups excel.

Regarding new material in the third edition, Steve Dewhurst worked with me to come up with an initial set of candidate Items. In Item 11, the idea of implementing operator= via copy-and-swap came from Herb Sutter's writings on the topic, e.g., Item 13 of his *Exceptional C++* (Addison-Wesley, 2000). RAII (see Item 13) is from Bjarne Stroustrup's *The C++ Programming Language* (Addison-Wesley, 2000). The idea behind Item 17 came from the "Best Practices" section of the Boost shared_ptr web page, http://boost.org/libs/smart_ptr/shared_ptr.htm#Best-Practices and was refined by Item 21 of Herb Sutter's *More Exceptional C++* (Addison-Wesley, 2002). Item 29 was strongly influenced by Herb Sutter's extensive writings on the topic, e.g., Items 8-19 of *Exceptional C++*, Items 17–23 of *More Exceptional C++*, and Items 11–13 of *Exceptional C++ Style* (Addison-Wesley, 2005); David Abrahams helped me better understand the three exception safety guarantees. The NVI idiom in Item 35 is from Herb Sutter's column, "Virtuality," in the September 2001 *C/C++ Users Journal*. In that same Item, the Template Method and Strategy design patterns are from *Design Patterns* (Addison-Wesley, 1995) by Erich Gamma, Richard Helm, Ralph Johnson, and John Vlissides. The idea of using the NVI idiom in Item 37 came from Hendrik Schober. David Smallberg contributed the motivation for writing a custom set implementation in Item 38. Item 39's observation that the EBO generally isn't available under multiple inheritance is from David Vandevoorde's and Nicolai M. Josuttis' *C++ Templates* (Addison-Wesley, 2003). In Item 42, my initial understanding about typename came from Greg Comeau's C++ and C FAQ (http://www.comeaucomputing.com/techtalk/#typename), and Leor Zolman helped me realize that my understanding was incorrect. (My fault, not Greg's.) The essence of Item 46 is from Dan Saks' talk, "Making New Friends." The idea at the end of Item 52 that if you declare one version of operator new, you should declare them all, is from Item 22 of Herb Sutter's *Exceptional C++ Style*. My understanding of the Boost review process (summarized in Item 55) was refined by David Abrahams.

Everything above corresponds to who or where *I* learned about something, not necessarily to who or where the thing was invented or first published.

My notes tell me that I also used information from Steve Clamage, Antoine Trux, Timothy Knox, and Mike Kaelbling, though, regrettably, the notes fail to tell me how or where.

Drafts of the first edition were reviewed by Tom Cargill, Glenn Carroll, Tony Davis, Brian Kernighan, Jak Kirman, Doug Lea, Moises Lejter, Eugene Santos, Jr., John Shewchuk, John Stasko, Bjarne Stroustrup, Barbara Tilly, and Nancy L. Urbano. I received suggestions for improvements that I was able to incorporate in later printings from Nancy L. Urbano, Chris Treichel, David Corbin, Paul Gibson, Steve Vinoski, Tom Cargill, Neil Rhodes, David Bern, Russ Williams, Robert Brazile, Doug Morgan, Uwe Steinmüller, Mark Somer, Doug Moore, David Smallberg, Seth Meltzer, Oleg Shteynbuk, David Papurt, Tony Hansen, Peter McCluskey, Stefan Kuhlins, David Braunegg, Paul Chisholm, Adam Zell, Clovis Tondo, Mike Kaelbling, Natraj Kini, Lars Nyman, Greg Lutz, Tim Johnson, John Lakos, Roger Scott, Scott Frohman, Alan Rooks, Robert Poor, Eric Nagler, Antoine Trux, Cade Roux, Chandrika Gokul, Randy Mangoba, and Glenn Teitelbaum.

Drafts of the second edition were reviewed by Derek Bosch, Tim Johnson, Brian Kernighan, Junichi Kimura, Scott Lewandowski, Laura Michaels, David Smallberg, Clovis Tondo, Chris Van Wyk, and Oleg Zabluda. Later printings benefited from comments from Daniel Steinberg, Arunprasad Marathe, Doug Stapp, Robert Hall, Cheryl Ferguson, Gary Bartlett, Michael Tamm, Kendall Beaman, Eric Nagler, Max Hailperin, Joe Gottman, Richard Weeks, Valentin Bonnard, Jun He, Tim King, Don Maier, Ted Hill, Mark Harrison, Michael Rubenstein, Mark Rodgers, David Goh, Brenton Cooper, Andy Thomas-Cramer,

Antoine Trux, John Wait, Brian Sharon, Liam Fitzpatrick, Bernd Mohr, Gary Yee, John O'Hanley, Brady Patterson, Christopher Peterson, Feliks Kluzniak, Isi Dunietz, Christopher Creutzi, Ian Cooper, Carl Harris, Mark Stickel, Clay Budin, Panayotis Matsinopoulos, David Smallberg, Herb Sutter, Pajo Misljencevic, Giulio Agostini, Fredrik Blomqvist, Jimmy Snyder, Byrial Jensen, Witold Kuzminski, Kazunobu Kuriyama, Michael Christensen, Jorge Yáñez Teruel, Mark Davis, Marty Rabinowitz, Ares Lagae, and Alexander Medvedev.

An early partial draft of this edition was reviewed by Brian Kernighan, Angelika Langer, Jesse Laeuchli, Roger E. Pedersen, Chris Van Wyk, Nicholas Stroustrup, and Hendrik Schober. Reviewers for a full draft were Leor Zolman, Mike Tsao, Eric Nagler, Gene Gutnik, David Abrahams, Gerhard Kreuzer, Drosos Kourounis, Brian Kernighan, Andrew Kirmse, Balog Pal, Emily Jagdhar, Eugene Kalenkovich, Mike Roze, Enrico Carrara, Benjamin Berck, Jack Reeves, Steve Schirripa, Martin Fallenstedt, Timothy Knox, Yun Bai, Michael Lanzetta, Philipp Janert, Guido Bartolucci, Michael Topic, Jeff Scherpelz, Chris Nauroth, Nishant Mittal, Jeff Somers, Hal Moroff, Vincent Manis, Brandon Chang, Greg Li, Jim Meehan, Alan Geller, Siddhartha Singh, Sam Lee, Sasan Dashtinezhad, Alex Marin, Steve Cai, Thomas Fruchterman, Cory Hicks, David Smallberg, Gunavardhan Kakulapati, Danny Rabbani, Jake Cohen, Hendrik Schober, Paco Viciana, Glenn Kennedy, Jeffrey D. Oldham, Nicholas Stroustrup, Matthew Wilson, Andrei Alexandrescu, Tim Johnson, Leon Matthews, Peter Dulimov, and Kevlin Henney. Drafts of some individual Items were reviewed by Herb Sutter and Attila F. Feher.

Reviewing an unpolished (possibly incomplete) manuscript is demanding work, and doing it under time pressure only makes it harder. I continue to be grateful that so many people have been willing to undertake it for me.

Reviewing is harder still if you have no background in the material being discussed and are expected to catch *every* problem in the manuscript. Astonishingly, some people still choose to be copy editors. Chrysta Meadowbrooke was the copy editor for this book, and her very thorough work exposed many problems that eluded everyone else.

Leor Zolman checked all the code examples against multiple compilers in preparation for the full review, then did it again after I revised the manuscript. If any errors remain, I'm responsible for them, not Leor.

Karl Wiegers and especially Tim Johnson offered rapid, helpful feedback on back cover copy.

Since publication of the first printing, I have incorporated revisions suggested by Jason Ross, Robert Yokota, Bernhard Merkle, Attila Feher, Gerhard Kreuzer, Marcin Sochacki, J. Daniel Smith, Idan Lupinsky, G. Wade Johnson, Clovis Tondo, Joshua Lehrer, T. David Hudson, Phillip Hellewell, Thomas Schell, Eldar Ronen, Ken Kobayashi, Cameron Mac Minn, John Hershberger, Alex Dumov, Vincent Stojanov, Andrew Henrick, Jiongxiong Chen, Balbir Singh, Fraser Ross, Niels Dekker, Harsh Gaurav Vangani, Vasily Poshehonov, Yukitoshi Fujimura, Alex Howlett, Ed Ji Xihuang, Mike Rizzi, Balog Pal, David Solomon, and Tony Oliver.

John Wait, my editor for the first two editions of this book, foolishly signed up for another tour of duty in that capacity. His assistant, Denise Mickelsen, adroitly handled my frequent pestering with a pleasant smile. (At least I think she's been smiling. I've never actually seen her.) Julie Nahil drew the short straw and hence became my production manager. She handled the overnight loss of six weeks in the production schedule with remarkable equanimity. John Fuller (her boss) and Marty Rabinowitz (his boss) helped out with production issues, too. Vanessa Moore's official job was to help with FrameMaker issues and PDF preparation, but she also added the entries to Appendix B and formatted it for printing on the inside cover. Solveig Haugland helped with index formatting. Sandra Schroeder and Chuti Prasertsith were responsible for cover design, though Chuti seems to have been the one who had to rework the cover each time I said, "But what about *this* photo with a stripe of *that* color...?" Chanda Leary-Coutu got tapped for the heavy lifting in marketing.

During the months I worked on the manuscript, the TV series *Buffy the Vampire Slayer* often helped me "de-stress" at the end of the day. Only with great restraint have I kept Buffyspeak out of the book.

Kathy Reed taught me programming in 1971, and I'm gratified that we remain friends to this day. Donald French hired me and Moises Lejter to create C++ training materials in 1989 (an act that led to my *really* knowing C++), and in 1991 he engaged me to present them at Stratus Computer. The students in that class encouraged me to write what ultimately became the first edition of this book. Don also introduced me to John Wait, who agreed to publish it.

My wife, Nancy L. Urbano, continues to encourage my writing, even after seven book projects, a CD adaptation, and a dissertation. She has unbelievable forbearance. I couldn't do what I do without her.

From start to finish, our dog, Persephone, has been a companion without equal. Sadly, for much of this project, her companionship has taken the form of an urn in the office. We really miss her.

Introduction

Learning the fundamentals of a programming language is one thing; learning how to design and implement *effective* programs in that language is something else entirely. This is especially true of C++, a language boasting an uncommon range of power and expressiveness. Properly used, C++ can be a joy to work with. An enormous variety of designs can be directly expressed and efficiently implemented. A judiciously chosen and carefully crafted set of classes, functions, and templates can make application programming easy, intuitive, efficient, and nearly error-free. It isn't unduly difficult to write effective C++ programs, *if* you know how to do it. Used without discipline, however, C++ can lead to code that is incomprehensible, unmaintainable, inextensible, inefficient, and just plain wrong.

The purpose of this book is to show you how to use C++ *effectively*. I assume you already know C++ as a *language* and that you have some experience in its use. What I provide here is a guide to using the language so that your software is comprehensible, maintainable, portable, extensible, efficient, and likely to behave as you expect.

The advice I proffer falls into two broad categories: general design strategies, and the nuts and bolts of specific language features. The design discussions concentrate on how to choose between different approaches to accomplishing something in C++. How do you choose between inheritance and templates? Between public and private inheritance? Between private inheritance and composition? Between member and non-member functions? Between pass-by-value and pass-by-reference? It's important to make these decisions correctly at the outset, because a poor choice may not become apparent until much later in the development process, at which point rectifying it is often difficult, time-consuming, and expensive.

Even when you know exactly what you want to do, getting things just right can be tricky. What's the proper return type for assignment operators? When should a destructor be virtual? How should operator new behave when it can't find enough memory? It's crucial to sweat details like these, because failure to do so almost always leads to unexpected, possibly mystifying program behavior. This book will help you avoid that.

This is not a comprehensive reference for C++. Rather, it's a collection of 55 specific suggestions (I call them *Items*) for how you can improve your programs and designs. Each Item stands more or less on its own, but most also contain references to other Items. One way to read the book, then, is to start with an Item of interest, then follow its references to see where they lead you.

The book isn't an introduction to C++, either. In Chapter 2, for example, I'm eager to tell you all about the proper implementations of constructors, destructors, and assignment operators, but I assume you already know or can go elsewhere to find out what these functions do and how they are declared. A number of C++ books contain information such as that.

The purpose of *this* book is to highlight those aspects of C++ programming that are often overlooked. Other books describe the different parts of the language. This book tells you how to combine those parts so you end up with effective programs. Other books tell you how to get your programs to compile. This book tells you how to avoid problems that compilers won't tell you about.

At the same time, this book limits itself to *standard* C++. Only features in the official language standard have been used here. Portability is a key concern in this book, so if you're looking for platform-dependent hacks and kludges, this is not the place to find them.

Another thing you won't find in this book is the C++ Gospel, the One True Path to perfect C++ software. Each of the Items in this book provides guidance on how to develop better designs, how to avoid common problems, or how to achieve greater efficiency, but none of the Items is universally applicable. Software design and implementation is a complex task, one colored by the constraints of the hardware, the operating system, and the application, so the best I can do is provide *guidelines* for creating better programs.

If you follow all the guidelines all the time, you are unlikely to fall into the most common traps surrounding C++, but guidelines, by their nature, have exceptions. That's why each Item has an explanation. The explanations are the most important part of the book. Only by understanding the rationale behind an Item can you determine whether it applies to the software you are developing and to the unique constraints under which you toil.

The best use of this book is to gain insight into how C++ behaves, why it behaves that way, and how to use its behavior to your advantage. Blind application of the Items in this book is clearly inappropriate, but at the same time, you probably shouldn't violate any of the guidelines without a good reason.

Terminology

There is a small C++ vocabulary that every programmer should understand. The following terms are important enough that it is worth making sure we agree on what they mean.

A ***declaration*** tells compilers about the name and type of something, but it omits certain details. These are declarations:

```
extern int x;                          // object declaration

std::size_t numDigits(int number);     // function declaration

class Widget;                          // class declaration

template<typename T>                   // template declaration
class GraphNode;                       // (see Item 42 for info on
                                       // the use of "typename")
```

Note that I refer to the integer x as an "object," even though it's of built-in type. Some people reserve the name "object" for variables of user-defined type, but I'm not one of them. Also note that the function numDigits' return type is std::size_t, i.e., the type size_t in namespace std. That namespace is where virtually everything in C++'s standard library is located. However, because C's standard library (the one from C89, to be precise) can also be used in C++, symbols inherited from C (such as size_t) may exist at global scope, inside std, or both, depending on which headers have been #included. In this book, I assume that C++ headers have been #included, and that's why I refer to std::size_t instead of just size_t. When referring to components of the standard library in prose, I typically omit references to std, relying on you to recognize that things like size_t, vector, and cout are in std. In example code, I always include std, because real code won't compile without it.

size_t, by the way, is just a typedef for some unsigned type that C++ uses when counting things (e.g., the number of characters in a char*-based string, the number of elements in an STL container, etc.). It's also the type taken by the operator[] functions in vector, deque, and string, a convention we'll follow when defining our own operator[] functions in Item 3.

Each function's declaration reveals its ***signature***, i.e., its parameter and return types. A function's signature is the same as its type. In the case of numDigits, the signature is std::size_t (int), i.e., "function taking an int and returning a std::size_t." The official C++ definition of "signature" excludes the function's return type, but in this book, it's more useful to have the return type be considered part of the signature.

A **definition** provides compilers with the details a declaration omits. For an object, the definition is where compilers set aside memory for the object. For a function or a function template, the definition provides the code body. For a class or a class template, the definition lists the members of the class or template:

```cpp
int x;                                  // object definition

std::size_t numDigits(int number)       // function definition.
{                                       // (This function returns
    std::size_t digitsSoFar = 1;        // the number of digits
                                        // in its parameter.)
    while ((number /= 10) != 0) ++digitsSoFar;

    return digitsSoFar;
}
class Widget {                          // class definition
public:
    Widget();
    ~Widget();
    ...
};
template<typename T>                    // template definition
class GraphNode {
public:
    GraphNode();
    ~GraphNode();
    ...
};
```

Initialization is the process of giving an object its first value. For objects generated from structs and classes, initialization is performed by constructors. A **default constructor** is one that can be called without any arguments. Such a constructor either has no parameters or has a default value for every parameter:

```cpp
class A {
public:
    A();                               // default constructor
};
class B {
public:
    explicit B(int x = 0, bool b = true);   // default constructor; see below
};                                          // for info on "explicit"
```

```
class C {
public:
    explicit C(int x);                    // not a default constructor
};
```

The constructors for classes B and C are declared explicit here. That prevents them from being used to perform implicit type conversions, though they may still be used for explicit type conversions:

```
void doSomething(B bObject);          // a function taking an object of
                                      // type B

B bObj1;                              // an object of type B

doSomething(bObj1);                   // fine, passes a B to doSomething

B bObj2(28);                          // fine, creates a B from the int 28
                                      // (the bool defaults to true)

doSomething(28);                      // error! doSomething takes a B,
                                      // not an int, and there is no
                                      // implicit conversion from int to B

doSomething(B(28));                   // fine, uses the B constructor to
                                      // explicitly convert (i.e., cast) the
                                      // int to a B for this call. (See
                                      // Item 27 for info on casting.)
```

Constructors declared explicit are usually preferable to non-explicit ones, because they prevent compilers from performing unexpected (often unintended) type conversions. Unless I have a good reason for allowing a constructor to be used for implicit type conversions, I declare it explicit. I encourage you to follow the same policy.

Please note how I've highlighted the cast in the example above. Throughout this book, I use such highlighting to call your attention to material that is particularly noteworthy. (I also highlight chapter numbers, but that's just because I think it looks nice.)

The **copy constructor** is used to initialize an object with a different object of the same type, and the **copy assignment operator** is used to copy the value from one object to another of the same type:

```
class Widget {
public:
    Widget();                              // default constructor
    Widget(const Widget& rhs);             // copy constructor
    Widget& operator=(const Widget& rhs);  // copy assignment operator
    ...
};

Widget w1;                             // invoke default constructor

Widget w2(w1);                         // invoke copy constructor

w1 = w2;                               // invoke copy
                                      // assignment operator
```

Read carefully when you see what appears to be an assignment, because the "=" syntax can also be used to call the copy constructor:

```
Widget w3 = w2;                          // invoke copy constructor!
```

Fortunately, copy construction is easy to distinguish from copy assignment. If a new object is being defined (such as w3 in the statement above), a constructor has to be called; it can't be an assignment. If no new object is being defined (such as in the "w1 = w2" statement above), no constructor can be involved, so it's an assignment.

The copy constructor is a particularly important function, because it defines how an object is passed by value. For example, consider this:

```
bool hasAcceptableQuality(Widget w);

...

Widget aWidget;
if (hasAcceptableQuality(aWidget)) ...
```

The parameter w is passed to hasAcceptableQuality by value, so in the call above, aWidget is copied into w. The copying is done by Widget's copy constructor. Pass-by-value *means* "call the copy constructor." (However, it's generally a bad idea to pass user-defined types by value. Pass-by-reference-to-const is typically a better choice. For details, see Item 20.)

The **STL** is the Standard Template Library, the part of C++'s standard library devoted to containers (e.g., vector, list, set, map, etc.), iterators (e.g., vector<int>::iterator, set<string>::iterator, etc.), algorithms (e.g., for_each, find, sort, etc.), and related functionality. Much of that related functionality has to do with **_function objects_**: objects that act like functions. Such objects come from classes that overload operator(), the function call operator. If you're unfamiliar with the STL, you'll want to have a decent reference available as you read this book, because the STL is too useful for me not to take advantage of it. Once you've used it a little, you'll feel the same way.

Programmers coming to C++ from languages like Java or C# may be surprised at the notion of **_undefined behavior_**. For a variety of reasons, the behavior of some constructs in C++ is literally not defined: you can't reliably predict what will happen at runtime. Here are two examples of code with undefined behavior:

```
int *p = 0;              // p is a null pointer

std::cout << *p;         // dereferencing a null pointer
                         // yields undefined behavior
```

```
char name[] = "Darla";          // name is an array of size 6 (don't
                                // forget the trailing null!)
char c = name[10];              // referring to an invalid array index
                                // yields undefined behavior
```

To emphasize that the results of undefined behavior are not predictable and may be very unpleasant, experienced C++ programmers often say that programs with undefined behavior can erase your hard drive. It's true: a program with undefined behavior *could* erase your hard drive. But it's not probable. More likely is that the program will behave erratically, sometimes running normally, other times crashing, still other times producing incorrect results. Effective C++ programmers do their best to steer clear of undefined behavior. In this book, I point out a number of places where you need to be on the lookout for it.

Another term that may confuse programmers coming to C++ from another language is **interface**. Java and the .NET languages offer Interfaces as a language element, but there is no such thing in C++, though Item 31 discusses how to approximate them. When I use the term "interface," I'm generally talking about a function's signature, about the accessible elements of a class (e.g., a class's "public interface," "protected interface," or "private interface"), or about the expressions that must be valid for a template's type parameter (see Item 41). That is, I'm talking about interfaces as a fairly general design idea.

A **client** is someone or something that uses the code (typically the interfaces) you write. A function's clients, for example, are its users: the parts of the code that call the function (or take its address) as well as the humans who write and maintain such code. The clients of a class or a template are the parts of the software that use the class or template, as well as the programmers who write and maintain that code. When discussing clients, I typically focus on programmers, because programmers can be confused, misled, or annoyed by bad interfaces. The code they write can't be.

You may not be used to thinking about clients, but I'll spend a good deal of time trying to convince you to make their lives as easy as you can. After all, you are a client of the software other people develop. Wouldn't you want those people to make things easy for you? Besides, at some point you'll almost certainly find yourself in the position of being your own client (i.e., using code you wrote), and at that point, you'll be glad you kept client concerns in mind when developing your interfaces.

In this book, I often gloss over the distinction between functions and function templates and between classes and class templates. That's because what's true about one is often true about the other. In situations where this is not the case, I distinguish among classes, functions, and the templates that give rise to classes and functions.

When referring to constructors and destructors in code comments, I sometimes use the abbreviations **ctor** and **dtor**.

Naming Conventions

I have tried to select meaningful names for objects, classes, functions, templates, etc., but the meanings behind some of my names may not be immediately apparent. Two of my favorite parameter names, for example, are lhs and rhs. They stand for "left-hand side" and "right-hand side," respectively. I often use them as parameter names for functions implementing binary operators, e.g., operator== and operator*. For example, if a and b are objects representing rational numbers, and if Rational objects can be multiplied via a non-member operator* function (as Item 24 explains is likely to be the case), the expression

    a * b

is equivalent to the function call

    operator*(a, b)

In Item 24, I declare operator* like this:

    const Rational operator*(const Rational& lhs, const Rational& rhs);

As you can see, the left-hand operand, a, is known as lhs inside the function, and the right-hand operand, b, is known as rhs.

For member functions, the left-hand argument is represented by the this pointer, so sometimes I use the parameter name rhs by itself. You may have noticed this in the declarations for some Widget member functions on page 5. Which reminds me. I often use the Widget class in examples. "Widget" doesn't mean anything. It's just a name I sometimes use when I need an example class name. It has nothing to do with widgets in GUI toolkits.

I often name pointers following the rule that a pointer to an object of type T is called pt, "pointer to T." Here are some examples:

```
Widget *pw;                          // pw = ptr to Widget
class Airplane;
Airplane *pa;                        // pa = ptr to Airplane
```

```
class GameCharacter;
GameCharacter *pgc;                        // pgc = ptr to GameCharacter
```

I use a similar convention for references: rw might be a reference to a Widget and ra a reference to an Airplane.

I occasionally use the name mf when I'm talking about member functions.

Threading Considerations

As a language, C++ has no notion of threads — no notion of concurrency of any kind, in fact. Ditto for C++'s standard library. As far as C++ is concerned, multithreaded programs don't exist.

And yet they do. My focus in this book is on standard, portable C++, but I can't ignore the fact that thread safety is an issue many programmers confront. My approach to dealing with this chasm between standard C++ and reality is to point out places where the C++ constructs I examine are likely to cause problems in a threaded environment. That doesn't make this a book on multithreaded programming with C++. Far from it. Rather, it makes it a book on C++ programming that, while largely limiting itself to single-threaded considerations, acknowledges the existence of multithreading and tries to point out places where thread-aware programmers need to take particular care in evaluating the advice I offer.

If you're unfamiliar with multithreading or have no need to worry about it, you can ignore my threading-related remarks. If you are programming a threaded application or library, however, remember that my comments are little more than a starting point for the issues you'll need to address when using C++.

TR1 and Boost

You'll find references to TR1 and Boost throughout this book. Each has an Item that describes it in some detail (Item 54 for TR1, Item 55 for Boost), but, unfortunately, these Items are at the end of the book. (They're there because it works better that way. Really. I tried them in a number of other places.) If you like, you can turn to those Items and read them now, but if you'd prefer to start the book at the beginning instead of the end, the following executive summary will tide you over:

- TR1 ("Technical Report 1") is a specification for new functionality being added to C++'s standard library. This functionality takes the form of new class and function templates for things like hash tables, reference-counting smart pointers, regular expressions, and more. All TR1 components are in the namespace tr1 that's nested inside the namespace std.

- Boost is an organization and a web site (http://boost.org) offering portable, peer-reviewed, open source C++ libraries. Most TR1 functionality is based on work done at Boost, and until compiler vendors include TR1 in their C++ library distributions, the Boost web site is likely to remain the first stop for developers looking for TR1 implementations. Boost offers more than is available in TR1, however, so it's worth knowing about in any case.

Accustoming Yourself to C++

Regardless of your programming background, C++ is likely to take a little getting used to. It's a powerful language with an enormous range of features, but before you can harness that power and make effective use of those features, you have to accustom yourself to C++'s way of doing things. This entire book is about how to do that, but some things are more fundamental than others, and this chapter is about some of the most fundamental things of all.

Item 1: View C++ as a federation of languages.

In the beginning, C++ was just C with some object-oriented features tacked on. Even C++'s original name, "C with Classes," reflected this simple heritage.

As the language matured, it grew bolder and more adventurous, adopting ideas, features, and programming strategies different from those of C with Classes. Exceptions required different approaches to structuring functions (see Item 29). Templates gave rise to new ways of thinking about design (see Item 41), and the STL defined an approach to extensibility unlike any most people had ever seen.

Today's C++ is a *multiparadigm programming language*, one supporting a combination of procedural, object-oriented, functional, generic, and metaprogramming features. This power and flexibility make C++ a tool without equal, but can also cause some confusion. All the "proper usage" rules seem to have exceptions. How are we to make sense of such a language?

The easiest way is to view C++ not as a single language but as a federation of related languages. Within a particular sublanguage, the rules tend to be simple, straightforward, and easy to remember. When you move from one sublanguage to another, however, the rules may change. To make sense of C++, you have to recognize its primary sub-languages. Fortunately, there are only four:

- **C.** Way down deep, C++ is still based on C. Blocks, statements, the preprocessor, built-in data types, arrays, pointers, etc., all come from C. In many cases, C++ offers approaches to problems that are superior to their C counterparts (e.g., see Items 2 (alternatives to the preprocessor) and 13 (using objects to manage resources)), but when you find yourself working with the C part of C++, the rules for effective programming reflect C's more limited scope: no templates, no exceptions, no overloading, etc.

- **Object-Oriented C++.** This part of C++ is what C with Classes was all about: classes (including constructors and destructors), encapsulation, inheritance, polymorphism, virtual functions (dynamic binding), etc. This is the part of C++ to which the classic rules for object-oriented design most directly apply.

- **Template C++.** This is the generic programming part of C++, the one that most programmers have the least experience with. Template considerations pervade C++, and it's not uncommon for rules of good programming to include special template-only clauses (e.g., see Item 46 on facilitating type conversions in calls to template functions). In fact, templates are so powerful, they give rise to a completely new programming paradigm, *template metaprogramming* (TMP). Item 48 provides an overview of TMP, but unless you're a hard-core template junkie, you need not worry about it. The rules for TMP rarely interact with mainstream C++ programming.

- **The STL.** The STL is a template library, of course, but it's a very special template library. Its conventions regarding containers, iterators, algorithms, and function objects mesh beautifully, but templates and libraries can be built around other ideas, too. The STL has particular ways of doing things, and when you're working with the STL, you need to be sure to follow its conventions.

Keep these four sublanguages in mind, and don't be surprised when you encounter situations where effective programming requires that you change strategy when you switch from one sublanguage to another. For example, pass-by-value is generally more efficient than pass-by-reference for built-in (i.e., C-like) types, but when you move from the C part of C++ to Object-Oriented C++, the existence of user-defined constructors and destructors means that pass-by-reference-to-const is usually better. This is especially the case when working in Template C++, because there, you don't even know the type of object you're dealing with. When you cross into the STL, however, you know that iterators and function objects are modeled on pointers in C, so for iterators and function objects in the STL, the old C pass-by-value rule applies again. (For all the details on choosing among parameter-passing options, see Item 20.)

C++, then, isn't a unified language with a single set of rules; it's a federation of four sublanguages, each with its own conventions. Keep these sublanguages in mind, and you'll find that C++ is a lot easier to understand.

Things to Remember

✦ Rules for effective C++ programming vary, depending on the part of C++ you are using.

Item 2:   Prefer consts, enums, and inlines to #defines.

This Item might better be called "prefer the compiler to the preprocessor," because #define may be treated as if it's not part of the language *per se*. That's one of its problems. When you do something like this,

```
#define ASPECT_RATIO 1.653
```

the symbolic name ASPECT_RATIO may never be seen by compilers; it may be removed by the preprocessor before the source code ever gets to a compiler. As a result, the name ASPECT_RATIO may not get entered into the symbol table. This can be confusing if you get an error during compilation involving the use of the constant, because the error message may refer to 1.653, not ASPECT_RATIO. If ASPECT_RATIO were defined in a header file you didn't write, you'd have no idea where that 1.653 came from, and you'd waste time tracking it down. This problem can also crop up in a symbolic debugger, because, again, the name you're programming with may not be in the symbol table.

The solution is to replace the macro with a constant:

```
const double AspectRatio = 1.653;      // uppercase names are usually for
                                       // macros, hence the name change
```

As a language constant, AspectRatio is definitely seen by compilers and is certainly entered into their symbol tables. In addition, in the case of a floating point constant (such as in this example), use of the constant may yield smaller code than using a #define. That's because the preprocessor's blind substitution of the macro name ASPECT_RATIO with 1.653 could result in multiple copies of 1.653 in your object code, while the use of the constant AspectRatio should never result in more than one copy.

When replacing #defines with constants, two special cases are worth mentioning. The first is defining constant pointers. Because constant definitions are typically put in header files (where many different source files will include them), it's important that the *pointer* be declared const, usually in addition to what the pointer points to. To define a constant char*-based string in a header file, for example, you have to write const *twice*:

```
const char * const authorName = "Scott Meyers";
```

For a complete discussion of the meanings and uses of const, especially in conjunction with pointers, see Item 3. However, it's worth reminding you here that string objects are generally preferable to their char*-based progenitors, so authorName is often better defined this way:

```
const std::string authorName("Scott Meyers");
```

The second special case concerns class-specific constants. To limit the scope of a constant to a class, you must make it a member, and to ensure there's at most one copy of the constant, you must make it a *static* member:

```
class GamePlayer {
private:
    static const int NumTurns = 5;        // constant declaration
    int scores[NumTurns];                  // use of constant
    ...
};
```

What you see above is a *declaration* for NumTurns, not a definition. Usually, C++ requires that you provide a definition for anything you use, but class-specific constants that are static and of integral type (e.g., integers, chars, bools) are an exception. As long as you don't take their address, you can declare them and use them without providing a definition. If you do take the address of a class constant, or if your compiler incorrectly insists on a definition even if you don't take the address, you provide a separate definition like this:

```
const int GamePlayer::NumTurns;       // definition of NumTurns; see
                                       // below for why no value is given
```

You put this in an implementation file, not a header file. Because the initial value of class constants is provided where the constant is declared (e.g., NumTurns is initialized to 5 when it is declared), no initial value is permitted at the point of definition.

Note, by the way, that there's no way to create a class-specific constant using a #define, because #defines don't respect scope. Once a macro is defined, it's in force for the rest of the compilation (unless it's

#undefed somewhere along the line). Which means that not only can't #defines be used for class-specific constants, they also can't be used to provide any kind of encapsulation, i.e., there is no such thing as a "private" #define. Of course, const data members can be encapsulated; NumTurns is.

Older compilers may not accept the syntax above, because it used to be illegal to provide an initial value for a static class member at its point of declaration. Furthermore, in-class initialization is allowed only for integral types and only for constants. In cases where the above syntax can't be used, you put the initial value at the point of definition:

```
class CostEstimate {
private:
    static const double FudgeFactor;        // declaration of static class
    ...                                     // constant; goes in header file
};

const double                                // definition of static class
    CostEstimate::FudgeFactor = 1.35;       // constant; goes in impl. file
```

This is all you need almost all the time. The only exception is when you need the value of a class constant during compilation of the class, such as in the declaration of the array GamePlayer::scores above (where compilers insist on knowing the size of the array during compilation). Then the accepted way to compensate for compilers that (incorrectly) forbid the in-class specification of initial values for static integral class constants is to use what is affectionately (and non-pejoratively) known as "the enum hack." This technique takes advantage of the fact that the values of an enumerated type can be used where ints are expected, so GamePlayer could just as well be defined like this:

```
class GamePlayer {
private:
    enum { NumTurns = 5 };          // "the enum hack" — makes
                                    // NumTurns a symbolic name for 5

    int scores[NumTurns];           // fine

    ...
};
```

The enum hack is worth knowing about for several reasons. First, the enum hack behaves in some ways more like a #define than a const does, and sometimes that's what you want. For example, it's legal to take the address of a const, but it's not legal to take the address of an enum, and it's typically not legal to take the address of a #define, either. If you don't want to let people get a pointer or reference to one of your integral constants, an enum is a good way to enforce that constraint. (For more on enforcing design constraints through coding decisions, consult Item 18.) Also, though good compilers won't set aside storage for const objects of integral types (unless you create a pointer or reference to the object), sloppy compilers may, and you may not be willing to set aside memory for such objects. Like #defines, enums never result in that kind of unnecessary memory allocation.

A second reason to know about the enum hack is purely pragmatic. Lots of code employs it, so you need to recognize it when you see it. In fact, the enum hack is a fundamental technique of template metaprogramming (see Item 48).

Getting back to the preprocessor, another common (mis)use of the #define directive is using it to implement macros that look like functions but that don't incur the overhead of a function call. Here's a macro that calls some function f with the greater of the macro's arguments:

```
// call f with the maximum of a and b
#define CALL_WITH_MAX(a, b) f((a) > (b) ? (a) : (b))
```

Macros like this have so many drawbacks, just thinking about them is painful.

Whenever you write this kind of macro, you have to remember to parenthesize all the arguments in the macro body. Otherwise you can run into trouble when somebody calls the macro with an expression. But even if you get that right, look at the weird things that can happen:

```
int a = 5, b = 0;

CALL_WITH_MAX(++a, b);           // a is incremented twice
CALL_WITH_MAX(++a, b+10);        // a is incremented once
```

Here, the number of times that a is incremented before calling f depends on what it is being compared with!

Fortunately, you don't need to put up with this nonsense. You can get all the efficiency of a macro plus all the predictable behavior and type safety of a regular function by using a template for an inline function (see Item 30):

```
template<typename T>                          // because we don't
inline void callWithMax(const T& a, const T& b)   // know what T is, we
{                                             // pass by reference-to-
  f(a > b ? a : b);                           // const — see Item 20
}
```

This template generates a whole family of functions, each of which takes two objects of the same type and calls f with the greater of the two objects. There's no need to parenthesize parameters inside the function body, no need to worry about evaluating parameters multiple times, etc. Furthermore, because callWithMax is a real function, it obeys scope and access rules. For example, it makes perfect sense to talk about an inline function that is private to a class. In general, there's just no way to do that with a macro.

Given the availability of consts, enums, and inlines, your need for the preprocessor (especially #define) is reduced, but it's not eliminated. #include remains essential, and #ifdef/#ifndef continue to play important roles in controlling compilation. It's not yet time to retire the preprocessor, but you should definitely give it long and frequent vacations.

Things to Remember

✦ For simple constants, prefer const objects or enums to #defines.

✦ For function-like macros, prefer inline functions to #defines.

Item 3:   Use const **whenever possible.**

The wonderful thing about const is that it allows you to specify a semantic constraint — a particular object should *not* be modified — and compilers will enforce that constraint. It allows you to communicate to both compilers and other programmers that a value should remain invariant. Whenever that is true, you should be sure to say so, because that way you enlist your compilers' aid in making sure the constraint isn't violated.

The const keyword is remarkably versatile. Outside of classes, you can use it for constants at global or namespace scope (see Item 2), as well as for objects declared static at file, function, or block scope. Inside classes, you can use it for both static and non-static data members. For pointers, you can specify whether the pointer itself is const, the data it points to is const, both, or neither:

```
char greeting[] = "Hello";
char *p = greeting;                    // non-const pointer,
                                       // non-const data
const char *p = greeting;              // non-const pointer,
                                       // const data
char * const p = greeting;             // const pointer,
                                       // non-const data
const char * const p = greeting;       // const pointer,
                                       // const data
```

This syntax isn't as capricious as it may seem. If the word const appears to the left of the asterisk, what's *pointed to* is constant; if the word const appears to the right of the asterisk, the *pointer itself* is constant; if const appears on both sides, both are constant.[†]

When what's pointed to is constant, some programmers list const before the type. Others list it after the type but before the asterisk. There is no difference in meaning, so the following functions take the same parameter type:

```
void f1(const Widget *pw);        // f1 takes a pointer to a
                                  // constant Widget object

void f2(Widget const *pw);        // so does f2
```

Because both forms exist in real code, you should accustom yourself to both of them.

STL iterators are modeled on pointers, so an iterator acts much like a T* pointer. Declaring an iterator const is like declaring a pointer const (i.e., declaring a T* const pointer): the iterator isn't allowed to point to something different, but the thing it points to may be modified. If you want an iterator that points to something that can't be modified (i.e., the STL analogue of a const T* pointer), you want a const_iterator:

```
std::vector<int> vec;
...
const std::vector<int>::iterator iter =    // iter acts like a T* const
    vec.begin();
*iter = 10;                                // OK, changes what iter points to
++iter;                                    // error! iter is const

std::vector<int>::const_iterator cIter =   //cIter acts like a const T*
    vec.begin();
*cIter = 10;                               // error! *cIter is const
++cIter;                                   // fine, changes cIter
```

Some of the most powerful uses of const stem from its application to function declarations. Within a function declaration, const can refer to the function's return value, to individual parameters, and, for member functions, to the function as a whole.

Having a function return a constant value often makes it possible to reduce the incidence of client errors without giving up safety or efficiency. For example, consider the declaration of the operator* function for rational numbers that is explored in Item 24:

```
class Rational { ... };

const Rational operator*(const Rational& lhs, const Rational& rhs);
```

---

† Some people find it helpful to read pointer declarations right to left, e.g., to read const char * const p as "p is a constant pointer to constant chars."

Many programmers squint when they first see this. Why should the result of operator* be a const object? Because if it weren't, clients would be able to commit atrocities like this:

```
Rational a, b, c;

...

(a * b) = c;                          // invoke operator= on the
                                      // result of a*b!
```

I don't know why any programmer would want to make an assignment to the product of two numbers, but I do know that many programmers have tried to do it without wanting to. All it takes is a simple typo (and a type that can be implicitly converted to bool):

```
if (a * b = c) ...                    // oops, meant to do a comparison!
```

Such code would be flat-out illegal if a and b were of a built-in type. One of the hallmarks of good user-defined types is that they avoid gratuitous incompatibilities with the built-ins (see also Item 18), and allowing assignments to the product of two numbers seems pretty gratuitous to me. Declaring operator*'s return value const prevents it, and that's why it's The Right Thing To Do.

There's nothing particularly new about const parameters — they act just like local const objects, and you should use both whenever you can. Unless you need to be able to modify a parameter or local object, be sure to declare it const. It costs you only the effort to type six characters, and it can save you from annoying errors such as the "I meant to type '==' but I accidentally typed '='" mistake we just saw.

const Member Functions

The purpose of const on member functions is to identify which member functions may be invoked on const objects. Such member functions are important for two reasons. First, they make the interface of a class easier to understand. It's important to know which functions may modify an object and which may not. Second, they make it possible to work with const objects. That's a critical aspect of writing efficient code, because, as Item 20 explains, one of the fundamental ways to improve a C++ program's performance is to pass objects by reference-to-const. That technique is viable only if there are const member functions with which to manipulate the resulting const-qualified objects.

Many people overlook the fact that member functions differing *only* in their constness can be overloaded, but this is an important feature of C++. Consider a class for representing a block of text:

```
class TextBlock {
public:

    ...

    const char& operator[](std::size_t position) const    // operator[] for
    { return text[position]; }                              // const objects

    char& operator[](std::size_t position)                 // operator[] for
    { return text[position]; }                              // non-const objects

private:
    std::string text;
};
```

TextBlock's operator[]s can be used like this:

```
TextBlock tb("Hello");
std::cout << tb[0];                         // calls non-const
                                            // TextBlock::operator[]

const TextBlock ctb("World");
std::cout << ctb[0];                        // calls const TextBlock::operator[]
```

Incidentally, const objects most often arise in real programs as a result of being passed by pointer- or reference-to-const. The example of ctb above is artificial. This is more realistic:

```
void print(const TextBlock& ctb)           // in this function, ctb is const
{
    std::cout << ctb[0];                    // calls const TextBlock::operator[]

    ...

}
```

By overloading operator[] and giving the different versions different return types, you can have const and non-const TextBlocks handled differently:

```
std::cout << tb[0];                         // fine — reading a
                                            // non-const TextBlock

tb[0] = 'x';                                // fine — writing a
                                            // non-const TextBlock

std::cout << ctb[0];                        // fine — reading a
                                            // const TextBlock

ctb[0] = 'x';                               // error! — writing a
                                            // const TextBlock
```

Note that the error here has only to do with the *return type* of the operator[] that is called; the calls to operator[] themselves are all fine. The error arises out of an attempt to make an assignment to a const char&, because that's the return type from the const version of operator[].

Also note that the return type of the non-const operator[] is a *reference* to a char — a char itself would not do. If operator[] did return a simple char, statements like this wouldn't compile:

```
tb[0] = 'x';
```

That's because it's never legal to modify the return value of a function that returns a built-in type. Even if it were legal, the fact that C++ returns objects by value (see Item 20) would mean that a *copy* of tb.text[0] would be modified, not tb.text[0] itself, and that's not the behavior you want.

Let's take a brief time-out for philosophy. What does it mean for a member function to be const? There are two prevailing notions: *bitwise constness* (also known as *physical constness*) and *logical constness*.

The bitwise const camp believes that a member function is const if and only if it doesn't modify any of the object's data members (excluding those that are static), i.e., if it doesn't modify any of the bits inside the object. The nice thing about bitwise constness is that it's easy to detect violations: compilers just look for assignments to data members. In fact, bitwise constness is C++'s definition of constness, and a const member function isn't allowed to modify any of the non-static data members of the object on which it is invoked.

Unfortunately, many member functions that don't act very const pass the bitwise test. In particular, a member function that modifies what a pointer *points to* frequently doesn't act const. But if only the *pointer* is in the object, the function is bitwise const, and compilers won't complain. That can lead to counterintuitive behavior. For example, suppose we have a TextBlock-like class that stores its data as a char* instead of a string, because it needs to communicate through a C API that doesn't understand string objects.

```
class CTextBlock {
public:
    ...
    char& operator[](std::size_t position) const     // inappropriate (but bitwise
    { return pText[position]; }                       // const) declaration of
                                                      // operator[]
private:
    char *pText;
};
```

This class (inappropriately) declares operator[] as a const member function, even though that function returns a reference to the object's internal data (a topic treated in depth in Item 28). Set that aside and note that operator[]'s implementation doesn't modify pText in any way. As a result, compilers will happily generate code for operator[]; it is, after all, bitwise const, and that's all compilers check for. But look what it allows to happen:

```
const CTextBlock cctb("Hello");      // declare constant object

char *pc = &cctb[0];                 // call the const operator[] to get a
                                     // pointer to cctb's data

*pc = 'J';                           // cctb now has the value "Jello"
```

Surely there is something wrong when you create a constant object with a particular value and you invoke only const member functions on it, yet you still change its value!

This leads to the notion of logical constness. Adherents to this philosophy — and you should be among them — argue that a const member function might modify some of the bits in the object on which it's invoked, but only in ways that clients cannot detect. For example, your CTextBlock class might want to cache the length of the textblock whenever it's requested:

```
class CTextBlock {
public:
   ...
    std::size_t length() const;

private:
    char *pText;
    std::size_t textLength;          // last calculated length of textblock
    bool lengthIsValid;              // whether length is currently valid
};
std::size_t CTextBlock::length() const
{
    if (!lengthIsValid) {
        textLength = std::strlen(pText);   // error! can't assign to textLength
        lengthIsValid = true;              // and lengthIsValid in a const
    }                                      // member function

    return textLength;
}
```

This implementation of length is certainly not bitwise const — both textLength and lengthIsValid may be modified — yet it seems as though it should be valid for const CTextBlock objects. Compilers disagree. They insist on bitwise constness. What to do?

The solution is simple: take advantage of C++'s const-related wiggle room known as mutable. mutable frees non-static data members from the constraints of bitwise constness:

```
class CTextBlock {
public:

   ...

   std::size_t length() const;

private:
   char *pText;

   mutable std::size_t textLength;        // these data members may
   mutable bool lengthIsValid;            // always be modified, even in
};                                        // const member functions

std::size_t CTextBlock::length() const
{
   if (!lengthIsValid) {
      textLength = std::strlen(pText);    // now fine
      lengthIsValid = true;               // also fine
   }

   return textLength;
}
```

Avoiding Duplication in const and Non-const Member Functions

mutable is a nice solution to the bitwise-constness-is-not-what-I-had-in-mind problem, but it doesn't solve all const-related difficulties. For example, suppose that operator[] in TextBlock (and CTextBlock) not only returned a reference to the appropriate character, it also performed bounds checking, logged access information, maybe even did data integrity validation. Putting all this in both the const and the non-const operator[] functions (and not fretting that we now have implicitly inline functions of nontrivial length — see Item 30) yields this kind of monstrosity:

```
class TextBlock {
public:

   ...

   const char& operator[](std::size_t position) const
   {
      ...                                 // do bounds checking
      ...                                 // log access data
      ...                                 // verify data integrity
      return text[position];
   }

   char& operator[](std::size_t position)
   {
      ...                                 // do bounds checking
      ...                                 // log access data
      ...                                 // verify data integrity
      return text[position];
   }

private:
   std::string text;
};
```

Ouch! Can you say code duplication, along with its attendant compilation time, maintenance, and code-bloat headaches? Sure, it's possible to move all the code for bounds checking, etc. into a separate member function (private, naturally) that both versions of operator[] call, but you've still got the duplicated calls to that function and you've still got the duplicated return statement code.

What you really want to do is implement operator[] functionality once and use it twice. That is, you want to have one version of operator[] call the other one. And that brings us to casting away constness.

As a general rule, casting is such a bad idea, I've devoted an entire Item to telling you not to do it (Item 27), but code duplication is no picnic, either. In this case, the const version of operator[] does exactly what the non-const version does, it just has a const-qualified return type. Casting away the const on the return value is safe, in this case, because whoever called the non-const operator[] must have had a non-const object in the first place. Otherwise they couldn't have called a non-const function. So having the non-const operator[] call the const version is a safe way to avoid code duplication, even though it requires a cast. Here's the code, but it may be clearer after you read the explanation that follows:

```cpp
class TextBlock {
public:

  ...

  const char& operator[](std::size_t position) const      // same as before
  {
    ...
    ...
    ...
    return text[position];
  }
  char& operator[](std::size_t position)                  // now just calls const op[]
  {
    return
      const_cast<char&>(                                  // cast away const on
                                                          // op[]'s return type;
          static_cast<const TextBlock&>(*this)            // add const to *this's type;
            [position]                                    // call const version of op[]
      );
  }
  ...
};
```

As you can see, the code has two casts, not one. We want the non-const operator[] to call the const one, but if, inside the non-const operator[], we just call operator[], we'll recursively call ourselves. That's only entertaining the first million or so times. To avoid infinite recursion, we have to specify that we want to call the const operator[], but there's no direct way to do that. Instead, we cast *this from its native type of TextBlock& to const TextBlock&. Yes, we use a cast to *add* const! So we have two casts: one to add const to *this (so that our call to operator[] will call the const version), the second to remove the const from the const operator[]'s return value.

The cast that adds const is just forcing a safe conversion (from a non-const object to a const one), so we use a static_cast for that. The one that removes const can be accomplished only via a const_cast, so we don't really have a choice there. (Technically, we do. A C-style cast would also work, but, as I explain in Item 27, such casts are rarely the right choice. If you're unfamiliar with static_cast or const_cast, Item 27 contains an overview.)

On top of everything else, we're calling an operator in this example, so the syntax is a little strange. The result may not win any beauty contests, but it has the desired effect of avoiding code duplication by implementing the non-const version of operator[] in terms of the const version. Whether achieving that goal is worth the ungainly syntax is something only you can determine, but the technique of implementing a non-const member function in terms of its const twin is definitely worth knowing.

Even more worth knowing is that trying to do things the other way around — avoiding duplication by having the const version call the non-const version — is *not* something you want to do. Remember, a const member function promises never to change the logical state of its object, but a non-const member function makes no such promise. If you were to call a non-const function from a const one, you'd run the risk that the object you'd promised not to modify would be changed. That's why having a const member function call a non-const one is wrong: the object could be changed. In fact, to get the code to compile, you'd have to use a const_cast to get rid of the const on *this, a clear sign of trouble. The reverse calling sequence — the one we used above — is safe: the non-const member function can do whatever it wants with an object, so calling a const member function imposes no risk. That's why a static_cast works on *this in that case: there's no const-related danger.

As I noted at the beginning of this Item, const is a wonderful thing. On pointers and iterators; on the objects referred to by pointers, iterators, and references; on function parameters and return types; on local variables; and on member functions, const is a powerful ally. Use it whenever you can. You'll be glad you did.

Things to Remember

✦ Declaring something const helps compilers detect usage errors. const can be applied to objects at any scope, to function parameters and return types, and to member functions as a whole.

✦ Compilers enforce bitwise constness, but you should program using logical constness.

✦ When const and non-const member functions have essentially identical implementations, code duplication can be avoided by having the non-const version call the const version.

Item 4:   Make sure that objects are initialized before they're used.

C++ can seem rather fickle about initializing the values of objects. For example, if you say this,

```
int x;
```

in some contexts, x is guaranteed to be initialized (to zero), but in others, it's not. If you say this,

```
class Point {
  int x, y;
};

...

Point p;
```

p's data members are sometimes guaranteed to be initialized (to zero), but sometimes they're not. If you're coming from a language where uninitialized objects can't exist, pay attention, because this is important.

Reading uninitialized values yields undefined behavior. On some platforms, the mere act of reading an uninitialized value can halt your program. More typically, the result of the read will be semi-random bits, which will then pollute the object you read the bits into, eventually leading to inscrutable program behavior and a lot of unpleasant debugging.

Now, there are rules that describe when object initialization is guaranteed to take place and when it isn't. Unfortunately, the rules are complicated — too complicated to be worth memorizing, in my opinion. In general, if you're in the C part of C++ (see Item 1) and initialization would probably incur a runtime cost, it's not guaranteed to take place. If you cross into the non-C parts of C++, things sometimes change. This explains why an array (from the C part of C++) isn't necessarily guaranteed to have its contents initialized, but a vector (from the STL part of C++) is.

The best way to deal with this seemingly indeterminate state of affairs is to *always* initialize your objects before you use them. For non-member objects of built-in types, you'll need to do this manually. For example:

```
int x = 0;                         // manual initialization of an int

const char * text = "A C-style string";   // manual initialization of a
                                          // pointer (see also Item 3)

double d;                          // "initialization" by reading from
std::cin >> d;                     // an input stream
```

For almost everything else, the responsibility for initialization falls on constructors. The rule there is simple: make sure that all constructors initialize everything in the object.

The rule is easy to follow, but it's important not to confuse assignment with initialization. Consider a constructor for a class representing entries in an address book:

```
class PhoneNumber { ... };

class ABEntry {                         // ABEntry = "Address Book Entry"
public:
    ABEntry(const std::string& name, const std::string& address,
            const std::list<PhoneNumber>& phones);
private:
    std::string theName;
    std::string theAddress;
    std::list<PhoneNumber> thePhones;
    int numTimesConsulted;
};

ABEntry::ABEntry(const std::string& name, const std::string& address,
                 const std::list<PhoneNumber>& phones)
{
    theName = name;                     // these are all assignments,
    theAddress = address;               // not initializations
    thePhones = phones;
    numTimesConsulted = 0;
}
```

This will yield ABEntry objects with the values you expect, but it's still not the best approach. The rules of C++ stipulate that data members of an object are initialized *before* the body of a constructor is entered. Inside the ABEntry constructor, theName, theAddress, and thePhones aren't being initialized, they're being *assigned*. Initialization took place earlier — when their default constructors were automatically called prior to entering the body of the ABEntry constructor. This isn't true for numTimesConsulted, because it's a built-in type. For it, there's no guarantee it was initialized at all prior to its assignment.

A better way to write the ABEntry constructor is to use the member initialization list instead of assignments:

```
ABEntry::ABEntry(const std::string& name, const std::string& address,
                const std::list<PhoneNumber>& phones)
: theName(name),
  theAddress(address),                    // these are now all initializations
  thePhones(phones),
  numTimesConsulted(0)
{}                                        // the ctor body is now empty
```

This constructor yields the same end result as the one above, but it will often be more efficient. The assignment-based version first called default constructors to initialize theName, theAddress, and thePhones, then promptly assigned new values on top of the default-constructed ones. All the work performed in those default constructions was therefore wasted. The member initialization list approach avoids that problem, because the arguments in the initialization list are used as constructor arguments for the various data members. In this case, theName is copy-constructed from name, theAddress is copy-constructed from address, and thePhones is copy-constructed from phones. For most types, a single call to a copy constructor is more efficient — sometimes *much* more efficient — than a call to the default constructor followed by a call to the copy assignment operator.

For objects of built-in type like numTimesConsulted, there is no difference in cost between initialization and assignment, but for consistency, it's often best to initialize everything via member initialization. Similarly, you can use the member initialization list even when you want to default-construct a data member; just specify nothing as an initialization argument. For example, if ABEntry had a constructor taking no parameters, it could be implemented like this:

```
ABEntry::ABEntry()
: theName(),                    // call theName's default ctor;
  theAddress(),                 // do the same for theAddress;
  thePhones(),                  // and for thePhones;
  numTimesConsulted(0)          // but explicitly initialize
{}                              // numTimesConsulted to zero
```

Because compilers will automatically call default constructors for data members of user-defined types when those data members have no initializers on the member initialization list, some programmers consider the above approach overkill. That's understandable, but having a policy of always listing every data member on the initialization list avoids having to remember which data members may go uninitialized if they are omitted. Because numTimesConsulted is of a built-in type, for example, leaving it off a member initialization list could open the door to undefined behavior.

Sometimes the initialization list *must* be used, even for built-in types. For example, data members that are const or are references must be initialized; they can't be assigned (see also Item 5). To avoid having to memorize when data members must be initialized in the member initialization list and when it's optional, the easiest choice is to *always* use the initialization list. It's sometimes required, and it's often more efficient than assignments.

Many classes have multiple constructors, and each constructor has its own member initialization list. If there are many data members and/or base classes, the existence of multiple initialization lists introduces undesirable repetition (in the lists) and boredom (in the programmers). In such cases, it's not unreasonable to omit entries in the lists for data members where assignment works as well as true initialization, moving the assignments to a single (typically private) function that all the constructors call. This approach can be especially helpful if the true initial values for the data members are to be read from a file or looked up in a database. In general, however, true member initialization (via an initialization list) is preferable to pseudo-initialization via assignment.

One aspect of C++ that isn't fickle is the order in which an object's data is initialized. This order is always the same: base classes are initialized before derived classes (see also Item 12), and within a class, data members are initialized in the order in which they are declared. In ABEntry, for example, theName will always be initialized first, theAddress second, thePhones third, and numTimesConsulted last. This is true even if they are listed in a different order on the member initialization list (something that's unfortunately legal). To avoid reader confusion, as well as the possibility of some truly obscure behavioral bugs, always list members in the initialization list in the same order as they're declared in the class.

Once you've taken care of explicitly initializing non-member objects of built-in types and you've ensured that your constructors initialize their base classes and data members using the member initialization list, there's only one more thing to worry about. That thing is — take a deep breath — the order of initialization of non-local static objects defined in different translation units.

Let's pick that phrase apart bit by bit.

A *static object* is one that exists from the time it's constructed until the end of the program. Stack and heap-based objects are thus excluded. Included are global objects, objects defined at namespace scope, objects declared static inside classes, objects declared static inside functions, and objects declared static at file scope. Static objects inside functions are known as *local static objects* (because they're local to a function), and the other kinds of static objects are known as *non-local static objects*. Static objects are destroyed when the program exits, i.e., their destructors are called when main finishes executing.

A *translation unit* is the source code giving rise to a single object file. It's basically a single source file, plus all of its #include files.

The problem we're concerned with, then, involves at least two separately compiled source files, each of which contains at least one non-local static object (i.e., an object that's global, at namespace scope, or static in a class or at file scope). And the actual problem is this: if initialization of a non-local static object in one translation unit uses a non-local static object in a different translation unit, the object it uses could be uninitialized, because *the relative order of initialization of non-local static objects defined in different translation units is undefined.*

An example will help. Suppose you have a FileSystem class that makes files on the Internet look like they're local. Since your class makes the world look like a single file system, you might create a special object at global or namespace scope representing the single file system:

```
class FileSystem {            // from your library's header file
public:
    ...
    std::size_t numDisks() const;    // one of many member functions
    ...
};
extern FileSystem tfs;        // declare object for clients to use
                              // ("tfs" = "the file system" ); definition
                              // is in some .cpp file in your library
```

A FileSystem object is decidedly non-trivial, so use of the tfs object before it has been constructed would be disastrous.

Now suppose some client creates a class for directories in a file system. Naturally, their class uses the tfs object:

```
class Directory {                          // created by library client
public:
    Directory( params );
    ...
};
Directory::Directory( params )
{
    ...
    std::size_t disks = tfs.numDisks();     // use the tfs object
    ...
}
```

Further suppose this client decides to create a single Directory object for temporary files:

```
Directory tempDir( params );               // directory for temporary files
```

Now the importance of initialization order becomes apparent: unless tfs is initialized before tempDir, tempDir's constructor will attempt to use tfs before it's been initialized. But tfs and tempDir were created by different people at different times in different source files — they're non-local static objects defined in different translation units. How can you be sure that tfs will be initialized before tempDir?

You can't. Again, *the relative order of initialization of non-local static objects defined in different translation units is undefined.* There is a reason for this. Determining the "proper" order in which to initialize non-local static objects is hard. Very hard. Unsolvably hard. In its most general form — with multiple translation units and non-local static objects generated through implicit template instantiations (which may themselves arise via implicit template instantiations) — it's not only impossible to determine the right order of initialization, it's typically not even worth looking for special cases where it *is* possible to determine the right order.

Fortunately, a small design change eliminates the problem entirely. All that has to be done is to move each non-local static object into its own function, where it's declared static. These functions return references to the objects they contain. Clients then call the functions instead of referring to the objects. In other words, non-local static objects are replaced with *local* static objects. (Aficionados of design patterns will recognize this as a common implementation of the Singleton pattern.[†])

This approach is founded on C++'s guarantee that local static objects are initialized when the object's definition is first encountered during a call to that function. So if you replace direct accesses to non-local

---

† Actually, it's only *part* of a Singleton implementation. An essential part of Singleton I ignore in this Item is preventing the creation of multiple objects of a particular type.

static objects with calls to functions that return references to local static objects, you're guaranteed that the references you get back will refer to initialized objects. As a bonus, if you never call a function emulating a non-local static object, you never incur the cost of constructing and destructing the object, something that can't be said for true non-local static objects.

Here's the technique applied to both tfs and tempDir:

```
class FileSystem { ... };        // as before

FileSystem& tfs()                // this replaces the tfs object; it could be
{                                // static in the FileSystem class

  static FileSystem fs;          // define and initialize a local static object
  return fs;                     // return a reference to it

}

class Directory { ... };         // as before

Directory::Directory( params )   // as before, except references to tfs are
{                                // now to tfs()

  ...
  std::size_t disks = tfs().numDisks();
  ...

}

Directory& tempDir()             // this replaces the tempDir object; it
{                                // could be static in the Directory class

  static Directory td( params ); // define/initialize local static object
  return td;                     // return reference to it

}
```

Clients of this modified system program exactly as they used to, except they now refer to tfs() and tempDir() instead of tfs and tempDir. That is, they use functions returning references to objects instead of using the objects themselves.

The reference-returning functions dictated by this scheme are always simple: define and initialize a local static object on line 1, return it on line 2. This simplicity makes them excellent candidates for inlining, especially if they're called frequently (see Item 30). On the other hand, the fact that these functions contain static objects makes them problematic in multithreaded systems. Then again, any kind of non-const static object — local or non-local — is trouble waiting to happen in the presence of multiple threads. One way to deal with such trouble is to manually invoke all the reference-returning functions during the single-threaded startup portion of the program. This eliminates initialization-related race conditions.

Of course, the idea of using reference-returning functions to prevent initialization order problems is dependent on there being a reasonable initialization order for your objects in the first place. If you have a system where object A must be initialized before object B, but A's initialization is dependent on B's having already been initialized, you are going to have problems, and frankly, you deserve them. If you steer clear of such pathological scenarios, however, the approach described here should serve you nicely, at least in single-threaded applications.

To avoid using objects before they're initialized, then, you need to do only three things. First, manually initialize non-member objects of built-in types. Second, use member initialization lists to initialize all parts of an object. Finally, design around the initialization order uncertainty that afflicts non-local static objects defined in separate translation units.

Things to Remember

- ✦ Manually initialize objects of built-in type, because C++ only sometimes initializes them itself.

- ✦ In a constructor, prefer use of the member initialization list to assignment inside the body of the constructor. List data members in the initialization list in the same order they're declared in the class.

- ✦ Avoid initialization order problems across translation units by replacing non-local static objects with local static objects.

Constructors, Destructors, and Assignment Operators

Almost every class you write will have one or more constructors, a destructor, and a copy assignment operator. Little wonder. These are your bread-and-butter functions, the ones that control the fundamental operations of bringing a new object into existence and making sure it's initialized, getting rid of an object and making sure it's properly cleaned up, and giving an object a new value. Making mistakes in these functions will lead to far-reaching — and unpleasant — repercussions throughout your classes, so it's vital that you get them right. In this chapter, I offer guidance on putting together the functions that comprise the backbone of well-formed classes.

Item 5: Know what functions C++ silently writes and calls.

When is an empty class not an empty class? When C++ gets through with it. If you don't declare them yourself, compilers will declare their own versions of a copy constructor, a copy assignment operator, and a destructor. Furthermore, if you declare no constructors at all, compilers will also declare a default constructor for you. All these functions will be both public and inline (see Item 30). As a result, if you write

```
class Empty{};
```

it's essentially the same as if you'd written this:

```
class Empty {
public:
    Empty() { ... }                          // default constructor
    Empty(const Empty& rhs) { ... }          // copy constructor

    ~Empty() { ... }                         // destructor — see below
                                             // for whether it's virtual

    Empty& operator=(const Empty& rhs) { ... } // copy assignment operator
};
```

These functions are generated only if they are needed, but it doesn't take much to need them. The following code will cause each function to be generated:

```
Empty e1;                    // default constructor;
                             // destructor

Empty e2(e1);                // copy constructor

e2 = e1;                     // copy assignment operator
```

Given that compilers are writing functions for you, what do the functions do? Well, the default constructor and the destructor primarily give compilers a place to put "behind the scenes" code such as invocation of constructors and destructors of base classes and non-static data members. Note that the generated destructor is non-virtual (see Item 7) unless it's for a class inheriting from a base class that itself declares a virtual destructor (in which case the function's virtualness comes from the base class).

As for the copy constructor and the copy assignment operator, the compiler-generated versions simply copy each non-static data member of the source object over to the target object. For example, consider a NamedObject template that allows you to associate names with objects of type T:

```
template<typename T>
class NamedObject {
public:
    NamedObject(const char *name, const T& value);
    NamedObject(const std::string& name, const T& value);

    ...

private:
    std::string nameValue;
    T objectValue;
};
```

Because a constructor is declared in NamedObject, compilers won't generate a default constructor. This is important. It means that if you've carefully engineered a class to require constructor arguments, you don't have to worry about compilers overriding your decision by blithely adding a constructor that takes no arguments.

NamedObject declares neither copy constructor nor copy assignment operator, so compilers will generate those functions (if they are needed). Look, then, at this use of the copy constructor:

```
NamedObject<int> no1("Smallest Prime Number", 2);

NamedObject<int> no2(no1);                 // calls copy constructor
```

The copy constructor generated by compilers must initialize no2.name-Value and no2.objectValue using no1.nameValue and no1.objectValue, respectively. The type of nameValue is string, and the standard string type has a copy constructor, so no2.nameValue will be initialized by calling the string copy constructor with no1.nameValue as its argument. On the other hand, the type of NamedObject<int>::objectValue is int (because T is int for this template instantiation), and int is a built-in type, so no2.objectValue will be initialized by copying the bits in no1.objectValue.

The compiler-generated copy assignment operator for NamedObject<int> would behave essentially the same way, but in general, compiler-generated copy assignment operators behave as I've described only when the resulting code is both legal and has a reasonable chance of making sense. If either of these tests fails, compilers will refuse to generate an operator= for your class.

For example, suppose NamedObject were defined like this, where nameValue is a *reference* to a string and objectValue is a *const* T:

```
template<typename T>
class NamedObject {
public:
    // this ctor no longer takes a const name, because nameValue
    // is now a reference-to-non-const string. The char* constructor
    // is gone, because we must have a string to refer to.
    NamedObject(std::string& name, const T& value);

    ...                              // as above, assume no
                                     // operator= is declared
private:
    std::string& nameValue;          // this is now a reference
    const T objectValue;             // this is now const
};
```

Now consider what should happen here:

```
std::string newDog("Persephone");
std::string oldDog("Satch");

NamedObject<int> p(newDog, 2);       // when I originally wrote this, our
                                     // dog Persephone was about to
                                     // have her second birthday

NamedObject<int> s(oldDog, 36);      // the family dog Satch (from my
                                     // childhood) would be 36 if she
                                     // were still alive

p = s;                               // what should happen to
                                     // the data members in p?
```

Before the assignment, both p.nameValue and s.nameValue refer to string objects, though not the same ones. How should the assignment affect p.nameValue? After the assignment, should p.nameValue refer to the string referred to by s.nameValue, i.e., should the reference itself be modified? If so, that breaks new ground, because C++ doesn't provide a way to make a reference refer to a different object. Alternatively, should the string object to which p.nameValue refers be modified, thus affecting other objects that hold pointers or references to that string, i.e., objects not directly involved in the assignment? Is that what the compiler-generated copy assignment operator should do?

Faced with this conundrum, C++ refuses to compile the code. If you want to support copy assignment in a class containing a reference member, you must define the copy assignment operator yourself. Compilers behave similarly for classes containing const members (such as objectValue in the modified class above). It's not legal to modify const members, so compilers are unsure how to treat them during an implicitly generated assignment function. Finally, compilers reject implicit copy assignment operators in derived classes that inherit from base classes declaring the copy assignment operator private. After all, compiler-generated copy assignment operators for derived classes are supposed to handle base class parts, too (see Item 12), but in doing so, they certainly can't invoke member functions the derived class has no right to call.

Things to Remember

✦ Compilers may implicitly generate a class's default constructor, copy constructor, copy assignment operator, and destructor.

Item 6: Explicitly disallow the use of compiler-generated functions you do not want.

Real estate agents sell houses, and a software system supporting such agents would naturally have a class representing homes for sale:

```
class HomeForSale { ... };
```

As every real estate agent will be quick to point out, every property is unique — no two are exactly alike. That being the case, the idea of making a *copy* of a HomeForSale object makes little sense. How can you copy something that's inherently unique? You'd thus like attempts to copy HomeForSale objects to not compile:

```
HomeForSale h1;
HomeForSale h2;

HomeForSale h3(h1);            // attempt to copy h1 — should
                              // not compile!

    h1 = h2;                  // attempt to copy h2 — should
                              // not compile!
```

Alas, preventing such compilation isn't completely straightforward. Usually, if you don't want a class to support a particular kind of functionality, you simply don't declare the function that would provide it. This strategy doesn't work for the copy constructor and copy assignment operator, because, as Item 5 points out, if you don't declare them and somebody tries to call them, compilers declare them for you.

This puts you in a bind. If you don't declare a copy constructor or a copy assignment operator, compilers may generate them for you. Your class thus supports copying. If, on the other hand, you do declare these functions, your class still supports copying. But the goal here is to *prevent* copying!

The key to the solution is that all the compiler generated functions are public. To prevent these functions from being generated, you must declare them yourself, but there is nothing that requires that *you* declare them public. Instead, declare the copy constructor and the copy assignment operator *private*. By declaring a member function explicitly, you prevent compilers from generating their own version, and by making the function private, you keep people from calling it.

Mostly. The scheme isn't foolproof, because member and friend functions can still call your private functions. *Unless*, that is, you are clever enough not to *define* them. Then if somebody inadvertently calls one, they'll get an error at link-time. This trick — declaring member functions private and deliberately not implementing them — is so well established, it's used to prevent copying in several classes in C++'s iostreams library. Take a look, for example, at the definitions of ios_base, basic_ios, and sentry in your standard library implementation. You'll find that in each case, both the copy constructor and the copy assignment operator are declared private and are not defined.

Applying the trick to HomeForSale is easy:

```
class HomeForSale {
public:
  ...
private:
  ...
  HomeForSale(const HomeForSale&);                    // declarations only
  HomeForSale& operator=(const HomeForSale&);
};
```

You'll note that I've omitted the names of the functions' parameters. This isn't required, it's just a common convention. After all, the functions will never be implemented, much less used, so what's the point in specifying parameter names?

With the above class definition, compilers will thwart client attempts to copy HomeForSale objects, and if you inadvertently try to do it in a member or a friend function, the linker will complain.

It's possible to move the link-time error up to compile time (always a good thing — earlier error detection is better than later) by declaring the copy constructor and copy assignment operator private not in HomeForSale itself, but in a base class specifically designed to prevent copying. The base class is simplicity itself:

```
class Uncopyable {
protected:                                    // allow construction
    Uncopyable() {}                           // and destruction of
    ~Uncopyable() {}                          // derived objects...

private:
    Uncopyable(const Uncopyable&);            // ...but prevent copying
    Uncopyable& operator=(const Uncopyable&);
};
```

To keep HomeForSale objects from being copied, all we have to do now is inherit from Uncopyable:

```
class HomeForSale: private Uncopyable {       // class no longer
    ...                                       // declares copy ctor or
};                                            // copy assign. operator
```

This works, because compilers will try to generate a copy constructor and a copy assignment operator if anybody — even a member or friend function — tries to copy a HomeForSale object. As Item 12 explains, the compiler-generated versions of these functions will try to call their base class counterparts, and those calls will be rejected, because the copying operations are private in the base class.

The implementation and use of Uncopyable include some subtleties, such as the fact that inheritance from Uncopyable needn't be public (see Items 32 and 39) and that Uncopyable's destructor need not be virtual (see Item 7). Because Uncopyable contains no data, it's eligible for the empty base class optimization described in Item 39, but because it's a base class, use of this technique could lead to multiple inheritance (see Item 40). Multiple inheritance, in turn, can some-times disable the empty base class optimization (again, see Item 39). In general, you can ignore these subtleties and just use Uncopyable as shown, because it works precisely as advertised. You can also use the version available at Boost (see Item 55). That class is named noncopy-able. It's a fine class, I just find the name a bit un-, er, *non*natural.

Things to Remember

✦ To disallow functionality automatically provided by compilers, de-clare the corresponding member functions private and give no imple-mentations. Using a base class like Uncopyable is one way to do this.

Item 7: Declare destructors virtual in polymorphic base classes.

There are lots of ways to keep track of time, so it would be reasonable to create a TimeKeeper base class along with derived classes for different approaches to timekeeping:

```
class TimeKeeper {
public:
  TimeKeeper();
  ~TimeKeeper();
  ...
};
class AtomicClock: public TimeKeeper { ... };

class WaterClock: public TimeKeeper { ... };

class WristWatch: public TimeKeeper { ... };
```

Many clients will want access to the time without worrying about the details of how it's calculated, so a *factory function* — a function that returns a base class pointer to a newly-created derived class object — can be used to return a pointer to a timekeeping object:

```
TimeKeeper* getTimeKeeper();        // returns a pointer to a dynamic-
                                    // ally allocated object of a class
                                    // derived from TimeKeeper
```

In keeping with the conventions of factory functions, the objects returned by getTimeKeeper are on the heap, so to avoid leaking memory and other resources, it's important that each returned object be properly deleted:

```
TimeKeeper *ptk = getTimeKeeper();  // get dynamically allocated object
                                    // from TimeKeeper hierarchy

...                                 // use it

delete ptk;                         // release it to avoid resource leak
```

Item 13 explains that relying on clients to perform the deletion is error-prone, and Item 18 explains how the interface to the factory function can be modified to prevent common client errors, but such concerns are secondary here, because in this Item we address a more fundamental weakness of the code above: even if clients do everything right, there is no way to know how the program will behave.

The problem is that getTimeKeeper returns a pointer to a derived class object (e.g., AtomicClock), that object is being deleted via a base class pointer (i.e., a TimeKeeper* pointer), and the base class (TimeKeeper) has a *non-virtual destructor*. This is a recipe for disaster, because C++

specifies that when a derived class object is deleted through a pointer to a base class with a non-virtual destructor, results are undefined. What typically happens at runtime is that the derived part of the object is never destroyed. If getTimeKeeper were to return a pointer to an AtomicClock object, the AtomicClock part of the object (i.e., the data members declared in the AtomicClock class) would probably not be destroyed, nor would the AtomicClock destructor run. However, the base class part (i.e., the TimeKeeper part) typically would be destroyed, thus leading to a curious "partially destroyed" object. This is an excellent way to leak resources, corrupt data structures, and spend a lot of time with a debugger.

Eliminating the problem is simple: give the base class a virtual destructor. Then deleting a derived class object will do exactly what you want. It will destroy the entire object, including all its derived class parts:

```
class TimeKeeper {
public:
  TimeKeeper();
  virtual ~TimeKeeper();
  ...
};
TimeKeeper *ptk = getTimeKeeper();

...

delete ptk;                              // now behaves correctly
```

Base classes like TimeKeeper generally contain virtual functions other than the destructor, because the purpose of virtual functions is to allow customization of derived class implementations (see Item 34). For example, TimeKeeper might have a virtual function, getCurrentTime, which would be implemented differently in the various derived classes. Any class with virtual functions should almost certainly have a virtual destructor.

If a class does *not* contain virtual functions, that often indicates it is not meant to be used as a base class. When a class is not intended to be a base class, making the destructor virtual is usually a bad idea. Consider a class for representing points in two-dimensional space:

```
class Point {                        // a 2D point
public:
  Point(int xCoord, int yCoord);
  ~Point();
private:
  int x, y;
};
```

If an int occupies 32 bits, a Point object can typically fit into a 64-bit register. Furthermore, such a Point object can be passed as a 64-bit quantity to functions written in other languages, such as C or FOR-TRAN. If Point's destructor is made virtual, however, the situation changes.

The implementation of virtual functions requires that objects carry information that can be used at runtime to determine which virtual functions should be invoked on the object. This information typically takes the form of a pointer called a vptr ("virtual table pointer"). The vptr points to an array of function pointers called a vtbl ("virtual table"); each class with virtual functions has an associated vtbl. When a virtual function is invoked on an object, the actual function called is determined by following the object's vptr to a vtbl and then looking up the appropriate function pointer in the vtbl.

The details of how virtual functions are implemented are unimportant. What *is* important is that if the Point class contains a virtual function, objects of that type will increase in size. On a 32-bit architecture, they'll go from 64 bits (for the two ints) to 96 bits (for the ints plus the vptr); on a 64-bit architecture, they may go from 64 to 128 bits, because pointers on such architectures are 64 bits in size. Addition of a vptr to Point will thus increase its size by 50–100%! No longer can Point objects fit in a 64-bit register. Furthermore, Point objects in C++ can no longer look like the same structure declared in another language such as C, because their foreign language counterparts will lack the vptr. As a result, it is no longer possible to pass Points to and from functions written in other languages unless you explicitly compensate for the vptr, which is itself an implementation detail and hence unportable.

The bottom line is that gratuitously declaring all destructors virtual is just as wrong as never declaring them virtual. In fact, many people summarize the situation this way: declare a virtual destructor in a class if and only if that class contains at least one virtual function.

It is possible to get bitten by the non-virtual destructor problem even in the complete absence of virtual functions. For example, the standard string type contains no virtual functions, but misguided programmers sometimes use it as a base class anyway:

```
class SpecialString: public std::string {      // bad idea! std::string has a
   ...                                          // non-virtual destructor
};
```

At first glance, this may look innocuous, but if anywhere in an application you somehow convert a pointer-to-SpecialString into a pointer-to-string and you then use delete on the string pointer, you are instantly transported to the realm of undefined behavior:

```
SpecialString *pss =new SpecialString("Impending Doom");
std::string *ps;

...

ps = pss;                          // SpecialString* ⇒ std::string*

...

delete ps;                         // undefined! In practice,
                                   // *ps's SpecialString resources
                                   // will be leaked, because the
                                   // SpecialString destructor won't
                                   // be called.
```

The same analysis applies to any class lacking a virtual destructor, including all the STL container types (e.g., vector, list, set, tr1::unordered_map (see Item 54), etc.). If you're ever tempted to inherit from a standard container or any other class with a non-virtual destructor, resist the temptation! (Unfortunately, C++ offers no derivation-prevention mechanism akin to Java's final classes or C#'s sealed classes.)

Occasionally it can be convenient to give a class a pure virtual destructor. Recall that pure virtual functions result in *abstract* classes — classes that can't be instantiated (i.e., you can't create objects of that type). Sometimes, however, you have a class that you'd like to be abstract, but you don't have any pure virtual functions. What to do? Well, because an abstract class is intended to be used as a base class, and because a base class should have a virtual destructor, and because a pure virtual function yields an abstract class, the solution is simple: declare a pure virtual destructor in the class you want to be abstract. Here's an example:

```
class AWOV {                       // AWOV = "Abstract w/o Virtuals"
public:
    virtual ~AWOV() = 0;           // declare pure virtual destructor
};
```

This class has a pure virtual function, so it's abstract, and it has a virtual destructor, so you won't have to worry about the destructor problem. There is one twist, however: you must provide a *definition* for the pure virtual destructor:

```
AWOV::~AWOV() {}                    // definition of pure virtual dtor
```

The way destructors work is that the most derived class's destructor is called first, then the destructor of each base class is called. Compilers will generate a call to ~AWOV from its derived classes' destructors, so you have to be sure to provide a body for the function. If you don't, the linker will complain.

The rule for giving base classes virtual destructors applies only to *polymorphic* base classes — to base classes designed to allow the manipulation of derived class types through base class interfaces. TimeKeeper is a polymorphic base class, because we expect to be able to manipulate AtomicClock and WaterClock objects, even if we have only TimeKeeper pointers to them.

Not all base classes are designed to be used polymorphically. Neither the standard string type, for example, nor the STL container types are designed to be base classes at all, much less polymorphic ones. Some classes are designed to be used as base classes, yet are not designed to be used polymorphically. Such classes — examples include Uncopyable from Item 6 and input_iterator_tag from the standard library (see Item 47) — are not designed to allow the manipulation of derived class objects via base class interfaces. As a result, they don't need virtual destructors.

Things to Remember

✦ Polymorphic base classes should declare virtual destructors. If a class has any virtual functions, it should have a virtual destructor.

✦ Classes not designed to be base classes or not designed to be used polymorphically should not declare virtual destructors.

Item 8: Prevent exceptions from leaving destructors.

C++ doesn't prohibit destructors from emitting exceptions, but it certainly discourages the practice. With good reason. Consider:

```cpp
class Widget {
public:
    ...
    ~Widget() { ... }              // assume this might emit an exception
};

void doSomething()
{
    std::vector<Widget> v;
    ...
}                                  // v is automatically destroyed here
```

When the vector v is destroyed, it is responsible for destroying all the Widgets it contains. Suppose v has ten Widgets in it, and during destruction of the first one, an exception is thrown. The other nine

Widgets still have to be destroyed (otherwise any resources they hold would be leaked), so v should invoke their destructors. But suppose that during those calls, a second Widget destructor throws an exception. Now there are two simultaneously active exceptions, and that's one too many for C++. Depending on the precise conditions under which such pairs of simultaneously active exceptions arise, program execution either terminates or yields undefined behavior. In this example, it yields undefined behavior. It would yield equally undefined behavior using any other standard library container (e.g., list, set), any container in TR1 (see Item 54), or even an array. Not that containers or arrays are required to get into trouble. Premature program termination or undefined behavior can result from destructors emitting exceptions even without using containers and arrays. C++ does *not* like destructors that emit exceptions!

That's easy enough to understand, but what should you do if your destructor needs to perform an operation that may fail by throwing an exception? For example, suppose you're working with a class for database connections:

```
class DBConnection {
public:
  ...
  static DBConnection create();      // function to return
                                     // DBConnection objects; params
                                     // omitted for simplicity

   void close();                     // close connection; throw an
};                                   // exception if closing fails
```

To ensure that clients don't forget to call close on DBConnection objects, a reasonable idea would be to create a resource-managing class for DBConnection that calls close in its destructor. Such resource-managing classes are explored in detail in Chapter 3, but here, it's enough to consider what the destructor for such a class would look like:

```
class DBConn {                       // class to manage DBConnection
public:                              // objects
  ...
  ~DBConn()                          // make sure database connections
  {                                  // are always closed
     db.close();
  }
private:
   DBConnection db;
};
```

That allows clients to program like this:

```
{                                           // open a block

    DBConn dbc(DBConnection::create());     // create DBConnection object
                                            // and turn it over to a DBConn
                                            // object to manage

    ...                                     // use the DBConnection object
                                            // via the DBConn interface

}                                           // at end of block, the DBConn
                                            // object is destroyed, thus
                                            // automatically calling close on
                                            // the DBConnection object
```

This is fine as long as the call to close succeeds, but if the call yields an exception, DBConn's destructor will propagate that exception, i.e., allow it to leave the destructor. That's a problem, because destructors that throw mean trouble.

There are two primary ways to avoid the trouble. DBConn's destructor could:

- **Terminate the program** if close throws, typically by calling abort:

```
DBConn::~DBConn()
{
  try { db.close(); }
  catch (...) {
    make log entry that the call to close failed;
    std::abort();
  }
}
```

This is a reasonable option if the program cannot continue to run after an error is encountered during destruction. It has the advantage that if allowing the exception to propagate from the destructor would lead to undefined behavior, this prevents that from happening. That is, calling abort may forestall undefined behavior.

- **Swallow the exception** arising from the call to close:

```
DBConn::~DBConn()
{
  try { db.close(); }
  catch (...) {
    make log entry that the call to close failed;
  }
}
```

In general, swallowing exceptions is a bad idea, because it suppresses important information — *something failed!* Sometimes, however, swallowing exceptions is preferable to running the risk of premature program termination or undefined behavior. For this to be a viable option, the program must be able to reliably continue execution even after an error has been encountered and ignored.

Neither of these approaches is especially appealing. The problem with both is that the program has no way to react to the condition that led to close throwing an exception in the first place.

A better strategy is to design DBConn's interface so that its clients have an opportunity to react to problems that may arise. For example, DBConn could offer a close function itself, thus giving clients a chance to handle exceptions arising from that operation. It could also keep track of whether its DBConnection had been closed, closing it itself in the destructor if not. That would prevent a connection from leaking. If the call to close were to fail in the DBConnection destructor, however, we'd be back to terminating or swallowing:

```
class DBConn {
public:
  ...
  void close()                              // new function for
  {                                         // client use
    db.close();
    closed = true;
  }

  ~DBConn()
  {
    if (!closed) {
      try {                                 // close the connection
        db.close();                         // if the client didn't
      }
      catch (...) {                         // if closing fails,
        make log entry that call to close failed;   // note that and
        ...                                 // terminate or swallow
      }
    }
  }

private:
  DBConnection db;
  bool closed;
};
```

Moving the responsibility for calling close from DBConn's destructor to DBConn's client (with DBConn's destructor containing a "backup" call) may strike you as an unscrupulous shift of burden. You might even view it as a violation of Item 18's advice to make interfaces easy to use correctly. In fact, it's neither. If an operation may fail by throwing an exception and there may be a need to handle that exception, the exception *has to come from some non-destructor function.* That's because destructors that emit exceptions are dangerous, always running the risk of premature program termination or undefined behavior. In this example, telling clients to call close themselves doesn't impose a burden on them; it gives them an opportunity to deal with errors they would otherwise have no chance to react to. If they don't find that opportunity useful (perhaps because they believe that no error will really occur), they can ignore it, relying on DBConn's destructor to call close for them. If an error occurs at that point — if close *does* throw — they're in no position to complain if DBConn swallows the exception or terminates the program. After all, they had first crack at dealing with the problem, and they chose not to use it.

Things to Remember

✦ Destructors should never emit exceptions. If functions called in a destructor may throw, the destructor should catch any exceptions, then swallow them or terminate the program.

✦ If class clients need to be able to react to exceptions thrown during an operation, the class should provide a regular (i.e., non-destructor) function that performs the operation.

Item 9:   Never call virtual functions during construction or destruction.

I'll begin with the recap: you shouldn't call virtual functions during construction or destruction, because the calls won't do what you think, and if they did, you'd still be unhappy. If you're a recovering Java or C# programmer, pay close attention to this Item, because this is a place where those languages zig, while C++ zags.

Suppose you've got a class hierarchy for modeling stock transactions, e.g., buy orders, sell orders, etc. It's important that such transactions be auditable, so each time a transaction object is created, an appropriate entry needs to be created in an audit log. This seems like a reasonable way to approach the problem:

```
class Transaction {                        // base class for all
public:                                    // transactions
  Transaction();

  virtual void logTransaction() const = 0; // make type-dependent
                                           // log entry

  ...
};
```

```
Transaction::Transaction()                         // implementation of
{                                                  // base class ctor
   ...
   logTransaction();                               // as final action, log this
}                                                  // transaction
class BuyTransaction: public Transaction {         // derived class
public:
   virtual void logTransaction() const;            // how to log trans-
                                                   // actions of this type
   ...

};
class SellTransaction: public Transaction {        // derived class
public:
   virtual void logTransaction() const;            // how to log trans-
                                                   // actions of this type
   ...

};
```

Consider what happens when this code is executed:

```
BuyTransaction b;
```

Clearly a BuyTransaction constructor will be called, but first, a Transaction constructor must be called; base class parts of derived class objects are constructed before derived class parts are. The last line of the Transaction constructor calls the virtual function logTransaction, but this is where the surprise comes in. The version of logTransaction that's called is the one in Transaction, *not* the one in BuyTransaction — even though the type of object being created is BuyTransaction. During base class construction, virtual functions never go down into derived classes. Instead, the object behaves as if it were of the base type. Informally speaking, during base class construction, virtual functions aren't.

There's a good reason for this seemingly counterintuitive behavior. Because base class constructors execute before derived class constructors, derived class data members have not been initialized when base class constructors run. If virtual functions called during base class construction went down to derived classes, the derived class functions would almost certainly refer to local data members, but those data members would not yet have been initialized. That would be a non-stop ticket to undefined behavior and late-night debugging sessions. Calling down to parts of an object that have not yet been initialized is inherently dangerous, so C++ gives you no way to do it.

It's actually more fundamental than that. During base class construction of a derived class object, the type of the object *is* that of the base class. Not only do virtual functions resolve to the base class, but the parts of the language using runtime type information (e.g., dynamic_cast (see Item 27) and typeid) treat the object as a base class type. In our example, while the Transaction constructor is running to initialize the base class part of a BuyTransaction object, the object is of type Transaction. That's how every part of C++ will treat it, and the treatment makes sense: the BuyTransaction-specific parts of the object haven't been initialized yet, so it's safest to treat them as if they didn't exist. An object doesn't become a derived class object until execution of a derived class constructor begins.

The same reasoning applies during destruction. Once a derived class destructor has run, the object's derived class data members assume undefined values, so C++ treats them as if they no longer exist. Upon entry to the base class destructor, the object becomes a base class object, and all parts of C++ — virtual functions, dynamic_casts, etc., — treat it that way.

In the example code above, the Transaction constructor made a direct call to a virtual function, a clear and easy-to-see violation of this Item's guidance. The violation is so easy to see, some compilers issue a warning about it. (Others don't. See Item 53 for a discussion of warnings.) Even without such a warning, the problem would almost certainly become apparent before runtime, because the logTransaction function is pure virtual in Transaction. Unless it had been defined (unlikely, but possible — see Item 34), the program wouldn't link: the linker would be unable to find the necessary implementation of Transaction::logTransaction.

It's not always so easy to detect calls to virtual functions during construction or destruction. If Transaction had multiple constructors, each of which had to perform some of the same work, it would be good software engineering to avoid code replication by putting the common initialization code, including the call to logTransaction, into a private non-virtual initialization function, say, init:

```
class Transaction {
public:
  Transaction()
    { init(); }                              // call to non-virtual...

  virtual void logTransaction() const = 0;

  ...

private:
  void init()
  {
    ...
    logTransaction();                        // ...that calls a virtual!
  }
};
```

This code is conceptually the same as the earlier version, but it's more insidious, because it will typically compile and link without complaint. In this case, because logTransaction is pure virtual in Transaction, most runtime systems will abort the program when the pure virtual is called (typically issuing a message to that effect). However, if logTransaction were a "normal" virtual function (i.e., not pure virtual) with an implementation in Transaction, that version would be called, and the program would merrily trot along, leaving you to figure out why the wrong version of logTransaction was called when a derived class object was created. The only way to avoid this problem is to make sure that none of your constructors or destructors call virtual functions on the object being created or destroyed and that all the functions they call obey the same constraint.

But how *do* you ensure that the proper version of logTransaction is called each time an object in the Transaction hierarchy is created? Clearly, calling a virtual function on the object from the Transaction constructor(s) is the wrong way to do it.

There are different ways to approach this problem. One is to turn logTransaction into a non-virtual function in Transaction, then require that derived class constructors pass the necessary log information to the Transaction constructor. That function can then safely call the non-virtual logTransaction. Like this:

```cpp
class Transaction {
public:
    explicit Transaction(const std::string& logInfo);
    void logTransaction(const std::string& logInfo) const;   // now a non-
                                                             // virtual func
    ...
};

Transaction::Transaction(const std::string& logInfo)
{
    ...
    logTransaction(logInfo);                                 // now a non-
}                                                            // virtual call

class BuyTransaction: public Transaction {
public:
    BuyTransaction( parameters )
        : Transaction(createLogString( parameters ))          // pass log info
        { ... }                                               // to base class
    ...                                                       // constructor
private:
    static std::string createLogString( parameters );
};
```

In other words, since you can't use virtual functions to call down from base classes during construction, you can compensate by having derived classes pass necessary construction information up to base class constructors instead.

In this example, note the use of the (private) static function createLog-String in BuyTransaction. Using a helper function to create a value to pass to a base class constructor is often more convenient (and more readable) than going through contortions in the member initialization list to give the base class what it needs. By making the function static, there's no danger of accidentally referring to the nascent BuyTransaction object's as-yet-uninitialized data members. That's important, because the fact that those data members will be in an undefined state is why calling virtual functions during base class construction and destruction doesn't go down into derived classes in the first place.

Things to Remember

✦ Don't call virtual functions during construction or destruction, because such calls will never go to a more derived class than that of the currently executing constructor or destructor.

Item 10: Have assignment operators return a reference to *this.

One of the interesting things about assignments is that you can chain them together:

```
int x, y, z;
x = y = z = 15;                          // chain of assignments
```

Also interesting is that assignment is right-associative, so the above assignment chain is parsed like this:

```
x = (y = (z = 15));
```

Here, 15 is assigned to z, then the result of that assignment (the updated z) is assigned to y, then the result of that assignment (the updated y) is assigned to x.

The way this is implemented is that assignment returns a reference to its left-hand argument, and that's the convention you should follow when you implement assignment operators for your classes:

```
class Widget {
public:
    ...
```

```
Widget& operator=(const Widget& rhs)    // return type is a reference to
{                                       // the current class
    ...
    return *this;                       // return the left-hand object
}
...
};
```

This convention applies to all assignment operators, not just the standard form shown above. Hence:

```
class Widget {
public:
    ...
    Widget& operator+=(const Widget& rhs)   // the convention applies to
    {                                       // +=, -=, *=, etc.
        ...
        return *this;
    }
    Widget& operator=(int rhs)              // it applies even if the
    {                                       // operator's parameter type
        ...                                 // is unconventional
        return *this;
    }
    ...
};
```

This is only a convention; code that doesn't follow it will compile. However, the convention is followed by all the built-in types as well as by all the types in (or soon to be in — see Item 54) the standard library (e.g., string, vector, complex, tr1::shared_ptr, etc.). Unless you have a good reason for doing things differently, don't.

Things to Remember

✦ Have assignment operators return a reference to *this.

Item 11: Handle assignment to self in operator=.

An assignment to self occurs when an object is assigned to itself:

```
class Widget { ... };
Widget w;
...
w = w;                                  // assignment to self
```

This looks silly, but it's legal, so rest assured that clients will do it. Besides, assignment isn't always so recognizable. For example,

```
a[i] = a[j];                          // potential assignment to self
```

is an assignment to self if i and j have the same value, and

```
*px = *py;                            // potential assignment to self
```

is an assignment to self if px and py happen to point to the same
thing. These less obvious assignments to self are the result of *aliasing*:
having more than one way to refer to an object. In general, code that
operates on references or pointers to multiple objects of the same type
needs to consider that the objects might be the same. In fact, the two
objects need not even be declared to be of the same type if they're from
the same hierarchy, because a base class reference or pointer can
refer or point to an object of a derived class type:

```
class Base { ... };

class Derived: public Base { ... };

void doSomething(const Base& rb,      // rb and *pd might actually be
                 Derived* pd);        // the same object
```

If you follow the advice of Items 13 and 14, you'll always use objects to
manage resources, and you'll make sure that the resource-managing
objects behave well when copied. When that's the case, your assignment operators will probably be self-assignment-safe without your
having to think about it. If you try to manage resources yourself, however (which you'd certainly have to do if you were writing a resource-
managing class), you can fall into the trap of accidentally releasing a
resource before you're done using it. For example, suppose you create
a class that holds a raw pointer to a dynamically allocated bitmap:

```
class Bitmap { ... };

class Widget {
    ...

private:
    Bitmap *pb;                       // ptr to a heap-allocated object
};
```

Here's an implementation of operator= that looks reasonable on the
surface but is unsafe in the presence of assignment to self. (It's also
not exception-safe, but we'll deal with that in a moment.)

```
Widget&
Widget::operator=(const Widget& rhs) // unsafe impl. of operator=
{
    delete pb;                        // stop using current bitmap
    pb = new Bitmap(*rhs.pb);         // start using a copy of rhs's bitmap

    return *this;                     // see Item 10
}
```

The self-assignment problem here is that inside operator=, *this (the target of the assignment) and rhs could be the same object. When they are, the delete not only destroys the bitmap for the current object, it destroys the bitmap for rhs, too. At the end of the function, the Widget — which should not have been changed by the assignment to self — finds itself holding a pointer to a deleted object!

The traditional way to prevent this error is to check for assignment to self via an *identity test* at the top of operator=:

```
Widget& Widget::operator=(const Widget& rhs)
{
    if (this == &rhs) return *this;          // identity test: if a self-assignment,
                                             // do nothing
    delete pb;
    pb = new Bitmap(*rhs.pb);

    return *this;
}
```

This works, but I mentioned above that the previous version of operator= wasn't just self-assignment-unsafe, it was also exception-unsafe, and this version continues to have exception trouble. In particular, if the "new Bitmap" expression yields an exception (either because there is insufficient memory for the allocation or because Bitmap's copy constructor throws one), the Widget will end up holding a pointer to a deleted Bitmap. Such pointers are toxic. You can't safely delete them. You can't even safely read them. About the only safe thing you can do with them is spend lots of debugging energy figuring out where they came from.

Happily, making operator= exception-safe typically renders it self-assignment-safe, too. As a result, it's increasingly common to deal with issues of self-assignment by ignoring them, focusing instead on achieving exception safety. Item 29 explores exception safety in depth, but in this Item, it suffices to observe that in many cases, a careful ordering of statements can yield exception-safe (and self-assignment-safe) code. Here, for example, we just have to be careful not to delete pb until after we've copied what it points to:

```
Widget& Widget::operator=(const Widget& rhs)
{
    Bitmap *pOrig = pb;                      // remember original pb
    pb = new Bitmap(*rhs.pb);                // make pb point to a copy of *pb
    delete pOrig;                            // delete the original pb

    return *this;
}
```

Now, if "new Bitmap" throws an exception, pb (and the Widget it's inside of) remains unchanged. Even without the identity test, this code handles assignment to self, because we make a copy of the original bitmap, delete the original bitmap, then point to the copy we made. It may not be the most efficient way to handle self-assignment, but it does work.

If you're concerned about efficiency, you could put the identity test back at the top of the function. Before doing that, however, ask yourself how often you expect self-assignments to occur, because the test isn't free. It makes the code (both source and object) a bit bigger, and it introduces a branch into the flow of control, both of which can decrease runtime speed. The effectiveness of instruction prefetching, caching, and pipelining can be reduced, for example.

An alternative to manually ordering statements in operator= to make sure the implementation is both exception- and self-assignment-safe is to use the technique known as "copy and swap." This technique is closely associated with exception safety, so it's described in Item 29. However, it's a common enough way to write operator= that it's worth seeing what such an implementation often looks like:

```
class Widget {
  ...
  void swap(Widget& rhs);         // exchange *this's and rhs's data;
  ...                             // see Item 29 for details
};
Widget& Widget::operator=(const Widget& rhs)
{
  Widget temp(rhs);               // make a copy of rhs's data
  swap(temp);                     // swap *this's data with the copy's
  return *this;
}
```

A variation on this theme takes advantage of the facts that (1) a class's copy assignment operator may be declared to take its argument by value and (2) passing something by value makes a *copy* of it (see Item 20):

```
Widget& Widget::operator=(Widget rhs)    // rhs is a copy of the object
{                                        // passed in — note pass by val
  swap(rhs);                             // swap *this's data with
                                         // the copy's
  return *this;
}
```

Personally, I worry that this approach sacrifices clarity at the altar of cleverness, but by moving the copying operation from the body of the function to construction of the parameter, it's a fact that compilers can sometimes generate more efficient code.

Things to Remember

✦ Make sure operator= is well-behaved when an object is assigned to itself. Techniques include comparing addresses of source and target objects, careful statement ordering, and copy-and-swap.

✦ Make sure that any function operating on more than one object behaves correctly if two or more of the objects are the same.

Item 12: Copy all parts of an object.

In well-designed object-oriented systems that encapsulate the internal parts of objects, only two functions copy objects: the aptly named copy constructor and copy assignment operator. We'll call these the *copying functions*. Item 5 observes that compilers will generate the copying functions, if needed, and it explains that the compiler-generated versions do precisely what you'd expect: they copy all the data of the object being copied.

When you declare your own copying functions, you are indicating to compilers that there is something about the default implementations you don't like. Compilers seem to take offense at this, and they retaliate in a curious fashion: they don't tell you when your implementations are almost certainly wrong.

Consider a class representing customers, where the copying functions have been manually written so that calls to them are logged:

```
void logCall(const std::string& funcName);          // make a log entry

class Customer {
public:
    ...
    Customer(const Customer& rhs);
    Customer& operator=(const Customer& rhs);
    ...
private:
    std::string name;
};
```

```
Customer::Customer(const Customer& rhs)
: name(rhs.name)                                  // copy rhs's data
{
  logCall("Customer copy constructor");
}

Customer& Customer::operator=(const Customer& rhs)
{
  logCall("Customer copy assignment operator");

  name = rhs.name;                                // copy rhs's data

  return *this;                                   // see Item 10
}
```

Everything here looks fine, and in fact everything is fine — until another data member is added to Customer:

```
class Date { ... };                               // for dates in time

class Customer {
public:
  ...                                             // as before

private:
  std::string name;
  Date lastTransaction;
};
```

At this point, the existing copying functions are performing a *partial copy*: they're copying the customer's name, but not its lastTransaction. Yet most compilers say nothing about this, not even at maximal warning level (see also Item 53). That's their revenge for your writing the copying functions yourself. You reject the copying functions they'd write, so they don't tell you if your code is incomplete. The conclusion is obvious: if you add a data member to a class, you need to make sure that you update the copying functions, too. (You'll also need to update all the constructors (see Items 4 and 45) as well as any non-standard forms of operator= in the class (Item 10 gives an example). If you forget, compilers are unlikely to remind you.)

One of the most insidious ways this issue can arise is through inheritance. Consider:

```
class PriorityCustomer: public Customer {         // a derived class
public:
  ...
  PriorityCustomer(const PriorityCustomer& rhs);
  PriorityCustomer& operator=(const PriorityCustomer& rhs);
  ...

private:
  int priority;
};
```

```
PriorityCustomer::PriorityCustomer(const PriorityCustomer& rhs)
: priority(rhs.priority)
{
  logCall("PriorityCustomer copy constructor");
}

PriorityCustomer&
PriorityCustomer::operator=(const PriorityCustomer& rhs)
{
  logCall("PriorityCustomer copy assignment operator");

  priority = rhs.priority;

  return *this;
}
```

PriorityCustomer's copying functions look like they're copying every-thing in PriorityCustomer, but look again. Yes, they copy the data mem-ber that PriorityCustomer declares, but every PriorityCustomer also contains a copy of the data members it inherits from Customer, and those data members are not being copied at all! PriorityCustomer's copy constructor specifies no arguments to be passed to its base class con-structor (i.e., it makes no mention of Customer on its member initial-ization list), so the Customer part of the PriorityCustomer object will be initialized by the Customer constructor taking no arguments — by the default constructor. (Assuming it has one. If not, the code won't com-pile.) That constructor will perform a *default* initialization for name and lastTransaction.

The situation is only slightly different for PriorityCustomer's copy assignment operator. It makes no attempt to modify its base class data members in any way, so they'll remain unchanged.

Any time you take it upon yourself to write copying functions for a derived class, you must take care to also copy the base class parts. Those parts are typically private, of course (see Item 22), so you can't access them directly. Instead, derived class copying functions must invoke their corresponding base class functions:

```
PriorityCustomer::PriorityCustomer(const PriorityCustomer& rhs)
: Customer(rhs),                    // invoke base class copy ctor
  priority(rhs.priority)
{
  logCall("PriorityCustomer copy constructor");
}

PriorityCustomer&
PriorityCustomer::operator=(const PriorityCustomer& rhs)
{
  logCall("PriorityCustomer copy assignment operator");

  Customer::operator=(rhs);         // assign base class parts
  priority = rhs.priority;

  return *this;
}
```

The meaning of "copy all parts" in this Item's title should now be clear. When you're writing a copying function, be sure to (1) copy all local data members and (2) invoke the appropriate copying function in all base classes, too.

In practice, the two copying functions will often have similar bodies, and this may tempt you to try to avoid code duplication by having one function call the other. Your desire to avoid code duplication is laudable, but having one copying function call the other is the wrong way to achieve it.

It makes no sense to have the copy assignment operator call the copy constructor, because you'd be trying to construct an object that already exists. This is so nonsensical, there's not even a syntax for it. There are syntaxes that *look* like you're doing it, but you're not; and there are syntaxes that *do* do it in a backwards kind of way, but they corrupt your object under some conditions. So I'm not going to show you any of those syntaxes. Simply accept that having the copy assignment operator call the copy constructor is something you don't want to do.

Trying things the other way around — having the copy constructor call the copy assignment operator — is equally nonsensical. A constructor initializes new objects, but an assignment operator applies only to objects that have already been initialized. Performing an assignment on an object under construction would mean doing something to a not-yet-initialized object that makes sense only for an initialized object. Nonsense! Don't try it.

Instead, if you find that your copy constructor and copy assignment operator have similar code bodies, eliminate the duplication by creating a third member function that both call. Such a function is typically private and is often named init. This strategy is a safe, proven way to eliminate code duplication in copy constructors and copy assignment operators.

Things to Remember

✦ Copying functions should be sure to copy all of an object's data members and all of its base class parts.

✦ Don't try to implement one of the copying functions in terms of the other. Instead, put common functionality in a third function that both call.

Resource Management

A resource is something that, once you're done using it, you need to return to the system. If you don't, bad things happen. In C++ programs, the most commonly used resource is dynamically allocated memory (if you allocate memory and never deallocate it, you've got a memory leak), but memory is only one of many resources you must manage. Other common resources include file descriptors, mutex locks, fonts and brushes in graphical user interfaces (GUIs), database connections, and network sockets. Regardless of the resource, it's important that it be released when you're finished with it.

Trying to ensure this by hand is difficult under any conditions, but when you consider exceptions, functions with multiple return paths, and maintenance programmers modifying software without fully comprehending the impact of their changes, it becomes clear that ad hoc ways of dealing with resource management aren't sufficient.

This chapter begins with a straightforward object-based approach to resource management built on C++'s support for constructors, destructors, and copying operations. Experience has shown that disciplined adherence to this approach can all but eliminate resource management problems. The chapter then moves on to Items dedicated specifically to memory management. These latter Items complement the more general Items that come earlier, because objects that manage memory have to know how to do it properly.

Item 13: Use objects to manage resources.

Suppose we're working with a library for modeling investments (e.g., stocks, bonds, etc.), where the various investment types inherit from a root class Investment:

```
class Investment { ... };          // root class of hierarchy of
                                   // investment types
```

Further suppose that the way the library provides us with specific Investment objects is through a factory function (see Item 7):

```
Investment* createInvestment();   // return ptr to dynamically allocated
                                  // object in the Investment hierarchy;
                                  // the caller must delete it
                                  // (parameters omitted for simplicity)
```

As the comment indicates, callers of createInvestment are responsible for deleting the object that function returns when they are done with it. Consider, then, a function f written to fulfill this obligation:

```
void f()
{
    Investment *pInv = createInvestment();       // call factory function

    ...                                          // use pInv

    delete pInv;                                 // release object
}
```

This looks okay, but there are several ways f could fail to delete the investment object it gets from createInvestment. There might be a premature return statement somewhere inside the "..." part of the function. If such a return were executed, control would never reach the delete statement. A similar situation would arise if the uses of createInvestment and delete were in a loop, and the loop was prematurely exited by a break or goto statement. Finally, some statement inside the "..." might throw an exception. If so, control would again not get to the delete. Regardless of how the delete were to be skipped, we'd leak not only the memory containing the investment object but also any resources held by that object.

Of course, careful programming could prevent these kinds of errors, but think about how the code might change over time. As the software gets maintained, somebody might add a return or continue statement without fully grasping the repercussions on the rest of the function's resource management strategy. Even worse, the "..." part of f might call a function that never used to throw an exception but suddenly starts doing so after it has been "improved." Relying on f always getting to its delete statement simply isn't viable.

To make sure that the resource returned by createInvestment is always released, we need to put that resource inside an object whose destructor will automatically release the resource when control leaves f. In fact, that's half the idea behind this Item: by putting resources inside objects, we can rely on C++'s automatic destructor invocation to make sure that the resources are released. (We'll discuss the other half of the idea in a moment.)

Many resources are dynamically allocated on the heap, are used only within a single block or function, and should be released when control leaves that block or function. The standard library's auto_ptr is tailor-made for this kind of situation. auto_ptr is a pointer-like object (a *smart pointer*) whose destructor automatically calls delete on what it points to. Here's how to use auto_ptr to prevent f's potential resource leak:

```
void f()
{
    std::auto_ptr<Investment> pInv(createInvestment());   // call factory
                                                          // function

    ...                                                   // use pInv as
                                                          // before

}                                                         // automatically
                                                          // delete pInv via
                                                          // auto_ptr's dtor
```

This simple example demonstrates the two critical aspects of using objects to manage resources:

- **Resources are acquired and immediately turned over to resource-managing objects.** Above, the resource returned by create-Investment is used to initialize the auto_ptr that will manage it. In fact, the idea of using objects to manage resources is often called *Resource Acquisition Is Initialization* (RAII), because it's so common to acquire a resource and initialize a resource-managing object in the same statement. Sometimes acquired resources are *assigned* to resource-managing objects instead of initializing them, but either way, every resource is immediately turned over to a resource-managing object at the time the resource is acquired.

- **Resource-managing objects use their destructors to ensure that resources are released.** Because destructors are called automatically when an object is destroyed (e.g., when an object goes out of scope), resources are correctly released, regardless of how control leaves a block. Things can get tricky when the act of releasing resources can lead to exceptions being thrown, but that's a matter addressed by Item 8, so we'll not worry about it here.

Because an auto_ptr automatically deletes what it points to when the auto_ptr is destroyed, it's important that there never be more than one auto_ptr pointing to an object. If there were, the object would be deleted more than once, and that would put your program on the fast track to undefined behavior. To prevent such problems, auto_ptrs have an unusual characteristic: copying them (via copy constructor or copy assignment operator) sets them to null, and the copying pointer assumes sole ownership of the resource!

```
std::auto_ptr<Investment>            // pInv1 points to the
    pInv1(createInvestment());       // object returned from
                                     // createInvestment

std::auto_ptr<Investment> pInv2(pInv1);  // pInv2 now points to the
                                         // object; pInv1 is now null

pInv1 = pInv2;                        // now pInv1 points to the
                                     // object, and pInv2 is null
```

This odd copying behavior, plus the underlying requirement that resources managed by auto_ptrs must never have more than one auto_ptr pointing to them, means that auto_ptrs aren't the best way to manage all dynamically allocated resources. For example, STL containers require that their contents exhibit "normal" copying behavior, so containers of auto_ptr aren't allowed.

An alternative to auto_ptr is a *reference-counting smart pointer* (RCSP). An RCSP is a smart pointer that keeps track of how many objects point to a particular resource and automatically deletes the resource when nobody is pointing to it any longer. As such, RCSPs offer behavior that is similar to that of garbage collection. Unlike garbage collection, however, RCSPs can't break cycles of references (e.g., two otherwise unused objects that point to one another).

TR1's tr1::shared_ptr (see Item 54) is an RCSP, so you could write f this way:

```
void f()
{
    ...
    std::tr1::shared_ptr<Investment>
        pInv(createInvestment());        // call factory function

    ...                                  // use pInv as before

}                                        // automatically delete
                                         // pInv via shared_ptr's dtor
```

This code looks almost the same as that employing auto_ptr, but copying shared_ptrs behaves much more naturally:

```
void f()
{
    ...
    std::tr1::shared_ptr<Investment>       // pInv1 points to the
        pInv1(createInvestment());         // object returned from
                                           // createInvestment
```

```
std::tr1::shared_ptr<Investment>        // both pInv1 and pInv2 now
   pInv2(pInv1);                        // point to the object

pInv1 = pInv2;                          // ditto — nothing has
                                        // changed

   ...                                  // pInv1 and pInv2 are
}                                       // destroyed, and the
                                        // object they point to is
                                        // automatically deleted
```

Because copying tr1::shared_ptrs works "as expected," they can be used in STL containers and other contexts where auto_ptr's unorthodox copying behavior is inappropriate.

Don't be misled, though. This Item isn't about auto_ptr, tr1::shared_ptr, or any other kind of smart pointer. It's about the importance of using objects to manage resources. auto_ptr and tr1::shared_ptr are just examples of objects that do that. (For more information on tr1:shared_ptr, consult Items 14, 18, and 54.)

Both auto_ptr and tr1::shared_ptr use delete in their destructors, not delete []. (Item 16 describes the difference.) That means that using auto_ptr or tr1::shared_ptr with dynamically allocated arrays is a bad idea, though, regrettably, one that will compile:

```
std::auto_ptr<std::string>              // bad idea! the wrong
   aps(new std::string[10]);            // delete form will be used

std::tr1::shared_ptr<int> spi(new int[1024]);   // same problem
```

You may be surprised to discover that there is nothing like auto_ptr or tr1::shared_ptr for dynamically allocated arrays in C++, not even in TR1. That's because vector and string can almost always replace dynamically allocated arrays. If you still think it would be nice to have auto_ptr- and tr1::shared_ptr-like classes for arrays, look to Boost (see Item 55). There you'll be pleased to find the boost::scoped_array and boost::shared_array classes that offer the behavior you're looking for.

This Item's guidance to use objects to manage resources suggests that if you're releasing resources manually (e.g., using delete other than in a resource-managing class), you're doing something wrong. Pre-canned resource-managing classes like auto_ptr and tr1::shared_ptr often make following this Item's advice easy, but sometimes you're using a resource where these pre-fab classes don't do what you need. When that's the case, you'll need to craft your own resource-managing classes. That's not terribly difficult to do, but it does involve some subtleties you'll need to consider. Those considerations are the topic of Items 14 and 15.

As a final comment, I have to point out that createInvestment's raw pointer return type is an invitation to a resource leak, because it's so easy for callers to forget to call delete on the pointer they get back. (Even if they use an auto_ptr or tr1::shared_ptr to perform the delete, they still have to remember to store createInvestment's return value in a smart pointer object.) Combatting that problem calls for an interface modification to createInvestment, a topic I address in Item 18.

Things to Remember

+ To prevent resource leaks, use RAII objects that acquire resources in their constructors and release them in their destructors.

+ Two commonly useful RAII classes are tr1::shared_ptr and auto_ptr. tr1::shared_ptr is usually the better choice, because its behavior when copied is intuitive. Copying an auto_ptr sets it to null.

Item 14: Think carefully about copying behavior in resource-managing classes.

Item 13 introduces the idea of *Resource Acquisition Is Initialization* (RAII) as the backbone of resource-managing classes, and it describes how auto_ptr and tr1::shared_ptr are manifestations of this idea for heap-based resources. Not all resources are heap-based, however, and for such resources, smart pointers like auto_ptr and tr1::shared_ptr are generally inappropriate as resource handlers. That being the case, you're likely to find yourself needing to create your own resource-managing classes from time to time.

For example, suppose you're using a C API to manipulate mutex objects of type Mutex offering functions lock and unlock:

```
void lock(Mutex *pm);          // lock mutex pointed to by pm
void unlock(Mutex *pm);        // unlock the mutex
```

To make sure that you never forget to unlock a Mutex you've locked, you'd like to create a class to manage locks. The basic structure of such a class is dictated by the RAII principle that resources are acquired during construction and released during destruction:

```
class Lock {
public:
    explicit Lock(Mutex *pm)
    : mutexPtr(pm)
    { lock(mutexPtr); }                    // acquire resource

    ~Lock() { unlock(mutexPtr); }          // release resource

private:
    Mutex *mutexPtr;
};
```

Clients use Lock in the conventional RAII fashion:

```
Mutex m;                              // define the mutex you need to use

...

{                                     // create block to define critical section
    Lock ml(&m);                      // lock the mutex

    ...                               // perform critical section operations

}                                     // automatically unlock mutex at end
                                      // of block
```

This is fine, but what should happen if a Lock object is copied?

```
Lock ml1(&m);                         // lock m
Lock ml2(ml1);                        // copy ml1 to ml2 — what should
                                      // happen here?
```

This is a specific example of a more general question, one that every RAII class author must confront: what should happen when an RAII object is copied? Most of the time, you'll want to choose one of the following possibilities:

- **Prohibit copying.** In many cases, it makes no sense to allow RAII objects to be copied. This is likely to be true for a class like Lock, because it rarely makes sense to have "copies" of synchronization primitives. When copying makes no sense for an RAII class, you should prohibit it. Item 6 explains how to do that: declare the copying operations private. For Lock, that could look like this:

  ```
  class Lock: private Uncopyable {     // prohibit copying — see
  public:                              // Item 6

      ...                              // as before

  };
  ```

- **Reference-count the underlying resource.** Sometimes it's desirable to hold on to a resource until the last object using it has been destroyed. When that's the case, copying an RAII object should increment the count of the number of objects referring to the resource. This is the meaning of "copy" used by tr1::shared_ptr.

  Often, RAII classes can implement reference-counting copying behavior by containing a tr1::shared_ptr data member. For example, if Lock wanted to employ reference counting, it could change the type of mutexPtr from Mutex* to tr1::shared_ptr<Mutex>. Unfortunately, tr1::shared_ptr's default behavior is to delete what it points to when the reference count goes to zero, and that's not what we want. When we're done with a Mutex, we want to unlock it, not delete it.

Fortunately, tr1::shared_ptr allows specification of a "deleter" — a function or function object to be called when the reference count goes to zero. (This functionality does not exist for auto_ptr, which *always* deletes its pointer.) The deleter is an optional second parameter to the tr1::shared_ptr constructor, so the code would look like this:

```
class Lock {
public:
    explicit Lock(Mutex *pm)         // init shared_ptr with the Mutex
    : mutexPtr(pm, unlock)           // to point to and the unlock func
    {                                // as the deleter

        lock(mutexPtr.get());        // see Item 15 for info on "get"
    }
private:
    std::tr1::shared_ptr<Mutex> mutexPtr;    // use shared_ptr
};                                           // instead of raw pointer
```

In this example, notice how the Lock class no longer declares a destructor. That's because there's no need to. Item 5 explains that a class's destructor (regardless of whether it is compiler-generated or user-defined) automatically invokes the destructors of the class's non-static data members. In this example, that's mutexPtr. But mutexPtr's destructor will automatically call the tr1::shared_ptr's deleter — unlock, in this case — when the mutex's reference count goes to zero. (People looking at the class's source code would probably appreciate a comment indicating that you didn't forget about destruction, you're just relying on the default compiler-generated behavior.)

- **Copy the underlying resource.** Sometimes you can have as many copies of a resource as you like, and the only reason you need a resource-managing class is to make sure that each copy is released when you're done with it. In that case, copying the resource-managing object should also copy the resource it wraps. That is, copying a resource-managing object performs a "deep copy."

Some implementations of the standard string type consist of pointers to heap memory, where the characters making up the string are stored. Objects of such strings contain a pointer to the heap memory. When a string object is copied, a copy is made of both the pointer and the memory it points to. Such strings exhibit deep copying.

- **Transfer ownership of the underlying resource.** On rare occasion, you may wish to make sure that only one RAII object refers to a raw resource and that when the RAII object is copied, owner-ship of the resource is transferred from the copied object to the copying object. As explained in Item 13, this is the meaning of "copy" used by auto_ptr.

The copying functions (copy constructor and copy assignment opera-tor) may be generated by compilers, so unless the compiler-generated versions will do what you want (Item 5 explains the default behavior), you'll need to write them yourself. In some cases, you'll also want to support generalized versions of these functions. Such versions are described in Item 45.

Things to Remember

✦ Copying an RAII object entails copying the resource it manages, so the copying behavior of the resource determines the copying behav-ior of the RAII object.

✦ Common RAII class copying behaviors are disallowing copying and performing reference counting, but other behaviors are possible.

Item 15: Provide access to raw resources in resource-managing classes.

Resource-managing classes are wonderful. They're your bulwark against resource leaks, the absence of such leaks being a fundamen-tal characteristic of well-designed systems. In a perfect world, you'd rely on such classes for all your interactions with resources, never sullying your hands with direct access to raw resources. But the world is not perfect. Many APIs refer to resources directly, so unless you plan to foreswear use of such APIs (something that's rarely practical), you'll have to bypass resource-managing objects and deal with raw resources from time to time.

For example, Item 13 introduces the idea of using smart pointers like auto_ptr or tr1::shared_ptr to hold the result of a call to a factory func-tion like createInvestment:

```
std::tr1::shared_ptr<Investment> pInv(createInvestment());    // from Item 13
```

Suppose that a function you'd like to use when working with Invest-ment objects is this:

```
int daysHeld(const Investment *pi);          // return number of days
                                             // investment has been held
```

You'd like to call it like this,

```
int days = daysHeld(pInv);                      // error!
```

but the code won't compile: daysHeld wants a raw Investment* pointer, but you're passing an object of type tr1::shared_ptr<Investment>.

You need a way to convert an object of the RAII class (in this case, tr1::shared_ptr) into the raw resource it contains (e.g., the underlying Investment*). There are two general ways to do it: explicit conversion and implicit conversion.

tr1::shared_ptr and auto_ptr both offer a get member function to perform an explicit conversion, i.e., to return (a copy of) the raw pointer inside the smart pointer object:

```
int days = daysHeld(pInv.get());                // fine, passes the raw pointer
                                                // in pInv to daysHeld
```

Like virtually all smart pointer classes, tr1::shared_ptr and auto_ptr also overload the pointer dereferencing operators (operator-> and operator*), and this allows implicit conversion to the underlying raw pointers:

```
class Investment {                              // root class for a hierarchy
public:                                         // of investment types
  bool isTaxFree() const;

  ...
};

Investment* createInvestment();                 // factory function

std::tr1::shared_ptr<Investment>                // have tr1::shared_ptr
  pi1(createInvestment());                      // manage a resource

bool taxable1 = !(pi1->isTaxFree());            // access resource
                                                // via operator->

...

std::auto_ptr<Investment> pi2(createInvestment());  // have auto_ptr
                                                    // manage a
                                                    // resource

bool taxable2 = !((*pi2).isTaxFree());          // access resource
                                                // via operator*

...
```

Because it is sometimes necessary to get at the raw resource inside an RAII object, some RAII class designers grease the skids by offering an implicit conversion function. For example, consider this RAII class for fonts that are native to a C API:

```
FontHandle getFont();                           // from C API — params omitted
                                                // for simplicity

void releaseFont(FontHandle fh);                // from the same C API
```

```
class Font {                              // RAII class
public:
    explicit Font(FontHandle fh)          // acquire resource;
    : f(fh)                               // use pass-by-value, because the
    {}                                    // C API does

    ~Font() { releaseFont(f); }           // release resource

    ...                                   // handle copying (see Item 14)
private:
    FontHandle f;                         // the raw font resource
};
```

Assuming there's a large font-related C API that deals entirely with FontHandles, there will be a frequent need to convert from Font objects to FontHandles. The Font class could offer an explicit conversion function such as get:

```
class Font {
public:
    ...
    FontHandle get() const { return f; }    // explicit conversion function
    ...
};
```

Unfortunately, this would require that clients call get every time they want to communicate with the API:

```
void changeFontSize(FontHandle f, int newSize);      // from the C API

Font f(getFont());
int newFontSize;

...

changeFontSize(f.get(), newFontSize);                // explicitly convert
                                                     // Font to FontHandle
```

Some programmers might find the need to explicitly request such conversions off-putting enough to avoid using the class. That, in turn, would increase the chances of leaking fonts, the very thing the Font class is designed to prevent.

The alternative is to have Font offer an implicit conversion function to its FontHandle:

```
class Font {
public:
    ...
    operator FontHandle() const          // implicit conversion function
    { return f; }
    ...
};
```

That makes calling into the C API easy and natural:

```
Font f(getFont());
int newFontSize;

...

changeFontSize(f, newFontSize);        // implicitly convert Font
                                       // to FontHandle
```

The downside is that implicit conversions increase the chance of errors. For example, a client might accidently create a FontHandle when a Font was intended:

```
Font f1(getFont());

...

FontHandle f2 = f1;                     // oops! meant to copy a Font
                                        // object, but instead implicitly
                                        // converted f1 into its underlying
                                        // FontHandle, then copied that
```

Now the program has a FontHandle being managed by the Font object f1, but the FontHandle is also available for direct use as f2. That's almost never good. For example, when f1 is destroyed, the font will be released, and f2 will dangle.

The decision about whether to offer explicit conversion from an RAII class to its underlying resource (e.g., via a get member function) or whether to allow implicit conversion is one that depends on the specific task the RAII class is designed to perform and the circumstances in which it is intended to be used. The best design is likely to be the one that adheres to Item 18's advice to make interfaces easy to use correctly and hard to use incorrectly. Often, an explicit conversion function like get is the preferable path, because it minimizes the chances of unintended type conversions. Sometime, however, the naturalness of use arising from implicit type conversions will tip the scales in that direction.

It may have occurred to you that functions returning the raw resource inside an RAII class are contrary to encapsulation. That's true, but it's not the design disaster it may at first appear. RAII classes don't exist to encapsulate something; they exist to ensure that a particular action — resource release — takes place. If desired, encapsulation of the resource can be layered on top of this primary functionality, but it's not necessary. Furthermore, some RAII classes combine true encapsulation of implementation with very loose encapsulation of the underlying resource. For example, tr1::shared_ptr encapsulates all its reference-counting machinery, but it still offers easy access to the raw pointer it contains. Like most well-designed classes, it hides what clients don't need to see, but it makes available those things that clients honestly need to access.

Things to Remember

✦ APIs often require access to raw resources, so each RAII class should offer a way to get at the resource it manages.

✦ Access may be via explicit conversion or implicit conversion. In general, explicit conversion is safer, but implicit conversion is more convenient for clients.

Item 16: Use the same form in corresponding uses of new and delete.

What's wrong with this picture?

```
std::string *stringArray = new std::string[100];

...

delete stringArray;
```

Everything appears to be in order. The new is matched with a delete. Still, something is quite wrong. The program's behavior is undefined. At the very least, 99 of the 100 string objects pointed to by stringArray are unlikely to be properly destroyed, because their destructors will probably never be called.

When you employ a *new expression* (i.e., dynamic creation of an object via a use of new), two things happen. First, memory is allocated (via a function named operator new — see Items 49 and 51). Second, one or more constructors are called for that memory. When you employ a *delete expression* (i.e., use delete), two other things happen: one or more destructors are called for the memory, then the memory is deallocated (via a function named operator delete — see Item 51). The big question for delete is this: *how many* objects reside in the memory being deleted? The answer to that determines how many destructors must be called.

Actually, the question is simpler: does the pointer being deleted point to a single object or to an array of objects? It's a critical question, because the memory layout for single objects is generally different from the memory layout for arrays. In particular, the memory for an array usually includes the size of the array, thus making it easy for delete to know how many destructors to call. The memory for a single object lacks this information. You can think of the different layouts as looking like this, where n is the size of the array:

Single Object	Object

Array	n	Object	Object	Object	...

This is just an example, of course. Compilers aren't required to implement things this way, though many do.

When you use delete on a pointer, the only way for delete to know whether the array size information is there is for you to tell it. If you use brackets in your use of delete, delete assumes an array is pointed to. Otherwise, it assumes that a single object is pointed to:

```
std::string *stringPtr1 = new std::string;

std::string *stringPtr2 = new std::string[100];

...

delete stringPtr1;               // delete an object
delete [] stringPtr2;            // delete an array of objects
```

What would happen if you used the "[]" form on stringPtr1? The result is undefined, but it's unlikely to be pretty. Assuming the layout above, delete would read some memory and interpret what it read as an array size, then start invoking that many destructors, oblivious to the fact that the memory it's working on not only isn't in the array, it's also probably not holding objects of the type it's busy destructing.

What would happen if you didn't use the "[]" form on stringPtr2? Well, that's undefined too, but you can see how it would lead to too few destructors being called. Furthermore, it's undefined (and sometimes harmful) for built-in types like ints, too, even though such types lack destructors.

The rule is simple: if you use [] in a new expression, you must use [] in the corresponding delete expression. If you don't use [] in a new expression, don't use [] in the matching delete expression.

This is a particularly important rule to bear in mind when you are writing a class containing a pointer to dynamically allocated memory and also offering multiple constructors, because then you must be careful to use the *same form* of new in all the constructors to initialize the pointer member. If you don't, how will you know what form of delete to use in your destructor?

This rule is also noteworthy for the typedef-inclined, because it means that a typedef's author must document which form of delete should be employed when new is used to conjure up objects of the typedef type. For example, consider this typedef:

```
typedef std::string AddressLines[4];     // a person's address has 4 lines,
                                         // each of which is a string
```

Because AddressLines is an array, this use of new,

```
std::string *pal = new AddressLines;     // note that "new AddressLines"
                                         // returns a string*, just like
                                         // "new string[4]" would
```

must be matched with the *array* form of delete:

```
delete pal;                              // undefined!

delete [] pal;                           // fine
```

To avoid such confusion, abstain from typedefs for array types. That's easy, because the standard C++ library (see Item 54) includes string and vector, and those templates reduce the need for dynamically allocated arrays to nearly zero. Here, for example, AddressLines could be defined to be a vector of strings, i.e., the type vector<string>.

Things to Remember

✦ If you use [] in a new expression, you must use [] in the corresponding delete expression. If you don't use [] in a new expression, you mustn't use [] in the corresponding delete expression.

Item 17: Store newed objects in smart pointers in standalone statements.

Suppose we have a function to reveal our processing priority and a second function to do some processing on a dynamically allocated Widget in accord with a priority:

```
int priority();

void processWidget(std::tr1::shared_ptr<Widget> pw, int priority);
```

Mindful of the wisdom of using objects to manage resources (see Item 13), processWidget uses a smart pointer (here, a tr1::shared_ptr) for the dynamically allocated Widget it processes.

Consider now a call to processWidget:

```
processWidget(new Widget, priority());
```

Wait, don't consider that call. It won't compile. tr1::shared_ptr's constructor taking a raw pointer is explicit, so there's no implicit conversion from the raw pointer returned by the expression "new Widget" to the tr1::shared_ptr required by processWidget. The following code, however, will compile:

```
processWidget(std::tr1::shared_ptr<Widget>(new Widget), priority());
```

Surprisingly, although we're using object-managing resources everywhere here, this call may leak resources. It's illuminating to see how.

Before compilers can generate a call to processWidget, they have to evaluate the arguments being passed as its parameters. The second argument is just a call to the function priority, but the first argument, ("std::tr1::shared_ptr<Widget>(new Widget)") consists of two parts:

- Execution of the expression "new Widget".

- A call to the tr1::shared_ptr constructor.

Before processWidget can be called, then, compilers must generate code to do these three things:

- Call priority.

- Execute "new Widget".

- Call the tr1::shared_ptr constructor.

C++ compilers are granted considerable latitude in determining the order in which these things are to be done. (This is different from the way languages like Java and C# work, where function parameters are always evaluated in a particular order.) The "new Widget" expression must be executed before the tr1::shared_ptr constructor can be called, because the result of the expression is passed as an argument to the tr1::shared_ptr constructor, but the call to priority can be performed first, second, or third. If compilers choose to perform it second (something that may allow them to generate more efficient code), we end up with this sequence of operations:

1. Execute "new Widget".

2. Call priority.

3. Call the tr1::shared_ptr constructor.

But consider what will happen if the call to priority yields an exception. In that case, the pointer returned from "new Widget" will be lost, because it won't have been stored in the tr1::shared_ptr we were expecting would guard against resource leaks. A leak in the call to process-Widget can arise because an exception can intervene between the time a resource is created (via "new Widget") and the time that resource is turned over to a resource-managing object.

The way to avoid problems like this is simple: use a separate state-ment to create the Widget and store it in a smart pointer, then pass the smart pointer to processWidget:

```
std::tr1::shared_ptr<Widget> pw(new Widget);   // store newed object
                                               // in a smart pointer in a
                                               // standalone statement

processWidget(pw, priority());                 // this call won't leak
```

This works because compilers are given less leeway in reordering operations *across* statements than *within* them. In this revised code, the "new Widget" expression and the call to the tr1::shared_ptr construc-tor are in a different statement from the one calling priority, so compil-ers are not allowed to move the call to priority between them.

Things to Remember

✦ Store newed objects in smart pointers in standalone statements. Failure to do this can lead to subtle resource leaks when exceptions are thrown.

Designs and Declarations

Software designs — approaches to getting the software to do what you want it to do — typically begin as fairly general ideas, but they eventually become detailed enough to allow for the development of specific interfaces. These interfaces must then be translated into C++ declarations. In this chapter, we attack the problem of designing and declaring good C++ interfaces. We begin with perhaps the most important guideline about designing interfaces of any kind: that they should be easy to use correctly and hard to use incorrectly. That sets the stage for a number of more specific guidelines addressing a wide range of topics, including correctness, efficiency, encapsulation, maintainability, extensibility, and conformance to convention.

The material that follows isn't everything you need to know about good interface design, but it highlights some of the most important considerations, warns about some of the most frequent errors, and provides solutions to problems often encountered by class, function, and template designers.

Item 18: Make interfaces easy to use correctly and hard to use incorrectly.

C++ is awash in interfaces. Function interfaces. Class interfaces. Template interfaces. Each interface is a means by which clients interact with your code. Assuming you're dealing with reasonable people, those clients are trying to do a good job. They *want* to use your interfaces correctly. That being the case, if they use one incorrectly, your interface is at least partially to blame. Ideally, if an attempted use of an interface won't do what the client expects, the code won't compile; and if the code does compile, it will do what the client wants.

Developing interfaces that are easy to use correctly and hard to use incorrectly requires that you consider the kinds of mistakes that clients might make. For example, suppose you're designing the constructor for a class representing dates in time:

```
class Date {
public:
   Date(int month, int day, int year);
   ...
};
```

At first glance, this interface may seem reasonable (at least in the USA), but there are at least two errors that clients might easily make. First, they might pass parameters in the wrong order:

```
Date d(30, 3, 1995);          // Oops! Should be "3, 30" , not "30, 3"
```

Second, they might pass an invalid month or day number:

```
Date d(3, 40, 1995);          // Oops! Should be "3, 30" , not "3, 40"
```

(This last example may look silly, but remember that on a keyboard, 4 is next to 3. Such "off by one" typing errors are not uncommon.)

Many client errors can be prevented by the introduction of new types. Indeed, the type system is your primary ally in preventing undesirable code from compiling. In this case, we can introduce simple wrapper types to distinguish days, months, and years, then use these types in the Date constructor:

```
struct Day {              struct Month {             struct Year {
   explicit Day(int d)       explicit Month(int m)      explicit Year(int y)
   : val(d) {}               : val(m) {}                : val(y){}

   int val;                  int val;                   int val;
};                        };                         };

class Date {
public:
   Date(const Month& m, const Day& d, const Year& y);
   ...
};
```

```
Date d(30, 3, 1995);                        // error! wrong types
Date d(Day(30), Month(3), Year(1995));      // error! wrong types
Date d(Month(3), Day(30), Year(1995));      // okay, types are correct
```

Making Day, Month, and Year full-fledged classes with encapsulated data would be better than the simple use of structs above (see Item 22), but even structs suffice to demonstrate that the judicious introduction of new types can work wonders for the prevention of interface usage errors.

Once the right types are in place, it can sometimes be reasonable to restrict the values of those types. For example, there are only 12 valid month values, so the Month type should reflect that. One way to do this would be to use an enum to represent the month, but enums are not as type-safe as we might like. For example, enums can be used like ints (see Item 2). A safer solution is to predefine the set of all valid Months:

```
class Month {
public:
    static Month Jan() { return Month(1); }     // functions returning all valid
    static Month Feb() { return Month(2); }     // Month values; see below for
    ...                                         // why these are functions, not
    static Month Dec() { return Month(12); }    // objects

    ...                                         // other member functions

private:
    explicit Month(int m);                      // prevent creation of new
                                                // Month values

    ...                                         // month-specific data
};

Date d(Month::Mar(), Day(30), Year(1995));
```

If the idea of using functions instead of objects to represent specific months strikes you as odd, it may be because you have forgotten that reliable initialization of non-local static objects can be problematic. Item 4 can refresh your memory.

Another way to prevent likely client errors is to restrict what can be done with a type. A common way to impose restrictions is to add const. For example, Item 3 explains how const-qualifying the return type from operator* can prevent clients from making this error for user-defined types:

```
if (a * b = c) ...                          // oops, meant to do a comparison!
```

In fact, this is just a manifestation of another general guideline for making types easy to use correctly and hard to use incorrectly: unless there's a good reason not to, have your types behave consistently with the built-in types. Clients already know how types like int behave, so you should strive to have your types behave the same way whenever reasonable. For example, assignment to a*b isn't legal if a and b are ints, so unless there's a good reason to diverge from this behavior, it should be illegal for your types, too. When in doubt, do as the ints do.

The real reason for avoiding gratuitous incompatibilities with the built-in types is to offer interfaces that behave consistently. Few characteristics lead to interfaces that are easy to use correctly as much as consistency, and few characteristics lead to aggravating interfaces as much as inconsistency. The interfaces to STL containers are largely (though not perfectly) consistent, and this helps make them fairly easy to use. For example, every STL container has a member function named size that tells how many objects are in the container. Contrast this with Java, where you use the length *property* for arrays, the length *method* for Strings, and the size *method* for Lists; and with .NET, where Arrays have a property named Length, while ArrayLists have a property named Count. Some developers think that integrated development environments (IDEs) render such inconsistencies unimportant, but they are mistaken. Inconsistency imposes mental friction into a developer's work that no IDE can fully remove.

Any interface that requires that clients remember to do something is prone to incorrect use, because clients can forget to do it. For example, Item 13 introduces a factory function that returns pointers to dynamically allocated objects in an Investment hierarchy:

```
Investment* createInvestment();    // from Item 13; parameters omitted
                                   // for simplicity
```

To avoid resource leaks, the pointers returned from createInvestment must eventually be deleted, but that creates an opportunity for at least two types of client errors: failure to delete a pointer, and deletion of the same pointer more than once.

Item 13 shows how clients can store createInvestment's return value in a smart pointer like auto_ptr or tr1::shared_ptr, thus turning over to the smart pointer the responsibility for using delete. But what if clients forget to use the smart pointer? In many cases, a better interface decision would be to preempt the problem by having the factory function return a smart pointer in the first place:

```
std::tr1::shared_ptr<Investment> createInvestment();
```

This essentially forces clients to store the return value in a tr1::shared_ptr, all but eliminating the possibility of forgetting to delete the underlying Investment object when it's no longer being used.

In fact, returning a tr1::shared_ptr makes it possible for an interface designer to prevent a host of other client errors regarding resource release, because, as Item 14 explains, tr1::shared_ptr allows a resource-release function — a "deleter" — to be bound to the smart pointer when the smart pointer is created. (auto_ptr has no such capability.)

Suppose clients who get an Investment* pointer from createInvestment are expected to pass that pointer to a function called getRidOfInvestment instead of using delete on it. Such an interface would open the door to a new kind of client error, one where clients use the wrong resource-destruction mechanism (i.e., delete instead of getRidOfInvest-ment). The implementer of createInvestment can forestall such prob-lems by returning a tr1::shared_ptr with getRidOfInvestment bound to it as its deleter.

tr1::shared_ptr offers a constructor taking two arguments: the pointer to be managed and the deleter to be called when the reference count goes to zero. This suggests that the way to create a null tr1::shared_ptr with getRidOfInvestment as its deleter is this:

```
std::tr1::shared_ptr<Investment>      // attempt to create a null
    pInv(0, getRidOfInvestment);      // shared_ptr with a custom deleter;
                                      // this won't compile
```

Alas, this isn't valid C++. The tr1::shared_ptr constructor insists on its first parameter being a *pointer*, and 0 isn't a pointer, it's an int. Yes, it's *convertible* to a pointer, but that's not good enough in this case; tr1::shared_ptr insists on an actual pointer. A cast solves the problem:

```
std::tr1::shared_ptr<Investment>            // create a null shared_ptr with
    pInv( static_cast<Investment*>(0),      // getRidOfInvestment as its
        getRidOfInvestment);                // deleter; see Item 27 for info on
                                            // static_cast
```

This means that the code for implementing createInvestment to return a tr1::shared_ptr with getRidOfInvestment as its deleter would look some-thing like this:

```
std::tr1::shared_ptr<Investment> createInvestment()
{
    std::tr1::shared_ptr<Investment> retVal(static_cast<Investment*>(0),
                                            getRidOfInvestment);

    retVal = ... ;                    // make retVal point to the
                                      // correct object

    return retVal;
}
```

Of course, if the raw pointer to be managed by retVal could be deter-mined prior to creating retVal, it would be better to pass the raw pointer to retVal's constructor instead of initializing retVal to null and then making an assignment to it. For details on why, consult Item 26.

An especially nice feature of tr1::shared_ptr is that it automatically uses its per-pointer deleter to eliminate another potential client error, the "cross-DLL problem." This problem crops up when an object is cre-ated using new in one dynamically linked library (DLL) but is deleted in a different DLL. On many platforms, such cross-DLL new/delete pairs lead to runtime errors. tr1::shared_ptr avoids the problem, because its default deleter uses delete from the same DLL where the tr1::shared_ptr is created. This means, for example, that if Stock is a class derived from Investment and createInvestment is implemented like this,

```
std::tr1::shared_ptr<Investment> createInvestment()
{
    return std::tr1::shared_ptr<Investment>(new Stock);
}
```

the returned tr1::shared_ptr can be passed among DLLs without concern for the cross-DLL problem. The tr1::shared_ptrs pointing to the Stock keep track of which DLL's delete should be used when the reference count for the Stock becomes zero.

This Item isn't about tr1::shared_ptr — it's about making interfaces easy to use correctly and hard to use incorrectly — but tr1::shared_ptr is such an easy way to eliminate some client errors, it's worth an overview of the cost of using it. The most common implementation of tr1::shared_ptr comes from Boost (see Item 55). Boost's shared_ptr is twice the size of a raw pointer, uses dynamically allocated memory for bookkeeping and deleter-specific data, uses a virtual function call when invoking its deleter, and incurs thread synchronization overhead when modifying the reference count in an application it believes is multithreaded. (You can disable multithreading support by defining a preprocessor symbol.) In short, it's bigger than a raw pointer, slower than a raw pointer, and uses auxiliary dynamic memory. In many applications, these additional runtime costs will be unnoticeable, but the reduction in client errors will be apparent to everyone.

Things to Remember

✦ Good interfaces are easy to use correctly and hard to use incorrectly. You should strive for these characteristics in all your interfaces.

✦ Ways to facilitate correct use include consistency in interfaces and behavioral compatibility with built-in types.

✦ Ways to prevent errors include creating new types, restricting operations on types, constraining object values, and eliminating client resource management responsibilities.

✦ tr1::shared_ptr supports custom deleters. This prevents the cross-DLL problem, can be used to automatically unlock mutexes (see Item 14), etc.

Item 19: Treat class design as type design.

In C++, as in other object-oriented programming languages, defining a new class defines a new type. Much of your time as a C++ developer will thus be spent augmenting your type system. This means you're not just a class designer, you're a *type* designer. Overloading functions and operators, controlling memory allocation and deallocation, defining object initialization and finalization — it's all in your hands. You should therefore approach class design with the same care that language designers lavish on the design of the language's built-in types.

Designing good classes is challenging because designing good types is challenging. Good types have a natural syntax, intuitive semantics, and one or more efficient implementations. In C++, a poorly planned class definition can make it impossible to achieve any of these goals. Even the performance characteristics of a class's member functions may be affected by how they are declared.

How, then, do you design effective classes? First, you must understand the issues you face. Virtually every class requires that you confront the following questions, the answers to which often lead to constraints on your design:

- **How should objects of your new type be created and destroyed?** How this is done influences the design of your class's constructors and destructor, as well as its memory allocation and deallocation functions (operator new, operator new[], operator delete, and operator delete[] — see Chapter 8), if you write them.

- **How should object initialization differ from object assignment?** The answer to this question determines the behavior of and the differences between your constructors and your assignment operators. It's important not to confuse initialization with assignment, because they correspond to different function calls (see Item 4).

- **What does it mean for objects of your new type to be passed by value?** Remember, the copy constructor defines how pass-by-value is implemented for a type.

- **What are the restrictions on legal values for your new type?** Usually, only some combinations of values for a class's data members are valid. Those combinations determine the invariants your class will have to maintain. The invariants determine the error checking you'll have to do inside your member functions, especially your constructors, assignment operators, and "setter" functions. It may also affect the exceptions your functions throw and, on the off chance you use them, your functions' exception specifications.

- **Does your new type fit into an inheritance graph?** If you inherit from existing classes, you are constrained by the design of those classes, particularly by whether their functions are virtual or non-virtual (see Items 34 and 36). If you wish to allow other classes to inherit from your class, that affects whether the functions you declare are virtual, especially your destructor (see Item 7).

- **What kind of type conversions are allowed for your new type?** Your type exists in a sea of other types, so should there be conversions between your type and other types? If you wish to allow objects of type T1 to be *implicitly* converted into objects of type T2, you will want to write either a type conversion function in class T1 (e.g., operator T2) or a non-explicit constructor in class T2 that can be called with a single argument. If you wish to allow *explicit* conversions only, you'll want to write functions to perform the conversions, but you'll need to avoid making them type conversion operators or non-explicit constructors that can be called with one argument. (For an example of both implicit and explicit conversion functions, see Item 15.)

- **What operators and functions make sense for the new type?** The answer to this question determines which functions you'll declare for your class. Some functions will be member functions, but some will not (see Items 23, 24, and 46).

- **What standard functions should be disallowed?** Those are the ones you'll need to declare private (see Item 6).

- **Who should have access to the members of your new type?** This question helps you determine which members are public, which are protected, and which are private. It also helps you determine which classes and/or functions should be friends, as well as whether it makes sense to nest one class inside another.

- **What is the "undeclared interface" of your new type?** What kind of guarantees does it offer with respect to performance, exception safety (see Item 29), and resource usage (e.g., locks and dynamic memory)? The guarantees you offer in these areas will impose constraints on your class implementation.

- **How general is your new type?** Perhaps you're not really defining a new type. Perhaps you're defining a whole *family* of types. If so, you don't want to define a new class, you want to define a new class *template*.

- **Is a new type really what you need?** If you're defining a new derived class only so you can add functionality to an existing class, perhaps you'd better achieve your goals by simply defining one or more non-member functions or templates.

These questions are difficult to answer, so defining effective classes can be challenging. Done well, however, user-defined classes in C++ yield types that are at least as good as the built-in types, and that makes all the effort worthwhile.

Things to Remember

✦ Class design is type design. Before defining a new type, be sure to consider all the issues discussed in this Item.

Item 20: Prefer pass-by-reference-to-const to pass-by-value.

By default, C++ passes objects to and from functions by value (a characteristic it inherits from C). Unless you specify otherwise, function parameters are initialized with *copies* of the actual arguments, and function callers get back a *copy* of the value returned by the function. These copies are produced by the objects' copy constructors. This can make pass-by-value an expensive operation. For example, consider the following class hierarchy:

```cpp
class Person {
public:
  Person();                    // parameters omitted for simplicity
  virtual ~Person();           // see Item 7 for why this is virtual
  ...
private:
  std::string name;
  std::string address;
};
class Student: public Person {
public:
  Student();                   // parameters again omitted
  virtual ~Student();
  ...
private:
  std::string schoolName;
  std::string schoolAddress;
};
```

Now consider the following code, in which we call a function, validate-Student, that takes a Student argument (by value) and returns whether it has been validated:

```
bool validateStudent(Student s);          // function taking a Student
                                          // by value

Student plato;                            // Plato studied under Socrates

bool platoIsOK = validateStudent(plato);  // call the function
```

What happens when this function is called?

Clearly, the Student copy constructor is called to initialize the parameter s from plato. Equally clearly, s is destroyed when validateStudent returns. So the parameter-passing cost of this function is one call to the Student copy constructor and one call to the Student destructor.

But that's not the whole story. A Student object has two string objects within it, so every time you construct a Student object you must also construct two string objects. A Student object also inherits from a Person object, so every time you construct a Student object you must also construct a Person object. A Person object has two additional string objects inside it, so each Person construction also entails two more string constructions. The end result is that passing a Student object by value leads to one call to the Student copy constructor, one call to the Person copy constructor, and four calls to the string copy constructor. When the copy of the Student object is destroyed, each constructor call is matched by a destructor call, so the overall cost of passing a Student by value is six constructors and six destructors!

Now, this is correct and desirable behavior. After all, you *want* all your objects to be reliably initialized and destroyed. Still, it would be nice if there were a way to bypass all those constructions and destructions. There is: pass by reference-to-const:

```
bool validateStudent(const Student& s);
```

This is much more efficient: no constructors or destructors are called, because no new objects are being created. The const in the revised parameter declaration is important. The original version of validate-Student took a Student parameter by value, so callers knew that they were shielded from any changes the function might make to the Student they passed in; validateStudent would be able to modify only a *copy* of it. Now that the Student is being passed by reference, it's necessary to also declare it const, because otherwise callers would have to worry about validateStudent making changes to the Student they passed in.

Passing parameters by reference also avoids the *slicing problem*. When a derived class object is passed (by value) as a base class object, the base class copy constructor is called, and the specialized features that make the object behave like a derived class object are "sliced" off. You're left with a simple base class object — little surprise, since a base class constructor created it. This is almost never what you want. For example, suppose you're working on a set of classes for implementing a graphical window system:

```
class Window {
public:
    ...
    std::string name() const;           // return name of window
    virtual void display() const;        // draw window and contents
};

class WindowWithScrollBars: public Window {
public:
    ...
    virtual void display() const;
};
```

All Window objects have a name, which you can get at through the name function, and all windows can be displayed, which you can bring about by invoking the display function. The fact that display is virtual tells you that the way in which simple base class Window objects are displayed is apt to differ from the way in which the fancier Window-WithScrollBars objects are displayed (see Items 34 and 36).

Now suppose you'd like to write a function to print out a window's name and then display the window. Here's the *wrong* way to write such a function:

```
void printNameAndDisplay( Window w)          // incorrect! parameter
{                                             // may be sliced!
    std::cout << w.name();
    w.display();
}
```

Consider what happens when you call this function with a Window-WithScrollBars object:

```
WindowWithScrollBars wwsb;

printNameAndDisplay(wwsb);
```

The parameter w will be constructed — it's passed by value, remember? — as a *Window* object, and all the specialized information that made wwsb act like a WindowWithScrollBars object will be sliced off. Inside printNameAndDisplay, w will always act like an object of class Window (because it *is* an object of class Window), regardless of the type of object passed to the function. In particular, the call to display inside printNameAndDisplay will *always* call Window::display, never Window-WithScrollBars::display.

The way around the slicing problem is to pass w by reference-to-const:

```
void printNameAndDisplay(const Window& w)      // fine, parameter won't
{                                              // be sliced
    std::cout << w.name();
    w.display();
}
```

Now w will act like whatever kind of window is actually passed in.

If you peek under the hood of a C++ compiler, you'll find that references are typically implemented as pointers, so passing something by reference usually means really passing a pointer. As a result, if you have an object of a built-in type (e.g., an int), it's often more efficient to pass it by value than by reference. For built-in types, then, when you have a choice between pass-by-value and pass-by-reference-to-const, it's not unreasonable to choose pass-by-value. This same advice applies to iterators and function objects in the STL, because, by convention, they are designed to be passed by value. Implementers of iterators and function objects are responsible for seeing to it that they are efficient to copy and are not subject to the slicing problem. (This is an example of how the rules change, depending on the part of C++ you are using — see Item 1.)

Built-in types are small, so some people conclude that all small types are good candidates for pass-by-value, even if they're user-defined. This is shaky reasoning. Just because an object is small doesn't mean that calling its copy constructor is inexpensive. Many objects — most STL containers among them — contain little more than a pointer, but copying such objects entails copying everything they point to. That can be *very* expensive.

Even when small objects have inexpensive copy constructors, there can be performance issues. Some compilers treat built-in and user-defined types differently, even if they have the same underlying representation. For example, some compilers refuse to put objects consisting of only a double into a register, even though they happily place naked doubles there on a regular basis. When that kind of thing happens, you can be better off passing such objects by reference, because compilers will certainly put pointers (the implementation of references) into registers.

Another reason why small user-defined types are not necessarily good pass-by-value candidates is that, being user-defined, their size is subject to change. A type that's small now may be bigger in a future release, because its internal implementation may change. Things can even change when you switch to a different C++ implementation. As I write this, for example, some implementations of the standard library's string type are *seven times* as big as others.

In general, the only types for which you can reasonably assume that pass-by-value is inexpensive are built-in types and STL iterator and function object types. For everything else, follow the advice of this Item and prefer pass-by-reference-to-const over pass-by-value.

Things to Remember

✦ Prefer pass-by-reference-to-const over pass-by-value. It's typically more efficient and it avoids the slicing problem.

✦ The rule doesn't apply to built-in types and STL iterator and function object types. For them, pass-by-value is usually appropriate.

Item 21: Don't try to return a reference when you must return an object.

Once programmers grasp the efficiency implications of pass-by-value for objects (see Item 20), many become crusaders, determined to root out the evil of pass-by-value wherever it may hide. Unrelenting in their pursuit of pass-by-reference purity, they invariably make a fatal mistake: they start to pass references to objects that don't exist. This is not a good thing.

Consider a class for representing rational numbers, including a function for multiplying two rationals together:

```
class Rational {
public:
    Rational(int numerator = 0,           // see Item 24 for why this
             int denominator = 1);        // ctor isn't declared explicit

    ...

private:
    int n, d;                             // numerator and denominator
    friend
        const Rational                    // see Item 3 for why the
            operator*(const Rational& lhs,   // return type is const
                      const Rational& rhs);
};
```

This version of operator* is returning its result object by value, and you'd be shirking your professional duties if you failed to worry about the cost of that object's construction and destruction. You don't want to pay for such an object if you don't have to. So the question is this: do you have to pay?

Well, you don't have to if you can return a reference instead. But remember that a reference is just a *name*, a name for some *existing* object. Whenever you see the declaration for a reference, you should immediately ask yourself what it is another name for, because it must be another name for *something*. In the case of operator*, if the function is to return a reference, it must return a reference to some Rational object that already exists and that contains the product of the two objects that are to be multiplied together.

There is certainly no reason to expect that such an object exists prior to the call to operator*. That is, if you have

```
Rational a(1, 2);                    // a = 1/2
Rational b(3, 5);                    // b = 3/5

Rational c = a * b;                  // c should be 3/10
```

it seems unreasonable to expect that there already happens to exist a rational number with the value three-tenths. No, if operator* is to return a reference to such a number, it must create that number object itself.

A function can create a new object in only two ways: on the stack or on the heap. Creation on the stack is accomplished by defining a local variable. Using that strategy, you might try to write operator* this way:

```
const Rational& operator*(const Rational& lhs,      // warning! bad code!
                          const Rational& rhs)
{
    Rational result(lhs.n * rhs.n, lhs.d * rhs.d);
    return result;
}
```

You can reject this approach out of hand, because your goal was to avoid a constructor call, and result will have to be constructed just like any other object. A more serious problem is that this function returns a reference to result, but result is a local object, and local objects are destroyed when the function exits. This version of operator*, then, doesn't return a reference to a Rational — it returns a reference to an *ex*-Rational; a *former* Rational; the empty, stinking, rotting carcass of what *used* to be a Rational but is no longer, because it has been destroyed. Any caller so much as *glancing* at this function's return value would instantly enter the realm of undefined behavior. The fact is, any function returning a reference to a local object is broken. (The same is true for any function returning a pointer to a local object.)

Let us consider, then, the possibility of constructing an object on the heap and returning a reference to it. Heap-based objects come into being through the use of new, so you might write a heap-based operator* like this:

```
const Rational& operator*(const Rational& lhs,     // warning! more bad
                          const Rational& rhs)     // code!
{
    Rational *result = new Rational(lhs.n * rhs.n, lhs.d * rhs.d);
    return *result;
}
```

Well, you *still* have to pay for a constructor call, because the memory allocated by new is initialized by calling an appropriate constructor, but now you have a different problem: who will apply delete to the object conjured up by your use of new?

Even if callers are conscientious and well intentioned, there's not much they can do to prevent leaks in reasonable usage scenarios like this:

```
Rational w, x, y, z;

w = x * y * z;                      // same as operator*(operator*(x, y), z)
```

Here, there are two calls to operator* in the same statement, hence two uses of new that need to be undone with uses of delete. Yet there is no reasonable way for clients of operator* to make those calls, because there's no reasonable way for them to get at the pointers hidden behind the references being returned from the calls to operator*. This is a guaranteed resource leak.

But perhaps you notice that both the on-the-stack and on-the-heap approaches suffer from having to call a constructor for each result returned from operator*. Perhaps you recall that our initial goal was to avoid such constructor invocations. Perhaps you think you know a way to avoid all but one constructor call. Perhaps the following implementation occurs to you, an implementation based on operator* returning a reference to a *static* Rational object, one defined *inside* the function:

```
const Rational& operator*(const Rational& lhs,     // warning! yet more
                          const Rational& rhs)     // bad code!
{
    static Rational result;               // static object to which a
                                          // reference will be returned

    result = ... ;                        // multiply lhs by rhs and put the
                                          // product inside result

    return result;
}
```

Like all designs employing the use of static objects, this one immediately raises our thread-safety hackles, but that's its more obvious weakness. To see its deeper flaw, consider this perfectly reasonable client code:

```
bool operator==(const Rational& lhs,          // an operator==
                const Rational& rhs);         // for Rationals
Rational a, b, c, d;

...

if ((a * b) == (c * d)) {

    do whatever's appropriate when the products are equal;

} else {

    do whatever's appropriate when they're not;

}
```

Guess what? The expression ((a*b) == (c*d)) will *always* evaluate to true, regardless of the values of a, b, c, and d!

This revelation is easiest to understand when the code is rewritten in its equivalent functional form:

```
if (operator==(operator*(a, b), operator*(c, d)))
```

Notice that when operator== is called, there will already be *two* active calls to operator*, each of which will return a reference to the static Rational object inside operator*. Thus, operator== will be asked to compare the value of the static Rational object inside operator* with the value of the static Rational object inside operator*. It would be surprising indeed if they did not compare equal. Always.

This should be enough to convince you that returning a reference from a function like operator* is a waste of time, but some of you are now thinking, "Well, if *one* static isn't enough, maybe a static *array* will do the trick...."

I can't bring myself to dignify this design with example code, but I can sketch why the notion should cause you to blush in shame. First, you must choose n, the size of the array. If n is too small, you may run out of places to store function return values, in which case you'll have gained nothing over the single-static design we just discredited. But if n is too big, you'll decrease the performance of your program, because *every* object in the array will be constructed the first time the function is called. That will cost you n constructors and n destructors[†], even if the function in question is called only once. If "optimization" is the process of improving software performance, this kind of thing should be called "pessimization." Finally, think about how you'd put the val-

---

† The destructors will be called once at program shutdown.

ues you need into the array's objects and what it would cost you to do it. The most direct way to move a value between objects is via assignment, but what is the cost of an assignment? For many types, it's about the same as a call to a destructor (to destroy the old value) plus a call to a constructor (to copy over the new value). But your goal is to avoid the costs of construction and destruction! Face it: this approach just isn't going to pan out. (No, using a vector instead of an array won't improve matters much.)

The right way to write a function that must return a new object is to have that function return a new object. For Rational's operator*, that means either the following code or something essentially equivalent:

```
inline const Rational operator*(const Rational& lhs, const Rational& rhs)
{
    return Rational(lhs.n * rhs.n, lhs.d * rhs.d);
}
```

Sure, you may incur the cost of constructing and destructing operator*'s return value, but in the long run, that's a small price to pay for correct behavior. Besides, the bill that so terrifies you may never arrive. Like all programming languages, C++ allows compiler implementers to apply optimizations to improve the performance of the generated code without changing its observable behavior, and it turns out that in some cases, construction and destruction of operator*'s return value can be safely eliminated. When compilers take advantage of that fact (and compilers often do), your program continues to behave the way it's supposed to, just faster than you expected.

It all boils down to this: when deciding between returning a reference and returning an object, your job is to make the choice that offers correct behavior. Let your compiler vendors wrestle with figuring out how to make that choice as inexpensive as possible.

Things to Remember

✦ Never return a pointer or reference to a local stack object, a reference to a heap-allocated object, or a pointer or reference to a local static object if there is a chance that more than one such object will be needed. (Item 4 provides an example of a design where returning a reference to a local static is reasonable, at least in single-threaded environments.)

Item 22: Declare data members private.

Okay, here's the plan. First, we're going to see why data members shouldn't be public. Then we'll see that all the arguments against public data members apply equally to protected ones. That will lead to the conclusion that data members should be private, and at that point, we'll be done.

So, public data members. Why not?

Let's begin with syntactic consistency (see also Item 18). If data members aren't public, the only way for clients to access an object is via member functions. If everything in the public interface is a function, clients won't have to scratch their heads trying to remember whether to use parentheses when they want to access a member of the class. They'll just do it, because everything is a function. Over the course of a lifetime, that can save a lot of head scratching.

But maybe you don't find the consistency argument compelling. How about the fact that using functions gives you much more precise control over the accessibility of data members? If you make a data member public, everybody has read-write access to it, but if you use functions to get or set its value, you can implement no access, read-only access, and read-write access. Heck, you can even implement write-only access if you want to:

```cpp
class AccessLevels {
public:
    ...
    int getReadOnly() const        { return readOnly; }
    void setReadWrite(int value)   { readWrite = value; }
    int getReadWrite() const       { return readWrite; }
    void setWriteOnly(int value)   { writeOnly = value; }
private:
    int noAccess;                  // no access to this int
    int readOnly;                  // read-only access to this int
    int readWrite;                 // read-write access to this int
    int writeOnly;                 // write-only access to this int
};
```

Such fine-grained access control is important, because many data members *should* be hidden. Rarely does every data member need a getter and setter.

Still not convinced? Then it's time to bring out the big gun: encapsulation. If you implement access to a data member through a function, you can later replace the data member with a computation, and nobody using your class will be any the wiser.

For example, suppose you are writing an application in which auto-mated equipment is monitoring the speed of passing cars. As each car passes, its speed is computed and the value added to a collection of all the speed data collected so far:

```
class SpeedDataCollection {
    ...
public:
    void addValue(int speed);          // add a new data value
    double averageSoFar() const;       // return average speed

    ...
};
```

Now consider the implementation of the member function averageSo-Far. One way to implement it is to have a data member in the class that is a running average of all the speed data so far collected. When-ever averageSoFar is called, it just returns the value of that data mem-ber. A different approach is to have averageSoFar compute its value anew each time it's called, something it could do by examining each data value in the collection.

The first approach (keeping a running average) makes each SpeedData-Collection object bigger, because you have to allocate space for the data members holding the running average, the accumulated total, and the number of data points. However, averageSoFar can be implemented very efficiently; it's just an inline function (see Item 30) that returns the value of the running average. Conversely, computing the average whenever it's requested will make averageSoFar run slower, but each SpeedDataCollection object will be smaller.

Who's to say which is best? On a machine where memory is tight (e.g., an embedded roadside device), and in an application where averages are needed only infrequently, computing the average each time is probably a better solution. In an application where averages are needed frequently, speed is of the essence, and memory is not an issue, keeping a running average will typically be preferable. The important point is that by accessing the average through a member function (i.e., by encapsulating it), you can interchange these different implementations (as well as any others you might think of), and cli-ents will, at most, only have to recompile. (You can eliminate even that inconvenience by following the techniques described in Item 31.)

Hiding data members behind functional interfaces can offer all kinds of implementation flexibility. For example, it makes it easy to notify other objects when data members are read or written, to verify class invariants and function pre- and postconditions, to perform synchronization in threaded environments, etc. Programmers coming to C++ from languages like Delphi and C# will recognize such capabilities as the equivalent of "properties" in these other languages, albeit with the need to type an extra set of parentheses.

The point about encapsulation is more important than it might initially appear. If you hide your data members from your clients (i.e., encapsulate them), you can ensure that class invariants are always maintained, because only member functions can affect them. Furthermore, you reserve the right to change your implementation decisions later. If you don't hide such decisions, you'll soon find that even if you own the source code to a class, your ability to change anything public is extremely restricted, because too much client code will be broken. Public means unencapsulated, and practically speaking, unencapsulated means unchangeable, especially for classes that are widely used. Yet widely used classes are most in need of encapsulation, because they are the ones that can most benefit from the ability to replace one implementation with a better one.

The argument against protected data members is similar. In fact, it's identical, though it may not seem that way at first. The reasoning about syntactic consistency and fine-grained access control is clearly as applicable to protected data as to public, but what about encapsulation? Aren't protected data members more encapsulated than public ones? Practically speaking, the surprising answer is that they are not.

Item 23 explains that something's encapsulation is inversely proportional to the amount of code that might be broken if that something changes. The encapsulatedness of a data member, then, is inversely proportional to the amount of code that might be broken if that data member changes, e.g., if it's removed from the class (possibly in favor of a computation, as in averageSoFar, above).

Suppose we have a public data member, and we eliminate it. How much code might be broken? All the client code that uses it, which is generally an *unknowably large* amount. Public data members are thus completely unencapsulated. But suppose we have a protected data member, and we eliminate it. How much code might be broken now? All the derived classes that use it, which is, again, typically an *unknowably large* amount of code. Protected data members are thus as unencapsulated as public ones, because in both cases, if the data members are changed, an unknowably large amount of client code is broken. This is unintuitive, but as experienced library implementers will tell you, it's still true. Once you've declared a data member public or protected and clients have started using it, it's very hard to change anything about that data member. Too much code has to be rewritten, retested, redocumented, or recompiled. From an encapsulation point of view, there are really only two access levels: private (which offers encapsulation) and everything else (which doesn't).

Things to Remember

✦ Declare data members private. It gives clients syntactically uniform access to data, affords fine-grained access control, allows invariants to be enforced, and offers class authors implementation flexibility.

✦ protected is no more encapsulated than public.

Item 23: Prefer non-member non-friend functions to member functions.

Imagine a class for representing web browsers. Among the many functions such a class might offer are those to clear the cache of downloaded elements, clear the history of visited URLs, and remove all cookies from the system:

```
class WebBrowser {
public:
  ...
  void clearCache();
  void clearHistory();
  void removeCookies();
  ...
};
```

Many users will want to perform all these actions together, so Web-Browser might also offer a function to do just that:

```
class WebBrowser {
public:
  ...
  void clearEverything();            // calls clearCache, clearHistory,
                                     // and removeCookies
  ...
};
```

Of course, this functionality could also be provided by a non-member function that calls the appropriate member functions:

```
void clearBrowser(WebBrowser& wb)
{
  wb.clearCache();
  wb.clearHistory();
  wb.removeCookies();
}
```

So which is better, the member function clearEverything or the non-member function clearBrowser?

Object-oriented principles dictate that data and the functions that operate on them should be bundled together, and that suggests that the member function is the better choice. Unfortunately, this suggestion is incorrect. It's based on a misunderstanding of what being object-oriented means. Object-oriented principles dictate that data should be as *encapsulated* as possible. Counterintuitively, the member function clearEverything actually yields *less* encapsulation than the non-member clearBrowser. Furthermore, offering the non-member function allows for greater packaging flexibility for WebBrowser-related functionality, and that, in turn, yields fewer compilation dependencies and an increase in WebBrowser extensibility. The non-member approach is thus better than a member function in many ways. It's important to understand why.

We'll begin with encapsulation. If something is encapsulated, it's hidden from view. The more something is encapsulated, the fewer things can see it. The fewer things can see it, the greater flexibility we have to change it, because our changes directly affect only those things that can see what we change. The greater something is encapsulated, then, the greater our ability to change it. That's the reason we value encapsulation in the first place: it affords us the flexibility to change things in a way that affects only a limited number of clients.

Consider the data associated with an object. The less code that can see the data (i.e., access it), the more the data is encapsulated, and the more freely we can change characteristics of an object's data, such as the number of data members, their types, etc. As a coarse-grained measure of how much code can see a piece of data, we can count the number of functions that can access that data: the more functions that can access it, the less encapsulated the data.

Item 22 explains that data members should be private, because if they're not, an unlimited number of functions can access them. They have no encapsulation at all. For data members that *are* private, the number of functions that can access them is the number of member functions of the class plus the number of friend functions, because only members and friends have access to private members. Given a choice between a member function (which can access not only the private data of a class, but also private functions, enums, typedefs, etc.) and a non-member non-friend function (which can access none of these things) providing the same functionality, the choice yielding greater encapsulation is the non-member non-friend function, because it doesn't increase the number of functions that can access the private parts of the class. This explains why clearBrowser (the non-member non-friend function) is preferable to clearEverything (the member function): it yields greater encapsulation in the WebBrowser class.

At this point, two things are worth noting. First, this reasoning applies only to non-member *non-friend* functions. Friends have the same access to a class's private members that member functions have, hence the same impact on encapsulation. From an encapsulation point of view, the choice isn't between member and non-member functions, it's between member functions and non-member non-friend functions. (Encapsulation isn't the only point of view, of course. Item 24 explains that when it comes to implicit type conversions, the choice *is* between member and non-member functions.)

The second thing to note is that just because concerns about encapsulation dictate that a function be a non-member of one class doesn't mean it can't be a member of another class. This may prove a mild salve to programmers accustomed to languages where all functions *must* be in classes (e.g., Eiffel, Java, C#, etc.). For example, we could make clearBrowser a static member function of some utility class. As long as it's not part of (or a friend of) WebBrowser, it doesn't affect the encapsulation of WebBrowser's private members.

In C++, a more natural approach would be to make clearBrowser a non-member function in the same namespace as WebBrowser:

```
namespace WebBrowserStuff {

    class WebBrowser { ... };

    void clearBrowser(WebBrowser& wb);

    ...

}
```

This has more going for it than naturalness, however, because namespaces, unlike classes, can be spread across multiple source files. That's important, because functions like clearBrowser are *convenience functions*. Being neither members nor friends, they have no special access to WebBrowser, so they can't offer any functionality a WebBrowser client couldn't already get in some other way. For example, if clearBrowser didn't exist, clients could just call clearCache, clearHistory, and removeCookies themselves.

A class like WebBrowser might have a large number of convenience functions, some related to bookmarks, others related to printing, still others related to cookie management, etc. As a general rule, most clients will be interested in only some of these sets of convenience functions. There's no reason for a client interested only in bookmark-related convenience functions to be compilation dependent on, e.g., cookie-related convenience functions. The straightforward way to separate them is to declare bookmark-related convenience functions in one header file, cookie-related convenience functions in a different header file, printing-related convenience functions in a third, etc.:

```
// header "webbrowser.h" — header for class WebBrowser itself
// as well as "core" WebBrowser-related functionality
namespace WebBrowserStuff {

    class WebBrowser { ... };

    ...                                 // "core" related functionality, e.g.
                                        // non-member functions almost
                                        // all clients need
}
// header "webbrowserbookmarks.h"
namespace WebBrowserStuff {
    ...                                 // bookmark-related convenience
}                                       // functions
// header "webbrowsercookies.h"
namespace WebBrowserStuff {
    ...                                 // cookie-related convenience
}                                       // functions

...
```

Note that this is exactly how the standard C++ library is organized. Rather than having a single monolithic <C++StandardLibrary> header containing everything in the std namespace, there are dozens of headers (e.g., <vector>, <algorithm>, <memory>, etc.), each declaring *some* of the functionality in std. Clients who use only vector-related functionality aren't required to #include <memory>; clients who don't use list don't have to #include <list>. This allows clients to be compilation dependent only on the parts of the system they actually use. (See Item 31 for a discussion of other ways to reduce compilation dependencies.) Partitioning functionality in this way is not possible when it comes from a class's member functions, because a class must be defined in its entirety; it can't be split into pieces.

Putting all convenience functions in multiple header files — but one namespace — also means that clients can easily *extend* the set of convenience functions. All they have to do is add more non-member non-friend functions to the namespace. For example, if a WebBrowser client decides to write convenience functions related to downloading images, he or she just needs to create a new header file containing the declarations of those functions in the WebBrowserStuff namespace. The new functions are now as available and as integrated as all other convenience functions. This is another feature classes can't offer, because class definitions are closed to extension by clients. Sure, clients can derive new classes, but derived classes have no access to encapsulated (i.e., private) members in the base class, so such "extended functionality" has second-class status. Besides, as Item 7 explains, not all classes are designed to be base classes.

Things to Remember

✦ Prefer non-member non-friend functions to member functions. Doing so increases encapsulation, packaging flexibility, and functional extensibility.

Item 24: Declare non-member functions when type conversions should apply to all parameters.

I noted in the Introduction to this book that having classes support implicit type conversions is generally a bad idea. Of course, there are exceptions to this rule, and one of the most common is when creating numerical types. For example, if you're designing a class to represent rational numbers, allowing implicit conversions from integers to rationals doesn't seem unreasonable. It's certainly no less reasonable than C++'s built-in conversion from int to double (and it's a lot more reasonable than C++'s built-in conversion from double to int). That being the case, you might start your Rational class this way:

```
class Rational {
public:
    Rational(int numerator = 0,      // ctor is deliberately not explicit;
             int denominator = 1);   // allows implicit int-to-Rational
                                     // conversions

    int numerator() const;           // accessors for numerator and
    int denominator() const;         // denominator — see Item 22

private:
    ...
};
```

You know you'd like to support arithmetic operations like addition, multiplication, etc., but you're unsure whether you should implement them via member functions, non-member functions, or, possibly, non-member functions that are friends. Your instincts tell you that when you're in doubt, you should be object-oriented. You know that, say, multiplication of rational numbers is related to the Rational class, so it seems natural to implement operator* for rational numbers inside the Rational class. Counterintuitively, Item 23 argues that the idea of putting functions inside the class they are associated with is sometimes *contrary* to object-oriented principles, but let's set that aside and investigate the idea of making operator* a member function of Rational:

```
class Rational {
public:
    ...
    const Rational operator*(const Rational& rhs) const;
};
```

(If you're unsure why this function is declared the way it is — returning a const by-value result, but taking a reference-to-const as its argument — consult Items 3, 20, and 21.)

This design lets you multiply rationals with the greatest of ease:

```
Rational oneEighth(1, 8);
Rational oneHalf(1, 2);

Rational result = oneHalf * oneEighth;          // fine

result = result * oneEighth;                    // fine
```

But you're not satisfied. You'd also like to support mixed-mode operations, where Rationals can be multiplied with, for example, ints. After all, few things are as natural as multiplying two numbers together, even if they happen to be different types of numbers.

When you try to do mixed-mode arithmetic, however, you find that it works only half the time:

```
result = oneHalf * 2;                           // fine
result = 2 * oneHalf;                           // error!
```

This is a bad omen. Multiplication is supposed to be commutative, remember?

The source of the problem becomes apparent when you rewrite the last two examples in their equivalent functional form:

```
result = oneHalf.operator*(2);                  // fine
result = 2.operator*(oneHalf);                  // error!
```

The object oneHalf is an instance of a class that contains an operator*, so compilers call that function. However, the integer 2 has no associated class, hence no operator* member function. Compilers will also look for non-member operator*s (i.e., ones at namespace or global scope) that can be called like this:

```
result = operator*(2, oneHalf);                 // error!
```

But in this example, there is no non-member operator* taking an int and a Rational, so the search fails.

Look again at the call that succeeds. You'll see that its second parameter is the integer 2, yet Rational::operator* takes a Rational object as its argument. What's going on here? Why does 2 work in one position and not in the other?

What's going on is implicit type conversion. Compilers know you're passing an int and that the function requires a Rational, but they also know they can conjure up a suitable Rational by calling the Rational constructor with the int you provided, so that's what they do. That is, they treat the call as if it had been written more or less like this:

```
const Rational temp(2);          // create a temporary
                                 // Rational object from 2

result = oneHalf * temp;         // same as oneHalf.operator*(temp);
```

Of course, compilers do this only because a non-explicit constructor is involved. If Rational's constructor were explicit, neither of these statements would compile:

```
result = oneHalf * 2;            // error! (with explicit ctor);
                                 // can't convert 2 to Rational

result = 2 * oneHalf;            // same error, same problem
```

That would fail to support mixed-mode arithmetic, but at least the behavior of the two statements would be consistent.

Your goal, however, is both consistency and support for mixed-mode arithmetic, i.e., a design where both of the above statements will compile. That brings us back to these two statements and why, even when Rational's constructor is not explicit, one compiles and one does not:

```
result = oneHalf * 2;            // fine (with non-explicit ctor)
result = 2 * oneHalf;            // error! (even with non-explicit ctor)
```

It turns out that parameters are eligible for implicit type conversion *only if they are listed in the parameter list.* The implicit parameter corresponding to the object on which the member function is invoked — the one this points to — is *never* eligible for implicit conversions. That's why the first call compiles and the second one does not. The first case involves a parameter listed in the parameter list, but the second one doesn't.

You'd still like to support mixed-mode arithmetic, however, and the way to do it is by now perhaps clear: make operator* a non-member function, thus allowing compilers to perform implicit type conversions on *all* arguments:

```
class Rational {
    ...                                         // contains no operator*
};
const Rational operator*(const Rational& lhs,   // now a non-member
                         const Rational& rhs)   // function
{
    return Rational(lhs.numerator() * rhs.numerator(),
                    lhs.denominator() * rhs.denominator());
}
Rational oneFourth(1, 4);
Rational result;

result = oneFourth * 2;                          // fine
result = 2 * oneFourth;                          // hooray, it works!
```

This is certainly a happy ending to the tale, but there is a nagging worry. Should operator* be made a friend of the Rational class?

In this case, the answer is no, because operator* can be implemented entirely in terms of Rational's public interface. The code above shows one way to do it. That leads to an important observation: the opposite of a member function is a *non-member* function, not a friend function. Too many C++ programmers assume that if a function is related to a class and should not be a member (due, for example, to a need for type conversions on all arguments), it should be a friend. This example demonstrates that such reasoning is flawed. Whenever you can avoid friend functions, you should, because, much as in real life, friends are often more trouble than they're worth. Sometimes friendship is warranted, of course, but the fact remains that just because a function shouldn't be a member doesn't automatically mean it should be a friend.

This Item contains the truth and nothing but the truth, but it's not the whole truth. When you cross the line from Object-Oriented C++ into Template C++ (see Item 1) and make Rational a class *template* instead of a class, there are new issues to consider, new ways to resolve them, and some surprising design implications. Such issues, resolutions, and implications are the topic of Item 46.

Things to Remember

✦ If you need type conversions on all parameters to a function (including the one that would otherwise be pointed to by the this pointer), the function must be a non-member.

Item 25: Consider support for a non-throwing swap.

swap is an interesting function. Originally introduced as part of the STL, it's since become a mainstay of exception-safe programming (see Item 29) and a common mechanism for coping with the possibility of assignment to self (see Item 11). Because swap is so useful, it's important to implement it properly, but along with its singular importance comes a set of singular complications. In this Item, we explore what they are and how to deal with them.

To *swap* the values of two objects is to give each the other's value. By default, swapping is accomplished via the standard swap algorithm. Its typical implementation is exactly what you'd expect:

```
namespace std {

  template<typename T>            // typical implementation of std::swap;
  void swap(T& a, T& b)           // swaps a's and b's values
  {
    T temp(a);
    a = b;
    b = temp;
  }

}
```

As long as your types support copying (via copy constructor and copy assignment operator), the default swap implementation will let objects of your types be swapped without your having to do any special work to support it.

However, the default swap implementation may not thrill you. It involves copying three objects: a to temp, b to a, and temp to b. For some types, none of these copies are really necessary. For such types, the default swap puts you on the fast track to the slow lane.

Foremost among such types are those consisting primarily of a pointer to another type that contains the real data. A common manifestation of this design approach is the "pimpl idiom" ("pointer to implementation" — see Item 31). A Widget class employing such a design might look like this:

```
class WidgetImpl {              // class for Widget data;
public:                         // details are unimportant

  ...

private:
  int a, b, c;                  // possibly lots of data —
  std::vector<double> v;        // expensive to copy!

  ...
};
```

```
class Widget {                          // class using the pimpl idiom
public:
  Widget(const Widget& rhs);

  Widget& operator=(const Widget& rhs)  // to copy a Widget, copy its
  {                                     // WidgetImpl object. For
    ...                                 // details on implementing
    *pImpl = *(rhs.pImpl);              // operator= in general,
    ...                                 // see Items 10, 11, and 12.
  }
  ...
private:
  WidgetImpl *pImpl;                    // ptr to object with this
};                                      // Widget's data
```

To swap the value of two Widget objects, all we really need to do is swap their pImpl pointers, but the default swap algorithm has no way to know that. Instead, it would copy not only three Widgets, but also three WidgetImpl objects. Very inefficient. Not a thrill.

What we'd like to do is tell std::swap that when Widgets are being swapped, the way to perform the swap is to swap their internal pImpl pointers. There is a way to say exactly that: specialize std::swap for Widget. Here's the basic idea, though it won't compile in this form:

```
namespace std {

  template<>                            // this is a specialized version
  void swap<Widget>(Widget& a,          // of std::swap for when T is
                    Widget& b)          // Widget; this won't compile
  {
    swap(a.pImpl, b.pImpl);             // to swap Widgets, just swap
  }                                     // their pImpl pointers

}
```

The "template<>" at the beginning of this function says that this is a *total template specialization* for std::swap, and the "<Widget>" after the name of the function says that the specialization is for when T is Widget. In other words, when the general swap template is applied to Widgets, this is the implementation that should be used. In general, we're not permitted to alter the contents of the std namespace, but we are allowed to totally specialize standard templates (like swap) for types of our own creation (such as Widget). That's what we're doing here.

As I said, though, this function won't compile. That's because it's trying to access the pImpl pointers inside a and b, and they're private. We could declare our specialization a friend, but the convention is different: it's to have Widget declare a public member function called swap that does the actual swapping, then specialize std::swap to call the member function:

```
class Widget {                      // same as above, except for the
public:                             // addition of the swap mem func
  ...
  void swap(Widget& other)
  {
    using std::swap;                // the need for this declaration
                                    // is explained later in this Item

    swap(pImpl, other.pImpl);       // to swap Widgets, swap their
  }                                 // pImpl pointers
  ...
};
namespace std {
  template<>                        // revised specialization of
  void swap<Widget>(Widget& a,      // std::swap
                    Widget& b)
  {
    a.swap(b);                      // to swap Widgets, call their
  }                                 // swap member function
}
```

Not only does this compile, it's also consistent with the STL containers, all of which provide both public swap member functions and versions of std::swap that call these member functions.

Suppose, however, that Widget and WidgetImpl were class *templates* instead of classes, possibly so we could parameterize the type of the data stored in WidgetImpl:

```
template<typename T>
class WidgetImpl { ... };

template<typename T>
class Widget { ... };
```

Putting a swap member function in Widget (and, if we need to, in WidgetImpl) is as easy as before, but we run into trouble with the specialization for std::swap. This is what we want to write:

```
namespace std {
  template<typename T>
  void swap<Widget<T> >(Widget<T>& a,          // error! illegal code!
                        Widget<T>& b)
  { a.swap(b); }
}
```

This looks perfectly reasonable, but it's not legal. We're trying to partially specialize a function template (std::swap), but though C++ allows partial specialization of class templates, it doesn't allow it for function templates. This code should not compile (though some compilers erroneously accept it).

When you want to "partially specialize" a function template, the usual approach is to simply add an overload. That would look like this:

```
namespace std {

    template<typename T>            // an overloading of std::swap
    void swap(Widget<T>& a,         // (note the lack of "<...>" after
            Widget<T>& b)           // "swap"), but see below for
    { a.swap(b); }                  // why this isn't valid code

}
```

In general, overloading function templates is fine, but std is a special namespace, and the rules governing it are special, too. It's okay to totally specialize templates in std, but it's not okay to add *new* templates (or classes or functions or anything else) to std. The contents of std are determined solely by the C++ standardization committee, and we're prohibited from augmenting what they've decided should go there. Alas, the form of the prohibition may dismay you. Programs that cross this line will almost certainly compile and run, but their behavior is undefined. If you want your software to have predictable behavior, you'll not add new things to std.

So what to do? We still need a way to let other people call swap and get our more efficient template-specific version. The answer is simple. We still declare a non-member swap that calls the member swap, we just don't declare the non-member to be a specialization or overloading of std::swap. For example, if all our Widget-related functionality is in the namespace WidgetStuff, it would look like this:

```
namespace WidgetStuff {

    ...                             // templatized WidgetImpl, etc.

    template<typename T>            // as before, including the swap
    class Widget { ... };           // member function

    ...

    template<typename T>            // non-member swap function;
    void swap(Widget<T>& a,         // not part of the std namespace
            Widget<T>& b)
    {
        a.swap(b);
    }

}
```

Now, if any code anywhere calls swap on two Widget objects, the name lookup rules in C++ (specifically the rules known as *argument-dependent lookup* or *Koenig lookup*) will find the Widget-specific version in WidgetStuff. Which is exactly what we want.

This approach works as well for classes as for class templates, so it seems like we should use it all the time. Unfortunately, there is a reason for specializing std::swap for classes (I'll describe it shortly), so if you want to have your class-specific version of swap called in as many contexts as possible (and you do), you need to write both a non-member version in the same namespace as your class and a specialization of std::swap.

By the way, if you're not using namespaces, everything above continues to apply (i.e., you still need a non-member swap that calls the member swap), but why are you clogging the global namespace with all your class, template, function, enum, enumerant, and typedef names? Have you no sense of propriety?

Everything I've written so far pertains to authors of swap, but it's worth looking at one situation from a client's point of view. Suppose you're writing a function template where you need to swap the values of two objects:

```
template<typename T>
void doSomething(T& obj1, T& obj2)
{
  ...
  swap(obj1, obj2);
  ...
}
```

Which swap should this call? The general one in std, which you know exists; a specialization of the general one in std, which may or may not exist; or a T-specific one, which may or may not exist and which may or may not be in a namespace (but should certainly not be in std)? What you desire is to call a T-specific version if there is one, but to fall back on the general version in std if there's not. Here's how you fulfill your desire:

```
template<typename T>
void doSomething(T& obj1, T& obj2)
{
  using std::swap;            // make std::swap available in this function
  ...
  swap(obj1, obj2);           // call the best swap for objects of type T
  ...
}
```

When compilers see the call to swap, they search for the right swap to invoke. C++'s name lookup rules ensure that this will find any T-specific swap at global scope or in the same namespace as the type T. (For example, if T is Widget in the namespace WidgetStuff, compilers will use argument-dependent lookup to find swap in WidgetStuff.) If no T-specific swap exists, compilers will use swap in std, thanks to the using declaration that makes std::swap visible in this function. Even then, however, compilers will prefer a T-specific specialization of std::swap over the general template, so if std::swap has been specialized for T, the specialized version will be used.

Getting the right swap called is therefore easy. The one thing you want to be careful of is to not qualify the call, because that will affect how C++ determines the function to invoke. For example, if you were to write the call to swap this way,

```
std::swap(obj1, obj2);              // the wrong way to call swap
```

you'd force compilers to consider only the swap in std (including any template specializations), thus eliminating the possibility of getting a more appropriate T-specific version defined elsewhere. Alas, some misguided programmers *do* qualify calls to swap in this way, and that's why it's important to totally specialize std::swap for your classes: it makes type-specific swap implementations available to code written in this misguided fashion. (Such code is present in some standard library implementations, so it's in your interest to help such code work as efficiently as possible.)

At this point, we've discussed the default swap, member swaps, non-member swaps, specializations of std::swap, and calls to swap, so let's summarize the situation.

First, if the default implementation of swap offers acceptable efficiency for your class or class template, you don't need to do anything. Anybody trying to swap objects of your type will get the default version, and that will work fine.

Second, if the default implementation of swap isn't efficient enough (which almost always means that your class or template is using some variation of the pimpl idiom), do the following:

1. Offer a public swap member function that efficiently swaps the value of two objects of your type. For reasons I'll explain in a moment, this function should never throw an exception.

2. Offer a non-member swap in the same namespace as your class or template. Have it call your swap member function.

3. If you're writing a class (not a class template), specialize std::swap for your class. Have it also call your swap member function.

Finally, if you're calling swap, be sure to include a using declaration to make std::swap visible in your function, then call swap without any namespace qualification.

The only loose end is my admonition to have the member version of swap never throw exceptions. That's because one of the most useful applications of swap is to help classes (and class templates) offer the strong exception-safety guarantee. Item 29 provides all the details, but the technique is predicated on the assumption that the member version of swap never throws. This constraint applies only to the member version! It can't apply to the non-member version, because the default version of swap is based on copy construction and copy assignment, and, in general, both of those functions are allowed to throw exceptions. When you write a custom version of swap, then, you are typically offering more than just an efficient way to swap values; you're also offering one that doesn't throw exceptions. As a general rule, these two swap characteristics go hand in hand, because highly efficient swaps are almost always based on operations on built-in types (such as the pointers underlying the pimpl idiom), and operations on built-in types never throw exceptions.

Things to Remember

✦ Provide a swap member function when std::swap would be inefficient for your type. Make sure your swap doesn't throw exceptions.

✦ If you offer a member swap, also offer a non-member swap that calls the member. For classes (not templates), specialize std::swap, too.

✦ When calling swap, employ a using declaration for std::swap, then call swap without namespace qualification.

✦ It's fine to totally specialize std templates for user-defined types, but never try to add something completely new to std.

5 Implementations

For the most part, coming up with appropriate definitions for your classes (and class templates) and appropriate declarations for your functions (and function templates) is the lion's share of the battle. Once you've got those right, the corresponding implementations are largely straightforward. Still, there are things to watch out for. Defining variables too soon can cause a drag on performance. Overuse of casts can lead to code that's slow, hard to maintain, and infected with subtle bugs. Returning handles to an object's internals can defeat encapsulation and leave clients with dangling handles. Failure to consider the impact of exceptions can lead to leaked resources and corrupted data structures. Overzealous inlining can cause code bloat. Excessive coupling can result in unacceptably long build times.

All of these problems can be avoided. This chapter explains how.

Item 26: Postpone variable definitions as long as possible.

Whenever you define a variable of a type with a constructor or destructor, you incur the cost of construction when control reaches the variable's definition, and you incur the cost of destruction when the variable goes out of scope. There's a cost associated with unused variables, so you want to avoid them whenever you can.

You're probably thinking that you never define unused variables, but you may need to think again. Consider the following function, which returns an encrypted version of a password, provided the password is long enough. If the password is too short, the function throws an exception of type logic_error, which is defined in the standard C++ library (see Item 54):

```
// this function defines the variable "encrypted" too soon
std::string encryptPassword(const std::string& password)
{
    using namespace std;

    string encrypted;

    if (password.length() < MinimumPasswordLength) {
        throw logic_error("Password is too short");
    }

    ...                             // do whatever is necessary to place an
                                    // encrypted version of password in encrypted

    return encrypted;
}
```

The object encrypted isn't *completely* unused in this function, but it's unused if an exception is thrown. That is, you'll pay for the construction and destruction of encrypted even if encryptPassword throws an exception. As a result, you're better off postponing encrypted's definition until you *know* you'll need it:

```
// this function postpones encrypted's definition until it's truly necessary
std::string encryptPassword(const std::string& password)
{
    using namespace std;

    if (password.length() < MinimumPasswordLength) {
        throw logic_error("Password is too short");
    }

    string encrypted;

    ...                             // do whatever is necessary to place an
                                    // encrypted version of password in encrypted

    return encrypted;
}
```

This code still isn't as tight as it might be, because encrypted is defined without any initialization arguments. That means its default constructor will be used. In many cases, the first thing you'll do to an object is give it some value, often via an assignment. Item 4 explains why default-constructing an object and then assigning to it is less efficient than initializing it with the value you really want it to have. That analysis applies here, too. For example, suppose the hard part of encryptPassword is performed in this function:

```
void encrypt(std::string& s);          // encrypts s in place
```

Then encryptPassword could be implemented like this, though it wouldn't be the best way to do it:

```
// this function postpones encrypted's definition until
// it's necessary, but it's still needlessly inefficient
std::string encryptPassword(const std::string& password)
{
    ...                              // import std and check length as above
    string encrypted;                // default-construct encrypted
    encrypted = password;            // assign to encrypted

    encrypt(encrypted);
    return encrypted;
}
```

A preferable approach is to initialize encrypted with password, thus skipping the pointless and potentially expensive default construction:

```
// finally, the best way to define and initialize encrypted
std::string encryptPassword(const std::string& password)
{
    ...                              // import std and check length
    string encrypted(password);      // define and initialize via copy
                                     // constructor

    encrypt(encrypted);
    return encrypted;
}
```

This suggests the real meaning of "as long as possible" in this Item's title. Not only should you postpone a variable's definition until right before you have to use the variable, you should also try to postpone the definition until you have initialization arguments for it. By doing so, you avoid constructing and destructing unneeded objects, and you avoid unnecessary default constructions. Further, you help document the purpose of variables by initializing them in contexts in which their meaning is clear.

"But what about loops?" you may wonder. If a variable is used only inside a loop, is it better to define it outside the loop and make an assignment to it on each loop iteration, or is it be better to define the variable inside the loop? That is, which of these general structures is better?

```
// Approach A: define outside loop      // Approach B: define inside loop
Widget w;
for (int i = 0; i < n; ++i) {           for (int i = 0; i < n; ++i) {
    w = some value dependent on i;          Widget w(some value dependent on i);
    ...                                     ...
}                                       }
```

Here I've switched from an object of type string to an object of type Widget to avoid any preconceptions about the cost of performing a construction, destruction, or assignment for the object.

In terms of Widget operations, the costs of these two approaches are as follows:

- Approach A: 1 constructor + 1 destructor + n assignments.

- Approach B: n constructors + n destructors.

For classes where an assignment costs less than a constructor-destructor pair, Approach A is generally more efficient. This is especially the case as n gets large. Otherwise, Approach B is probably better. Furthermore, Approach A makes the name w visible in a larger scope (the one containing the loop) than Approach B, something that's contrary to program comprehensibility and maintainability. As a result, unless you know that (1) assignment is less expensive than a constructor-destructor pair and (2) you're dealing with a performance-sensitive part of your code, you should default to using Approach B.

Things to Remember

✦ Postpone variable definitions as long as possible. It increases program clarity and improves program efficiency.

Item 27: Minimize casting.

The rules of C++ are designed to guarantee that type errors are impossible. In theory, if your program compiles cleanly, it's not trying to perform any unsafe or nonsensical operations on any objects. This is a valuable guarantee. You don't want to forgo it lightly.

Unfortunately, casts subvert the type system. That can lead to all kinds of trouble, some easy to recognize, some extraordinarily subtle. If you're coming to C++ from C, Java, or C#, take note, because casting in those languages is more necessary and less dangerous than in C++. But C++ is not C. It's not Java. It's not C#. In this language, casting is a feature you want to approach with great respect.

Let's begin with a review of casting syntax, because there are usually three different ways to write the same cast. C-style casts look like this:

    (T) expression   // cast expression to be of type T

Function-style casts use this syntax:

    T(expression)   // cast expression to be of type T

There is no difference in meaning between these forms; it's purely a matter of where you put the parentheses. I call these two forms *old-style casts*.

C++ also offers four new cast forms (often called *new-style* or *C++-style casts*):

```
const_cast<T>(expression)
dynamic_cast<T>(expression)
reinterpret_cast<T>(expression)
static_cast<T>(expression)
```

Each serves a distinct purpose:

- const_cast is typically used to cast away the constness of objects. It is the only C++-style cast that can do this.

- dynamic_cast is primarily used to perform "safe downcasting," i.e., to determine whether an object is of a particular type in an inheritance hierarchy. It is the only cast that cannot be performed using the old-style syntax. It is also the only cast that may have a significant runtime cost. (I'll provide details on this a bit later.)

- reinterpret_cast is intended for low-level casts that yield implementation-dependent (i.e., unportable) results, e.g., casting a pointer to an int. Such casts should be rare outside low-level code. I use it only once in this book, and that's only when discussing how you might write a debugging allocator for raw memory (see Item 50).

- static_cast can be used to force implicit conversions (e.g., non-const object to const object (as in Item 3), int to double, etc.). It can also be used to perform the reverse of many such conversions (e.g., void* pointers to typed pointers, pointer-to-base to pointer-to-derived), though it cannot cast from const to non-const objects. (Only const_cast can do that.)

The old-style casts continue to be legal, but the new forms are preferable. First, they're much easier to identify in code (both for humans and for tools like grep), thus simplifying the process of finding places in the code where the type system is being subverted. Second, the more narrowly specified purpose of each cast makes it possible for compilers to diagnose usage errors. For example, if you try to cast away constness using a new-style cast other than const_cast, your code won't compile.

About the only time I use an old-style cast is when I want to call an explicit constructor to pass an object to a function. For example:

```
class Widget {
public:
    explicit Widget(int size);

    ...
};

void doSomeWork(const Widget& w);
```

doSomeWork(Widget(15));	// create Widget from int // with function-style cast
doSomeWork(static_cast<Widget>(15));	// create Widget from int // with C++-style cast

Somehow, deliberate object creation doesn't "feel" like a cast, so I'd probably use the function-style cast instead of the static_cast in this case. Then again, code that leads to a core dump usually feels pretty reasonable when you write it, so perhaps you'd best ignore feelings and use new-style casts all the time.

Many programmers believe that casts do nothing but tell compilers to treat one type as another, but this is mistaken. Type conversions of any kind (either explicit via casts or implicit by compilers) often lead to code that is executed at runtime. For example, in this code fragment,

```
int x, y;
...
double d = static_cast<double>(x)/y;        // divide x by y, but use
                                             // floating point division
```

the cast of the int x to a double almost certainly generates code, because on most architectures, the underlying representation for an int is different from that for a double. That's perhaps not so surprising, but this example may widen your eyes a bit:

```
class Base { ... };

class Derived: public Base { ... };

Derived d;

Base *pb = &d;                  // implicitly convert Derived* ⟹ Base*
```

Here we're just creating a base class pointer to a derived class object, but sometimes, the two pointer values will not be the same. When that's the case, an offset is applied *at runtime* to the Derived* pointer to get the correct Base* pointer value.

This last example demonstrates that a single object (e.g., an object of type Derived) might have more than one address (e.g., its address when pointed to by a Base* pointer and its address when pointed to by a Derived* pointer). That can't happen in C. It can't happen in Java. It can't happen in C#. It *does* happen in C++. In fact, when multiple inheritance is in use, it happens virtually all the time, but it can happen under single inheritance, too. Among other things, that means you should generally avoid making assumptions about how things are laid out in C++, and you should certainly not perform casts based on such assumptions. For example, casting object addresses to char* pointers and then using pointer arithmetic on them almost always yields undefined behavior.

But note that I said that an offset is "sometimes" required. The way objects are laid out and the way their addresses are calculated varies from compiler to compiler. That means that just because your "I know how things are laid out" casts work on one platform doesn't mean they'll work on others. The world is filled with woeful programmers who've learned this lesson the hard way.

An interesting thing about casts is that it's easy to write something that looks right (and might be right in other languages) but is wrong. Many application frameworks, for example, require that virtual member function implementations in derived classes call their base class counterparts first. Suppose we have a Window base class and a SpecialWindow derived class, both of which define the virtual function onResize. Further suppose that SpecialWindow's onResize is expected to invoke Window's onResize first. Here's a way to implement this that looks like it does the right thing, but doesn't:

```
class Window {                              // base class
public:
  virtual void onResize() { ... }           // base onResize impl
  ...
};
class SpecialWindow: public Window {        // derived class
public:
  virtual void onResize() {                 // derived onResize impl;
    static_cast<Window>(*this).onResize();  // cast *this to Window,
                                            // then call its onResize;
                                            // this doesn't work!

                                            // do SpecialWindow-
  }                                         // specific stuff
  ...
};
```

I've highlighted the cast in the code. (It's a new-style cast, but using an old-style cast wouldn't change anything.) As you would expect, the code casts *this to a Window. The resulting call to onResize therefore invokes Window::onResize. What you might not expect is that it does not invoke that function on the current object! Instead, the cast cre-

ates a new, temporary *copy* of the base class part of *this, then invokes
onResize on the copy! The above code doesn't call Window::onResize on
the current object and then perform the SpecialWindow-specific
actions on that object — it calls Window::onResize on a *copy of the base
class part* of the current object before performing SpecialWindow-specific actions on the current object. If Window::onResize modifies the
current object (hardly a remote possibility, since onResize is a non-
const member function), the current object won't be modified. Instead,
a *copy* of that object will be modified. If SpecialWindow::onResize modifies the current object, however, the current object *will* be modified,
leading to the prospect that the code will leave the current object in an
invalid state, one where base class modifications have not been made,
but derived class ones have been.

The solution is to eliminate the cast, replacing it with what you really
want to say. You don't want to trick compilers into treating *this as a
base class object; you want to call the base class version of onResize on
the current object. So say that:

```
class SpecialWindow: public Window {
public:
  virtual void onResize() {
    Window::onResize();                        // call Window::onResize
    ...                                        // on *this
  }

  ...
};
```

This example also demonstrates that if you find yourself wanting to
cast, it's a sign that you could be approaching things the wrong way.
This is especially the case if your want is for dynamic_cast.

Before delving into the design implications of dynamic_cast, it's worth
observing that many implementations of dynamic_cast can be quite
slow. For example, at least one common implementation is based in
part on string comparisons of class names. If you're performing a
dynamic_cast on an object in a single-inheritance hierarchy four levels
deep, each dynamic_cast under such an implementation could cost you
up to four calls to strcmp to compare class names. A deeper hierarchy
or one using multiple inheritance would be more expensive. There are
reasons that some implementations work this way (they have to do
with support for dynamic linking). Nonetheless, in addition to being
leery of casts in general, you should be especially leery of
dynamic_casts in performance-sensitive code.

The need for dynamic_cast generally arises because you want to perform derived class operations on what you believe to be a derived class

object, but you have only a pointer- or reference-to-base through which to manipulate the object. There are two general ways to avoid this problem.

First, use containers that store pointers (often smart pointers — see Item 13) to derived class objects directly, thus eliminating the need to manipulate such objects through base class interfaces. For example, if, in our Window/SpecialWindow hierarchy, only SpecialWindows support blinking, instead of doing this:

```
class Window { ... };

class SpecialWindow: public Window {
public:
   void blink();

   ...
};

typedef                                          // see Item 13 for info
   std::vector<std::tr1::shared_ptr<Window> > VPW;  // on tr1::shared_ptr

VPW winPtrs;

...

for (VPW::iterator iter = winPtrs.begin();       // undesirable code:
     iter != winPtrs.end();                      // uses dynamic_cast
     ++iter) {
   if (SpecialWindow *psw = dynamic_cast<SpecialWindow*>(iter->get()))
      psw->blink();
}
```

try to do this instead:

```
typedef std::vector<std::tr1::shared_ptr<SpecialWindow> > VPSW;

VPSW winPtrs;

...

for (VPSW::iterator iter = winPtrs.begin();      // better code: uses
     iter != winPtrs.end();                      // no dynamic_cast
     ++iter)
   (*iter)->blink();
```

Of course, this approach won't allow you to store pointers to all possible Window derivatives in the same container. To work with different window types, you might need multiple type-safe containers.

An alternative that will let you manipulate all possible Window derivatives through a base class interface is to provide virtual functions in the base class that let you do what you need. For example, though only SpecialWindows can blink, maybe it makes sense to declare the function in the base class, offering a default implementation that does nothing:

```cpp
class Window {
public:
  virtual void blink() {}          // default impl is no-op;
                                   // see Item 34 for why
  ...                              // a default impl may be
};                                 // a bad idea

class SpecialWindow: public Window {
public:
  virtual void blink() { ... }     // in this class, blink
                                   // does something
  ...
};

typedef std::vector<std::tr1::shared_ptr<Window> > VPW;

VPW winPtrs;                       // container holds
                                   // (ptrs to) all possible
                                   // Window types
...

for (VPW::iterator iter = winPtrs.begin();
     iter != winPtrs.end();
     ++iter)                       // note lack of
  (*iter)->blink();                // dynamic_cast
```

Neither of these approaches — using type-safe containers or moving virtual functions up the hierarchy — is universally applicable, but in many cases, they provide a viable alternative to dynamic_casting. When they do, you should embrace them.

One thing you definitely want to avoid is designs that involve cascading dynamic_casts, i.e., anything that looks like this:

```cpp
class Window { ... };

...                                // derived classes are defined here

typedef std::vector<std::tr1::shared_ptr<Window> > VPW;

VPW winPtrs;

...

for (VPW::iterator iter = winPtrs.begin(); iter != winPtrs.end(); ++iter)
{
  if (SpecialWindow1 *psw1 =
       dynamic_cast<SpecialWindow1*>(iter->get())) { ... }

  else if (SpecialWindow2 *psw2 =
         dynamic_cast<SpecialWindow2*>(iter->get())) { ... }

  else if (SpecialWindow3 *psw3 =
         dynamic_cast<SpecialWindow3*>(iter->get())) { ... }

  ...
}
```

Such C++ generates code that's big and slow, plus it's brittle, because every time the Window class hierarchy changes, all such code has to be examined to see if it needs to be updated. (For example, if a new derived class gets added, a new conditional branch probably needs to be added to the above cascade.) Code that looks like this should almost always be replaced with something based on virtual function calls.

Good C++ uses very few casts, but it's generally not practical to get rid of all of them. The cast from int to double on page 118, for example, is a reasonable use of a cast, though it's not strictly necessary. (The code could be rewritten to declare a new variable of type double that's initialized with x's value.) Like most suspicious constructs, casts should be isolated as much as possible, typically hidden inside functions whose interfaces shield callers from the grubby work being done inside.

Things to Remember

✦ Avoid casts whenever practical, especially dynamic_casts in performance-sensitive code. If a design requires casting, try to develop a cast-free alternative.

✦ When casting is necessary, try to hide it inside a function. Clients can then call the function instead of putting casts in their own code.

✦ Prefer C++-style casts to old-style casts. They are easier to see, and they are more specific about what they do.

Item 28: Avoid returning "handles" to object internals.

Suppose you're working on an application involving rectangles. Each rectangle can be represented by its upper left corner and its lower right corner. To keep a Rectangle object small, you might decide that the points defining its extent shouldn't be stored in the Rectangle itself, but rather in an auxiliary struct that the Rectangle points to:

```
class Point {                              // class for representing points
public:
  Point(int x, int y);

  ...

  void setX(int newVal);
  void setY(int newVal);

  ...
};
```

```
struct RectData {                   // Point data for a Rectangle
    Point ulhc;                     // ulhc = " upper left-hand corner"
    Point lrhc;                     // lrhc = " lower right-hand corner"
};

class Rectangle {
    ...

private:
    std::tr1::shared_ptr<RectData> pData;       // see Item 13 for info on
};                                              // tr1::shared_ptr
```

Because Rectangle clients will need to be able to determine the extent of a Rectangle, the class provides the upperLeft and lowerRight functions. However, Point is a user-defined type, so, mindful of Item 20's observation that passing user-defined types by reference is typically more efficient than passing them by value, these functions return references to the underlying Point objects:

```
class Rectangle {
public:
    ...
    Point& upperLeft() const { return pData->ulhc; }
    Point& lowerRight() const { return pData->lrhc; }
    ...
};
```

This design will compile, but it's wrong. In fact, it's self-contradictory. On the one hand, upperLeft and lowerRight are declared to be const member functions, because they are designed only to offer clients a way to learn what the Rectangle's points are, not to let clients modify the Rectangle (see Item 3). On the other hand, both functions return references to private internal data — references that callers can use to modify that internal data! For example:

```
Point coord1(0, 0);
Point coord2(100, 100);

const Rectangle rec(coord1, coord2);        // rec is a const rectangle from
                                            // (0, 0) to (100, 100)

rec.upperLeft().setX(50);                   // now rec goes from
                                            // (50, 0) to (100, 100)!
```

Here, notice how the caller of upperLeft is able to use the returned reference to one of rec's internal Point data members to modify that member. But rec is supposed to be const!

This immediately leads to two lessons. First, a data member is only as encapsulated as the most accessible function returning a reference to it. In this case, though ulhc and lrhc are supposed to be private to their Rectangle, they're effectively public, because the public functions

upperLeft and lowerRight return references to them. Second, if a const
member function returns a reference to data associated with an object
that is stored outside the object itself, the caller of the function can
modify that data, (This is just a fallout of the limitations of bitwise
constness — see Item 3.)

Everything we've done has involved member functions returning references, but if they returned pointers or iterators, the same problems
would exist for the same reasons. References, pointers, and iterators
are all *handles* (ways to get at other objects), and returning a handle
to an object's internals always runs the risk of compromising an
object's encapsulation. As we've seen, it can also lead to const member
functions that allow an object's state to be modified.

We generally think of an object's "internals" as its data members, but
member functions not accessible to the general public (i.e., that are
protected or private) are part of an object's internals, too. As such, it's
important not to return handles to them. This means you should
never have a member function return a pointer to a less accessible
member function. If you do, the effective access level will be that of the
more accessible function, because clients will be able to get a pointer
to the less accessible function, then call that function through the
pointer.

Functions that return pointers to member functions are uncommon,
however, so let's turn our attention back to the Rectangle class and its
upperLeft and lowerRight member functions. Both of the problems
we've identified for those functions can be eliminated by simply applying const to their return types:

```
class Rectangle {
public:
   ...
   const Point& upperLeft() const { return pData->ulhc; }
   const Point& lowerRight() const { return pData->lrhc; }
   ...
};
```

With this altered design, clients can read the Points defining a rectangle, but they can't write them. This means that declaring upperLeft and
lowerRight as const is no longer a lie, because they no longer allow callers to modify the state of the object. As for the encapsulation problem,
we always intended to let clients see the Points making up a Rectangle,
so this is a deliberate relaxation of encapsulation. More importantly,
it's a *limited* relaxation: only read access is being granted by these
functions. Write access is still prohibited.

Even so, upperLeft and lowerRight are still returning handles to an
object's internals, and that can be problematic in other ways. In par-

ticular, it can lead to *dangling handles*: handles that refer to parts of objects that don't exist any longer. The most common source of such disappearing objects are function return values. For example, consider a function that returns the bounding box for a GUI object in the form of a rectangle:

```
class GUIObject { ... };

const Rectangle                            // returns a rectangle by
    boundingBox(const GUIObject& obj);     // value; see Item 3 for why
                                           //  return type is const
```

Now consider how a client might use this function:

```
GUIObject *pgo;                            // make pgo point to
...                                        // some GUIObject

const Point *pUpperLeft =                  // get a ptr to the upper
    &(boundingBox(*pgo).upperLeft());      // left point of its
                                           // bounding box
```

The call to boundingBox will return a new, temporary Rectangle object. That object doesn't have a name, so let's call it *temp*. upperLeft will then be called on *temp*, and that call will return a reference to an internal part of *temp*, in particular, to one of the Points making it up. pUpperLeft will then point to that Point object. So far, so good, but we're not done yet, because at the end of the statement, boundingBox's return value — *temp* — will be destroyed, and that will indirectly lead to the destruction of *temp*'s Points. That, in turn, will leave pUpperLeft pointing to an object that no longer exists; pUpperLeft will dangle by the end of the statement that created it!

This is why any function that returns a handle to an internal part of the object is dangerous. It doesn't matter whether the handle is a pointer, a reference, or an iterator. It doesn't matter whether it's qualified with const. It doesn't matter whether the member function returning the handle is itself const. All that matters is that a handle is being returned, because once that's being done, you run the risk that the handle will outlive the object it refers to.

This doesn't mean that you should *never* have a member function that returns a handle. Sometimes you have to. For example, operator[] allows you to pluck individual elements out of strings and vectors, and these operator[]s work by returning references to the data in the containers (see Item 3) — data that is destroyed when the containers themselves are. Still, such functions are the exception, not the rule.

Things to Remember

✦ Avoid returning handles (references, pointers, or iterators) to object internals. Not returning handles increases encapsulation, helps const member functions act const, and minimizes the creation of dangling handles.

Item 29: Strive for exception-safe code.

Exception safety is sort of like pregnancy...but hold that thought for a moment. We can't really talk reproduction until we've worked our way through courtship.

Suppose we have a class for representing GUI menus with background images. The class is designed to be used in a threaded environment, so it has a mutex for concurrency control:

```
class PrettyMenu {
public:
    ...
    void changeBackground(std::istream& imgSrc);   // change background
    ...                                            // image
private:
    Mutex mutex;                // mutex for this object

    Image *bgImage;             // current background image
    int imageChanges;          // # of times image has been changed
};
```

Consider this possible implementation of PrettyMenu's changeBackground function:

```
void PrettyMenu::changeBackground(std::istream& imgSrc)
{
    lock(&mutex);                       // acquire mutex (as in Item 14)

    delete bgImage;                     // get rid of old background
    ++imageChanges;                     // update image change count
    bgImage = new Image(imgSrc);        // install new background

    unlock(&mutex);                     // release mutex
}
```

From the perspective of exception safety, this function is about as bad as it gets. There are two requirements for exception safety, and this satisfies neither.

When an exception is thrown, exception-safe functions:

- **Leak no resources**. The code above fails this test, because if the "new Image(imgSrc)" expression yields an exception, the call to unlock never gets executed, and the mutex is held forever.

- **Don't allow data structures to become corrupted**. If "new Image(imgSrc)" throws, bgImage is left pointing to a deleted object. In addition, imageChanges has been incremented, even though it's not true that a new image has been installed. (On the other hand, the old image has definitely been eliminated, so I suppose you could argue that the image has been "changed.")

Addressing the resource leak issue is easy, because Item 13 explains how to use objects to manage resources, and Item 14 introduces the Lock class as a way to ensure that mutexes are released in a timely fashion:

```
void PrettyMenu::changeBackground(std::istream& imgSrc)
{
  Lock ml(&mutex);                      // from Item 14: acquire mutex and
                                        // ensure its later release

  delete bgImage;
  ++imageChanges;
  bgImage = new Image(imgSrc);
}
```

One of the best things about resource management classes like Lock is that they usually make functions shorter. See how the call to unlock is no longer needed? As a general rule, less code is better code, because there's less to go wrong and less to misunderstand when making changes.

With the resource leak behind us, we can turn our attention to the issue of data structure corruption. Here we have a choice, but before we can choose, we have to confront the terminology that defines our choices.

Exception-safe functions offer one of three guarantees:

- Functions offering **the basic guarantee** promise that if an exception is thrown, everything in the program remains in a valid state. No objects or data structures become corrupted, and all objects are in an internally consistent state (e.g., all class invariants are satisfied). However, the exact state of the program may not be predictable. For example, we could write changeBackground so that if an exception were thrown, the PrettyMenu object might continue to have the old background image, or it might have some default background image, but clients wouldn't be able to predict which. (To find out, they'd presumably have to call some member function that would tell them what the current background image was.)

- Functions offering **the strong guarantee** promise that if an exception is thrown, the state of the program is unchanged. Calls to such functions are *atomic* in the sense that if they succeed, they succeed completely, and if they fail, the program state is as if they'd never been called.

Working with functions offering the strong guarantee is easier than working with functions offering only the basic guarantee, because after calling a function offering the strong guarantee, there are only two possible program states: as expected following successful execution of the function, or the state that existed at the time the function was called. In contrast, if a call to a function offering only the basic guarantee yields an exception, the program could be in *any* valid state.

▪ Functions offering **the nothrow guarantee** promise never to throw exceptions, because they always do what they promise to do. All operations on built-in types (e.g., ints, pointers, etc.) are nothrow (i.e., offer the nothrow guarantee). This is a critical building block of exception-safe code.

It might seem reasonable to assume that functions with an empty exception specification are nothrow, but this isn't necessarily true. For example, consider this function:

```
int doSomething() throw();          // note empty exception spec.
```

This doesn't say that doSomething will never throw an exception; it says that *if* doSomething throws an exception, it's a serious error, and the unexpected function should be called.[†] In fact, doSomething may not offer any exception guarantee at all. The declaration of a function (including its exception specification, if it has one) doesn't tell you whether a function is correct or portable or efficient, and it doesn't tell you which, if any, exception safety guarantee it offers, either. All those characteristics are determined by the function's implementation, not its declaration.

Exception-safe code must offer one of the three guarantees above. If it doesn't, it's not exception-safe. The choice, then, is to determine which guarantee to offer for each of the functions you write. Other than when dealing with exception-unsafe legacy code (which we'll discuss later in this Item), offering no exception safety guarantee should be an option only if your crack team of requirements analysts has identified a need for your application to leak resources and run with corrupt data structures.

As a general rule, you want to offer the strongest guarantee that's practical. From an exception safety point of view, nothrow functions are wonderful, but it's hard to climb out of the C part of C++ without

---

† For information on the unexpected function, consult your favorite search engine or comprehensive C++ text. (You'll probably have better luck searching for set_unexpected, the function that specifies the unexpected function.)

calling functions that might throw. Anything using dynamically allocated memory (e.g., all STL containers) typically throws a bad_alloc
exception if it can't find enough memory to satisfy a request (see
Item 49). Offer the nothrow guarantee when you can, but for most
functions, the choice is between the basic and strong guarantees.

In the case of changeBackground, *almost* offering the strong guarantee
is not difficult. First, we change the type of PrettyMenu's bgImage data
member from a built-in Image* pointer to one of the smart resource-
managing pointers described in Item 13. Frankly, this is a good idea
purely on the basis of preventing resource leaks. The fact that it helps
us offer the strong exception safety guarantee simply reinforces
Item 13's argument that using objects (such as smart pointers) to
manage resources is fundamental to good design. In the code below, I
show use of tr1::shared_ptr, because its more intuitive behavior when
copied generally makes it preferable to auto_ptr.

Second, we reorder the statements in changeBackground so that we
don't increment imageChanges until the image has been changed. As a
general rule, it's a good policy not to change the status of an object to
indicate that something has happened until something actually has.

Here's the resulting code:

```
class PrettyMenu {
    ...
    std::tr1::shared_ptr<Image> bgImage;
    ...
};
void PrettyMenu::changeBackground(std::istream& imgSrc)
{
    Lock ml(&mutex);
    bgImage.reset(new Image(imgSrc));    // replace bgImage's internal
                                         // pointer with the result of the
                                         // "new Image" expression
    ++imageChanges;
}
```

Note that there's no longer a need to manually delete the old image,
because that's handled internally by the smart pointer. Furthermore,
the deletion takes place only if the new image is successfully created.
More precisely, the tr1::shared_ptr::reset function will be called only if its
parameter (the result of "new Image(imgSrc)") is successfully created.
delete is used only inside the call to reset, so if the function is never
entered, delete is never used. Note also that the use of an object (the
tr1::shared_ptr) to manage a resource (the dynamically allocated Image)
has again pared the length of changeBackground.

As I said, those two changes *almost* suffice to allow changeBackground
to offer the strong exception safety guarantee. What's the fly in the

ointment? The parameter imgSrc. If the Image constructor throws an exception, it's possible that the read marker for the input stream has been moved, and such movement would be a change in state visible to the rest of the program. Until changeBackground addresses that issue, it offers only the basic exception safety guarantee.

Let's set that aside, however, and pretend that changeBackground does offer the strong guarantee. (I'm confident you could come up with a way for it to do so, perhaps by changing its parameter type from an istream to the name of the file containing the image data.) There is a general design strategy that typically leads to the strong guarantee, and it's important to be familiar with it. The strategy is known as "copy and swap." In principle, it's very simple. Make a copy of the object you want to modify, then make all needed changes to the copy. If any of the modifying operations throws an exception, the original object remains unchanged. After all the changes have been successfully completed, swap the modified object with the original in a non-throwing operation.

This is usually implemented by putting all the per-object data from the "real" object into a separate implementation object, then giving the real object a pointer to its implementation object. This is often known as the "pimpl idiom," and Item 31 describes it in some detail. For PrettyMenu, it would typically look something like this:

```
struct PMImpl {                                    // PMImpl = "PrettyMenu
    std::tr1::shared_ptr<Image> bgImage;           // Impl."; see below for
    int imageChanges;                              // why it's a struct
};
class PrettyMenu {
    ...
private:
    Mutex mutex;
    std::tr1::shared_ptr<PMImpl> pImpl;
};
void PrettyMenu::changeBackground(std::istream& imgSrc)
{
    using std::swap;                               // see Item 25

    Lock ml(&mutex);                              // acquire the mutex

    std::tr1::shared_ptr<PMImpl>                   // copy obj. data
        pNew(new PMImpl(*pImpl));

    pNew->bgImage.reset(new Image(imgSrc));        // modify the copy
    ++pNew->imageChanges;

    swap(pImpl, pNew);                             // swap the new
                                                   // data into place
}                                                  // release the mutex
```

In this example, I've chosen to make PMImpl a struct instead of a class, because the encapsulation of PrettyMenu data is assured by pImpl being private. Making PMImpl a class would be at least as good, though somewhat less convenient. (It would also keep the object-oriented purists at bay.) If desired, PMImpl could be nested inside PrettyMenu, but packaging issues such as that are independent of writing exception-safe code, which is our concern here.

The copy-and-swap strategy is an excellent way to make all-or-nothing changes to an object's state, but, in general, it doesn't guarantee that the overall function is strongly exception-safe. To see why, consider an abstraction of changeBackground, someFunc, that uses copy-and-swap, but that includes calls to two other functions, f1 and f2:

```
void someFunc()
{
  ...                        // make copy of local state
  f1();
  f2();
  ...                        // swap modified state into place
}
```

It should be clear that if f1 or f2 is less than strongly exception-safe, it will be hard for someFunc to be strongly exception-safe. For example, suppose that f1 offers only the basic guarantee. For someFunc to offer the strong guarantee, it would have to write code to determine the state of the entire program prior to calling f1, catch all exceptions from f1, then restore the original state.

Things aren't really any better if both f1 and f2 *are* strongly exception safe. After all, if f1 runs to completion, the state of the program may have changed in arbitrary ways, so if f2 then throws an exception, the state of the program is not the same as it was when someFunc was called, even though f2 didn't change anything.

The problem is side effects. As long as functions operate only on local state (e.g., someFunc affects only the state of the object on which it's invoked), it's relatively easy to offer the strong guarantee. When functions have side effects on non-local data, it's much harder. If a side effect of calling f1, for example, is that a database is modified, it will be hard to make someFunc strongly exception-safe. There is, in general, no way to undo a database modification that has already been committed; other database clients may have already seen the new state of the database.

Issues such as these can prevent you from offering the strong guarantee for a function, even though you'd like to. Another issue is efficiency. The crux of copy-and-swap is the idea of modifying a copy of an object's data, then swapping the modified data for the original in a non-throwing operation. This requires making a copy of each object to be modified, which takes time and space you may be unable or unwilling to make available. The strong guarantee is highly desirable, and you should offer it when it's practical, but it's not practical 100% of the time.

When it's not, you'll have to offer the basic guarantee. In practice, you'll probably find that you can offer the strong guarantee for some functions, but the cost in efficiency or complexity will make it untenable for many others. As long as you've made a reasonable effort to offer the strong guarantee whenever it's practical, no one should be in a position to criticize you when you offer only the basic guarantee. For many functions, the basic guarantee is a perfectly reasonable choice.

Things are different if you write a function offering no exception-safety guarantee at all, because in this respect it's reasonable to assume that you're guilty until proven innocent. You *should* be writing exception-safe code. But you may have a compelling defense. Consider again the implementation of someFunc that calls the functions f1 and f2. Suppose f2 offers no exception safety guarantee at all, not even the basic guarantee. That means that if f2 emits an exception, the program may have leaked resources inside f2. It means that f2 may have corrupted data structures, e.g., sorted arrays might not be sorted any longer, objects being transferred from one data structure to another might have been lost, etc. There's no way that someFunc can compensate for those problems. If the functions someFunc calls offer no exception-safety guarantees, someFunc itself can't offer any guarantees.

Which brings me back to pregnancy. A female is either pregnant or she's not. It's not possible to be partially pregnant. Similarly, a software system is either exception-safe or it's not. There's no such thing as a partially exception-safe system. If a system has even a single function that's not exception-safe, the system as a whole is not exception-safe, because calls to that one function could lead to leaked resources and corrupted data structures. Unfortunately, much C++ legacy code was written without exception safety in mind, so many systems today are not exception-safe. They incorporate code that was written in an exception-unsafe manner.

There's no reason to perpetuate this state of affairs. When writing new code or modifying existing code, think carefully about how to make it exception-safe. Begin by using objects to manage resources. (Again, see Item 13.) That will prevent resource leaks. Follow that by determining which of the three exception safety guarantees is the strongest you can practically offer for each function you write, settling for no guarantee only if calls to legacy code leave you no choice. Document your decisions, both for clients of your functions and for future maintainers. A function's exception-safety guarantee is a visible part of its interface, so you should choose it as deliberately as you choose all other aspects of a function's interface.

Forty years ago, goto-laden code was considered perfectly good practice. Now we strive to write structured control flows. Twenty years ago, globally accessible data was considered perfectly good practice. Now we strive to encapsulate data. Ten years ago, writing functions without thinking about the impact of exceptions was considered perfectly good practice. Now we strive to write exception-safe code.

Time goes on. We live. We learn.

Things to Remember

✦ Exception-safe functions leak no resources and allow no data structures to become corrupted, even when exceptions are thrown. Such functions offer the basic, strong, or nothrow guarantees.

✦ The strong guarantee can often be implemented via copy-and-swap, but the strong guarantee is not practical for all functions.

✦ A function can usually offer a guarantee no stronger than the weakest guarantee of the functions it calls.

Item 30: Understand the ins and outs of inlining.

Inline functions — what a *wonderful* idea! They look like functions, they act like functions, they're ever so much better than macros (see Item 2), and you can call them without having to incur the overhead of a function call. What more could you ask for?

You actually get more than you might think, because avoiding the cost of a function call is only part of the story. Compiler optimizations are typically designed for stretches of code that lack function calls, so when you inline a function, you may enable compilers to perform context-specific optimizations on the body of the function. Most compilers never perform such optimizations on "outlined" function calls.

In programming, however, as in life, there is no free lunch, and inline functions are no exception. The idea behind an inline function is to replace each call of that function with its code body, and it doesn't take a Ph.D. in statistics to see that this is likely to increase the size of your object code. On machines with limited memory, overzealous inlining can give rise to programs that are too big for the available space. Even with virtual memory, inline-induced code bloat can lead to additional paging, a reduced instruction cache hit rate, and the performance penalties that accompany these things.

On the other hand, if an inline function body is *very* short, the code generated for the function body may be smaller than the code generated for a function call. If that is the case, inlining the function may actually lead to *smaller* object code and a higher instruction cache hit rate!

Bear in mind that inline is a *request* to compilers, not a command. The request can be given implicitly or explicitly. The implicit way is to define a function inside a class definition:

```
class Person {
public:
    ...
    int age() const { return theAge; }      // an implicit inline request: age is
    ...                                      // defined in a class definition
private:
    int theAge;
};
```

Such functions are usually member functions, but Item 46 explains that friend functions can also be defined inside classes. When they are, they're also implicitly declared inline.

The explicit way to declare an inline function is to precede its definition with the inline keyword. For example, this is how the standard max template (from <algorithm>) is often implemented:

```
template<typename T>                          // an explicit inline
inline const T& std::max(const T& a, const T& b)   // request: std::max is
{ return a < b ? b : a; }                     // preceded by "inline"
```

The fact that max is a template brings up the observation that both inline functions and templates are typically defined in header files. This leads some programmers to conclude that function templates must be inline. This conclusion is both invalid and potentially harmful, so it's worth looking into it a bit.

Inline functions must typically be in header files, because most build environments do inlining during compilation. In order to replace a function call with the body of the called function, compilers must know what the function looks like. (Some build environments can inline during linking, and a few — e.g., managed environments based on the .NET Common Language Infrastructure (CLI) — can actually inline at runtime. Such environments are the exception, however, not the rule. Inlining in most C++ programs is a compile-time activity.)

Templates are typically in header files, because compilers need to know what a template looks like in order to instantiate it when it's used. (Again, this is not universal. Some build environments perform template instantiation during linking. However, compile-time instantiation is more common.)

Template instantiation is independent of inlining. If you're writing a template and you believe that all the functions instantiated from the template should be inlined, declare the template inline; that's what's done with the std::max implementation above. But if you're writing a template for functions that you have no reason to want inlined, avoid declaring the template inline (either explicitly or implicitly). Inlining has costs, and you don't want to incur them without forethought. We've already mentioned how inlining can cause code bloat (a particularly important consideration for template authors — see Item 44), but there are other costs, too, which we'll discuss in a moment.

Before we do that, let's finish the observation that inline is a request that compilers may ignore. Most compilers refuse to inline functions they deem too complicated (e.g., those that contain loops or are recursive), and all but the most trivial calls to virtual functions defy inlining. This latter observation shouldn't be a surprise. virtual means "wait until runtime to figure out which function to call," and inline means "before execution, replace the call site with the called function." If compilers don't know which function will be called, you can hardly blame them for refusing to inline the function's body.

It all adds up to this: whether a given inline function is actually inlined depends on the build environment you're using — primarily on the compiler. Fortunately, most compilers have a diagnostic level that will result in a warning (see Item 53) if they fail to inline a function you've asked them to.

Sometimes compilers generate a function body for an inline function even when they are perfectly willing to inline the function. For example, if your program takes the address of an inline function, compilers must typically generate an outlined function body for it. How can they come up with a pointer to a function that doesn't exist? Coupled with the fact that compilers typically don't perform inlining across calls through function pointers, this means that calls to an inline function may or may not be inlined, depending on how the calls are made:

```
inline void f() {...}        // assume compilers are willing to inline calls to f
void (*pf)() = f;            // pf points to f

...

f();                         // this call will be inlined, because it's a "normal" call
```

pf();   // this call probably won't be, because it's through
                                       // a function pointer

The specter of un-inlined inline functions can haunt you even if you never use function pointers, because programmers aren't necessarily the only ones asking for pointers to functions. Sometimes compilers generate out-of-line copies of constructors and destructors so that they can get pointers to those functions for use during construction and destruction of objects in arrays.

In fact, constructors and destructors are often worse candidates for inlining than a casual examination would indicate. For example, consider the constructor for class Derived below:

```
class Base {
public:
  ...
private:
  std::string bm1, bm2;              // base members 1 and 2
};

class Derived: public Base {
public:
  Derived() {}                       // Derived's ctor is empty — or is it?
  ...
private:
  std::string dm1, dm2, dm3;         // derived members 1–3
};
```

This constructor looks like an excellent candidate for inlining, since it contains no code. But looks can be deceiving.

C++ makes various guarantees about things that happen when objects are created and destroyed. When you use new, for example, your dynamically created objects are automatically initialized by their constructors, and when you use delete, the corresponding destructors are invoked. When you create an object, each base class of and each data member in that object is automatically constructed, and the reverse process regarding destruction automatically occurs when an object is destroyed. If an exception is thrown during construction of an object, any parts of the object that have already been fully constructed are automatically destroyed. In all these scenarios, C++ says *what* must happen, but it doesn't say *how*. That's up to compiler implementers, but it should be clear that those things don't happen by themselves. There has to be some code in your program to make those things happen, and that code — the code written by compilers and inserted into your program during compilation — has to go somewhere. Sometimes it ends up in constructors and destructors, so we can imagine implementations generating code equivalent to the following for the allegedly empty Derived constructor above:

```
Derived::Derived()                       // conceptual implementation of
{                                        // "empty" Derived ctor

  Base::Base();                          // initialize Base part

  try { dm1.std::string::string(); }     // try to construct dm1
  catch (...) {                          // if it throws,
    Base::~Base();                       // destroy base class part and
    throw;                               // propagate the exception
  }

  try { dm2.std::string::string(); }     // try to construct dm2
  catch(...) {                           // if it throws,
    dm1.std::string::~string();          // destroy dm1,
    Base::~Base();                       // destroy base class part, and
    throw;                               // propagate the exception
  }

  try { dm3.std::string::string(); }     // construct dm3
  catch(...) {                           // if it throws,
    dm2.std::string::~string();          // destroy dm2,
    dm1.std::string::~string();          // destroy dm1,
    Base::~Base();                       // destroy base class part, and
    throw;                               // propagate the exception
  }

}
```

This code is unrepresentative of what real compilers emit, because real compilers deal with exceptions in more sophisticated ways. Still, this accurately reflects the behavior that Derived's "empty" constructor must offer. No matter how sophisticated a compiler's exception implementation, Derived's constructor must at least call constructors for its data members and base class, and those calls (which might themselves be inlined) could affect its attractiveness for inlining.

The same reasoning applies to the Base constructor, so if it's inlined, all the code inserted into it is also inserted into the Derived constructor (via the Derived constructor's call to the Base constructor). And if the string constructor also happens to be inlined, the Derived constructor will gain *five copies* of that function's code, one for each of the five strings in a Derived object (the two it inherits plus the three it declares itself). Perhaps now it's clear why it's not a no-brain decision whether to inline Derived's constructor. Similar considerations apply to Derived's destructor, which, one way or another, must see to it that all the objects initialized by Derived's constructor are properly destroyed.

Library designers must evaluate the impact of declaring functions inline, because it's impossible to provide binary upgrades to the client-visible inline functions in a library. In other words, if f is an inline function in a library, clients of the library compile the body of f into their applications. If a library implementer later decides to change f, all clients who've used f must recompile. This is often undesirable. On the other hand, if f is a non-inline function, a modification to f requires only that clients relink. This is a substantially less onerous burden than recompiling and, if the library containing the function is dynamically linked, one that may be absorbed in a way that's completely transparent to clients.

For purposes of program development, it is important to keep all these considerations in mind, but from a practical point of view during coding, one fact dominates all others: most debuggers have trouble with inline functions. This should be no great revelation. How do you set a breakpoint in a function that isn't there? Although some build environments manage to support debugging of inlined functions, many environments simply disable inlining for debug builds.

This leads to a logical strategy for determining which functions should be declared inline and which should not. Initially, don't inline anything, or at least limit your inlining to those functions that must be inline (see Item 46) or are truly trivial (such as Person::age on page 135). By employing inlines cautiously, you facilitate your use of a debugger, but you also put inlining in its proper place: as a hand-applied optimization. Don't forget the empirically determined rule of 80-20, which states that a typical program spends 80% of its time executing only 20% of its code. It's an important rule, because it reminds you that your goal as a software developer is to identify the 20% of your code that can increase your program's overall performance. You can inline and otherwise tweak your functions until the cows come home, but it's wasted effort unless you're focusing on the *right* functions.

Things to Remember

✦ Limit most inlining to small, frequently called functions. This facilitates debugging and binary upgradability, minimizes potential code bloat, and maximizes the chances of greater program speed.

✦ Don't declare function templates inline just because they appear in header files.

Item 31: Minimize compilation dependencies between files.

So you go into your C++ program and make a minor change to the implementation of a class. Not the class interface, mind you, just the implementation; only the private stuff. Then you rebuild the program, figuring that the exercise should take only a few seconds. After all, only one class has been modified. You click on Build or type make (or some equivalent), and you are astonished, then mortified, as you realize that the whole *world* is being recompiled and relinked! Don't you just *hate* it when that happens?

The problem is that C++ doesn't do a very good job of separating interfaces from implementations. A class definition specifies not only a class interface but also a fair number of implementation details. For example:

```
class Person {
public:
    Person(const std::string& name, const Date& birthday,
            const Address& addr);
    std::string name() const;
    std::string birthDate() const;
    std::string address() const;

    ...

private:
    std::string theName;        // implementation detail
    Date theBirthDate;          // implementation detail
    Address theAddress;         // implementation detail
};
```

Here, class Person can't be compiled without access to definitions for the classes the Person implementation uses, namely, string, Date, and Address. Such definitions are typically provided through #include directives, so in the file defining the Person class, you are likely to find something like this:

```
#include <string>
#include "date.h"
#include "address.h"
```

Unfortunately, this sets up a compilation dependency between the file defining Person and these header files. If any of these header files is changed, or if any of the header files *they* depend on changes, the file containing the Person class must be recompiled, as must any files that use Person. Such cascading compilation dependencies have caused many a project untold grief.

You might wonder why C++ insists on putting the implementation details of a class in the class definition. For example, why can't you define Person this way, specifying the implementation details of the class separately?

```
namespace std {
    class string;                   // forward declaration (an incorrect
}                                   // one — see below)

class Date;                         // forward declaration
class Address;                      // forward declaration

class Person {
public:
    Person(const std::string& name, const Date& birthday,
            const Address& addr);
    std::string name() const;
    std::string birthDate() const;
    std::string address() const;
    ...
};
```

If that were possible, clients of Person would have to recompile only if the interface to the class changed.

There are two problems with this idea. First, string is not a class, it's a typedef (for basic_string<char>). As a result, the forward declaration for string is incorrect. The proper forward declaration is substantially more complex, because it involves additional templates. That doesn't matter, however, because you shouldn't try to manually declare parts of the standard library. Instead, simply use the proper #includes and be done with it. Standard headers are unlikely to be a compilation bottleneck, especially if your build environment allows you to take advantage of precompiled headers. If parsing standard headers really is a problem, you may need to change your interface design to avoid using the parts of the standard library that give rise to the undesirable #includes.

The second (and more significant) difficulty with forward-declaring everything has to do with the need for compilers to know the size of objects during compilation. Consider:

```
int main()
{
    int x;                          // define an int

    Person p( params );             // define a Person
    ...
}
```

When compilers see the definition for x, they know they must allocate enough space (typically on the stack) to hold an int. No problem. Each

compiler knows how big an int is. When compilers see the definition
for p, they know they have to allocate enough space for a Person, but
how are they supposed to know how big a Person object is? The only
way they can get that information is to consult the class definition,
but if it were legal for a class definition to omit the implementation
details, how would compilers know how much space to allocate?

This question fails to arise in languages like Smalltalk and Java,
because, when an object is defined in such languages, compilers allocate only enough space for a *pointer* to an object. That is, they handle
the code above as if it had been written like this:

```
int main()
{
    int x;                          // define an int
    Person *p;                      // define a pointer to a Person
    ...
}
```

This, of course, is legal C++, so you can play the "hide the object
implementation behind a pointer" game yourself. One way to do that
for Person is to separate it into two classes, one offering only an interface, the other implementing that interface. If the implementation
class is named PersonImpl, Person would be defined like this:

```
#include <string>              // standard library components
                               // shouldn't be forward-declared

#include <memory>              // for tr1::shared_ptr; see below

class PersonImpl;              // forward decl of Person impl. class

class Date;                    // forward decls of classes used in
class Address;                 // Person interface

class Person {
public:
    Person(const std::string& name, const Date& birthday,
           const Address& addr);
    std::string name() const;
    std::string birthDate() const;
    std::string address() const;
    ...

private:                                    // ptr to implementation;
    std::tr1::shared_ptr<PersonImpl> pImpl; // see Item 13 for info on
};                                          // std::tr1::shared_ptr
```

Here, the main class (Person) contains as a data member nothing but a
pointer (here, a tr1::shared_ptr — see Item 13) to its implementation
class (PersonImpl). Such a design is often said to be using the *pimpl*

idiom ("pointer to implementation"). Within such classes, the name of the pointer is often pImpl, as it is above.

With this design, clients of Person are divorced from the details of dates, addresses, and persons. The implementations of those classes can be modified at will, but Person clients need not recompile. In addition, because they're unable to see the details of Person's implementation, clients are unlikely to write code that somehow depends on those details. This is a true separation of interface and implementation.

The key to this separation is replacement of dependencies on *definitions* with dependencies on *declarations*. That's the essence of minimizing compilation dependencies: make your header files self-sufficient whenever it's practical, and when it's not, depend on declarations in other files, not definitions. Everything else flows from this simple design strategy. Hence:

- **Avoid using objects when object references and pointers will do**. You may define references and pointers to a type with only a declaration for the type. Defining *objects* of a type necessitates the presence of the type's definition.

- **Depend on class declarations instead of class definitions whenever you can**. Note that you *never* need a class definition to declare a function using that class, not even if the function passes or returns the class type by value:

      class Date;   // class declaration

      Date today();   // fine — no definition
      void clearAppointments(Date d);   // of Date is needed

  Of course, pass-by-value is generally a bad idea (see Item 20), but if you find yourself using it for some reason, there's still no justification for introducing unnecessary compilation dependencies.

  The ability to declare today and clearAppointments without defining Date may surprise you, but it's not as curious as it seems. If anybody *calls* those functions, Date's definition must have been seen prior to the call. Why bother to declare functions that nobody calls, you wonder? Simple. It's not that *nobody* calls them, it's that *not everybody* calls them. If you have a library containing dozens of function declarations, it's unlikely that every client calls every function. By moving the onus of providing class definitions from your header file of function *declarations* to clients' files containing function *calls*, you eliminate artificial client dependencies on type definitions they don't really need.

- **Provide separate header files for declarations and definitions**. In order to facilitate adherence to the above guidelines, header files need to come in pairs: one for declarations, the other for definitions. These files must be kept consistent, of course. If a declaration is changed in one place, it must be changed in both. As a result, library clients should always #include a declaration file instead of forward-declaring something themselves, and library authors should provide both header files. For example, the Date client wishing to declare today and clearAppointments shouldn't manually forward-declare Date as shown above. Rather, it should #include the appropriate header of declarations:

      #include "datefwd.h"   // header file declaring (but not
                                      // defining) class Date

      Date today();   // as before
      void clearAppointments(Date d);

The name of the declaration-only header file "datefwd.h" is based on the header <iosfwd> from the standard C++ library (see Item 54). <iosfwd> contains declarations of iostream components whose corresponding definitions are in several different headers, including <sstream>, <streambuf>, <fstream>, and <iostream>.

<iosfwd> is instructive for another reason, and that's to make clear that the advice in this Item applies as well to templates as to non-templates. Although Item 30 explains that in many build environments, template definitions are typically found in header files, some build environments allow template definitions to be in non-header files, so it still makes sense to provide declaration-only headers for templates. <iosfwd> is one such header.

C++ also offers the export keyword to allow the separation of template declarations from template definitions. Unfortunately, compiler support for export is scanty, and real-world experience with export is scantier still. As a result, it's too early to say what role export will play in effective C++ programming.

Classes like Person that employ the pimpl idiom are often called *Handle classes*. Lest you wonder how such classes actually do anything, one way is to forward all their function calls to the corresponding implementation classes and have those classes do the real work. For example, here's how two of Person's member functions could be implemented:

      #include "Person.h"   // we're implementing the Person class,
                                     // so we must #include its class definition

```
#include "PersonImpl.h"          // we must also #include PersonImpl's class
                                  // definition, otherwise we couldn't call
                                  // its member functions; note that
                                  // PersonImpl has exactly the same
                                  // member functions as Person — their
                                  // interfaces are identical
Person::Person(const std::string& name, const Date& birthday,
               const Address& addr)
: pImpl(new PersonImpl(name, birthday, addr))
{}
std::string Person::name() const
{
    return pImpl->name();
}
```

Note how the Person constructor calls the PersonImpl constructor (by using new — see Item 16) and how Person::name calls PersonImpl::name. This is important. Making Person a Handle class doesn't change what Person does, it just changes the way it does it.

An alternative to the Handle class approach is to make Person a special kind of abstract base class called an *Interface class*. The purpose of such a class is to specify an interface for derived classes (see Item 34). As a result, it typically has no data members, no constructors, a virtual destructor (see Item 7), and a set of pure virtual functions that specify the interface.

Interface classes are akin to Java's and .NET's Interfaces, but C++ doesn't impose the restrictions on Interface classes that Java and .NET impose on Interfaces. Neither Java nor .NET allow data members or function implementations in Interfaces, for example, but C++ forbids neither of these things. C++'s greater flexibility can be useful. As Item 36 explains, the implementation of non-virtual functions should be the same for all classes in a hierarchy, so it makes sense to implement such functions as part of the Interface class that declares them.

An Interface class for Person could look like this:

```
class Person {
public:
    virtual ~Person();

    virtual std::string name() const = 0;
    virtual std::string birthDate() const = 0;
    virtual std::string address() const = 0;
    ...
};
```

Clients of this class must program in terms of Person pointers and references, because it's not possible to instantiate classes containing pure virtual functions. (It is, however, possible to instantiate classes *derived* from Person — see below.) Like clients of Handle classes, clients of Interface classes need not recompile unless the Interface class's interface is modified.

Clients of an Interface class must have a way to create new objects. They typically do it by calling a function that plays the role of the constructor for the derived classes that are actually instantiated. Such functions are typically called factory functions (see Item 13) or *virtual constructors*. They return pointers (preferably smart pointers — see Item 18) to dynamically allocated objects that support the Interface class's interface. Such functions are often declared static inside the Interface class:

```
class Person {
public:
    ...
    static std::tr1::shared_ptr<Person>      // return a tr1::shared_ptr to a new
        create(const std::string& name,      // Person initialized with the
            const Date& birthday,            // given params; see Item 18 for
            const Address& addr);            // why a tr1::shared_ptr is returned
    ...
};
```

Clients use them like this:

```
std::string name;
Date dateOfBirth;
Address address;
...

// create an object supporting the Person interface
std::tr1::shared_ptr<Person> pp(Person::create(name, dateOfBirth, address));

...

std::cout << pp->name()              // use the object via the
        << " was born on "           // Person interface
        << pp->birthDate()
        << " and now lives at "
        << pp->address();

    ...                              // the object is automatically
                                     // deleted when pp goes out of
                                     // scope — see Item 13
```

At some point, of course, concrete classes supporting the Interface class's interface must be defined and real constructors must be called. That all happens behind the scenes inside the files containing the implementations of the virtual constructors. For example, the Interface class Person might have a concrete derived class RealPerson that provides implementations for the virtual functions it inherits:

```
class RealPerson: public Person {
public:
  RealPerson(const std::string& name, const Date& birthday,
             const Address& addr)
   : theName(name), theBirthDate(birthday), theAddress(addr)
  {}

  virtual ~RealPerson() {}

  std::string name() const;          // implementations of these
  std::string birthDate() const;     // functions are not shown, but
  std::string address() const;       // they are easy to imagine
private:
  std::string theName;
  Date theBirthDate;
  Address theAddress;
};
```

Given RealPerson, it is truly trivial to write Person::create:

```
std::tr1::shared_ptr<Person> Person::create(const std::string& name,
                                            const Date& birthday,
                                            const Address& addr)
{
  return std::tr1::shared_ptr<Person>(new RealPerson(name, birthday,
                                                     addr));
}
```

A more realistic implementation of Person::create would create different types of derived class objects, depending on e.g., the values of additional function parameters, data read from a file or database, environment variables, etc.

RealPerson demonstrates one of the two most common mechanisms for implementing an Interface class: it inherits its interface specification from the Interface class (Person), then it implements the functions in the interface. A second way to implement an Interface class involves multiple inheritance, a topic explored in Item 40.

Handle classes and Interface classes decouple interfaces from implementations, thereby reducing compilation dependencies between files. Cynic that you are, I know you're waiting for the fine print. "What does all this hocus-pocus cost me?" you mutter. The answer is the usual one in computer science: it costs you some speed at runtime, plus some additional memory per object.

In the case of Handle classes, member functions have to go through the implementation pointer to get to the object's data. That adds one level of indirection per access. And you must add the size of this implementation pointer to the amount of memory required to store each object. Finally, the implementation pointer has to be initialized (in the Handle class's constructors) to point to a dynamically allocated implementation object, so you incur the overhead inherent in dynamic memory allocation (and subsequent deallocation) and the possibility of encountering bad_alloc (out-of-memory) exceptions.

For Interface classes, every function call is virtual, so you pay the cost of an indirect jump each time you make a function call (see Item 7). Also, objects derived from the Interface class must contain a virtual table pointer (again, see Item 7). This pointer may increase the amount of memory needed to store an object, depending on whether the Interface class is the exclusive source of virtual functions for the object.

Finally, neither Handle classes nor Interface classes can get much use out of inline functions. Item 30 explains why function bodies must typically be in header files in order to be inlined, but Handle and Interface classes are specifically designed to hide implementation details like function bodies.

It would be a serious mistake, however, to dismiss Handle classes and Interface classes simply because they have a cost associated with them. So do virtual functions, and you wouldn't want to forgo those, would you? (If so, you're reading the wrong book.) Instead, consider using these techniques in an evolutionary manner. Use Handle classes and Interface classes during development to minimize the impact on clients when implementations change. Replace Handle classes and Interface classes with concrete classes for production use when it can be shown that the difference in speed and/or size is significant enough to justify the increased coupling between classes.

Things to Remember

✦ The general idea behind minimizing compilation dependencies is to depend on declarations instead of definitions. Two approaches based on this idea are Handle classes and Interface classes.

✦ Library header files should exist in full and declaration-only forms. This applies regardless of whether templates are involved.

Inheritance and Object-Oriented Design

Object-oriented programming (OOP) has been the rage for almost two decades, so it's likely that you have some experience with the ideas of inheritance, derivation, and virtual functions. Even if you've been programming only in C, you've surely not escaped the OOP hoopla.

Still, OOP in C++ is probably a bit different from what you're used to. Inheritance can be single or multiple, and each inheritance link can be public, protected, or private. Each link can also be virtual or non-virtual. Then there are the member function options. Virtual? Non-virtual? Pure virtual? And the interactions with other language features. How do default parameter values interact with virtual functions? How does inheritance affect C++'s name lookup rules? And what about design options? If a class's behavior needs to be modifiable, is a virtual function the best way to do that?

This chapter sorts it all out. Furthermore, I explain what the different features in C++ really *mean* — what you are really *expressing* when you use a particular construct. For example, public inheritance means "is-a," and if you try to make it mean anything else, you'll run into trouble. Similarly, a virtual function means "interface must be inherited," while a non-virtual function means "both interface and implementation must be inherited." Failing to distinguish between these meanings has caused C++ programmers considerable grief.

If you understand the meanings of C++'s various features, you'll find that your outlook on OOP changes. Instead of it being an exercise in differentiating between language features, it will become a matter of determining what you want to say about your software system. And once you know what you want to say, the translation into C++ is not terribly demanding.

Item 32: Make sure public inheritance models "is-a."

In his book, *Some Must Watch While Some Must Sleep* (W. H. Freeman and Company, 1974), William Dement relates the story of his attempt to fix in the minds of his students the most important lessons of his course. It is claimed, he told his class, that the average British school-child remembers little more history than that the Battle of Hastings was in 1066. If a child remembers little else, Dement emphasized, he or she remembers the date 1066. For the students in *his* course, Dement went on, there were only a few central messages, including, interestingly enough, the fact that sleeping pills cause insomnia. He implored his students to remember these few critical facts even if they forgot everything else discussed in the course, and he returned to these fundamental precepts repeatedly during the term.

At the end of the course, the last question on the final exam was, "Write one thing from the course that you will surely remember for the rest of your life." When Dement graded the exams, he was stunned. Nearly everyone had written "1066."

It is thus with great trepidation that I proclaim to you now that the single most important rule in object-oriented programming with C++ is this: public inheritance means "is-a." Commit this rule to memory.

If you write that class D ("Derived") publicly inherits from class B ("Base"), you are telling C++ compilers (as well as human readers of your code) that every object of type D is also an object of type B, but *not vice versa.* You are saying that B represents a more general concept than D, that D represents a more specialized concept than B. You are asserting that anywhere an object of type B can be used, an object of type D can be used just as well, because every object of type D *is* an object of type B. On the other hand, if you need an object of type D, an object of type B will not do: every D is-a B, but not vice versa.

C++ enforces this interpretation of public inheritance. Consider this example:

```
class Person { ... };

class Student: public Person { ... };
```

We know from everyday experience that every student is a person, but not every person is a student. That is exactly what this hierarchy asserts. We expect that anything that is true of a person — for example, that he or she has a date of birth — is also true of a student. We do not expect that everything that is true of a student — that he or she is enrolled in a particular school, for instance — is true of people in general. The notion of a person is more general than is that of a student; a student is a specialized type of person.

Within the realm of C++, any function that expects an argument of type Person (or pointer-to-Person or reference-to-Person) will also take a Student object (or pointer-to-Student or reference-to-Student):

```
void eat(const Person& p);          // anyone can eat

void study(const Student& s);       // only students study

Person p;                           // p is a Person
Student s;                          // s is a Student

eat(p);                             // fine, p is a Person

eat(s);                             // fine, s is a Student,
                                    // and a Student is-a Person

study(s);                           // fine

study(p);                           // error! p isn't a Student
```

This is true only for *public* inheritance. C++ will behave as I've described only if Student is publicly derived from Person. Private inheritance means something entirely different (see Item 39), and protected inheritance is something whose meaning eludes me to this day.

The equivalence of public inheritance and is-a sounds simple, but sometimes your intuition can mislead you. For example, it is a fact that a penguin is a bird, and it is a fact that birds can fly. If we naively try to express this in C++, our effort yields:

```
class Bird {
public:
  virtual void fly();               // birds can fly

  ...

};

class Penguin: public Bird {        // penguins are birds

  ...

};
```

Suddenly we are in trouble, because this hierarchy says that penguins can fly, which we know is not true. What happened?

In this case, we are the victims of an imprecise language: English. When we say that birds can fly, we don't mean that *all* types of birds can fly, only that, in general, birds have the ability to fly. If we were more precise, we'd recognize that there are several types of non-flying

birds, and we would come up with the following hierarchy, which
models reality much better:

```
class Bird {
    ...                                     // no fly function is declared
};
class FlyingBird: public Bird {
public:
    virtual void fly();
    ...
};
class Penguin: public Bird {
    ...                                     // no fly function is declared
};
```

This hierarchy is much more faithful to what we really know than was
the original design.

Yet we're not finished with these fowl matters, because for some software systems, there may be no need to distinguish between flying and
non-flying birds. If your application has much to do with beaks and
wings and nothing to do with flying, the original two-class hierarchy
might be quite satisfactory. That's a simple reflection of the fact that
there is no one ideal design for all software. The best design depends
on what the system is expected to do, both now and in the future. If
your application has no knowledge of flying and isn't expected to ever
have any, failing to distinguish between flying and non-flying birds
may be a perfectly valid design decision. In fact, it may be preferable
to a design that does distinguish between them, because such a distinction would be absent from the world you are trying to model.

There is another school of thought on how to handle what I call the
"All birds can fly, penguins are birds, penguins can't fly, uh oh" problem. That is to redefine the fly function for penguins so that it generates a runtime error:

```
void error(const std::string& msg);      // defined elsewhere
class Penguin: public Bird {
public:
    virtual void fly() { error("Attempt to make a penguin fly!"); }
    ...
};
```

It's important to recognize that this says something different from what you might think. This does *not* say, "Penguins can't fly." This says, "Penguins can fly, but it's an error for them to actually try to do it."

How can you tell the difference? From the time at which the error is detected. The injunction, "Penguins can't fly," can be enforced by compilers, but violations of the rule, "It's an error for penguins to actually try to fly," can be detected only at runtime.

To express the constraint, "Penguins can't fly — *period*," you make sure that no such function is defined for Penguin objects:

```
class Bird {

    ...                                // no fly function is declared

};
class Penguin: public Bird {

    ...                                // no fly function is declared

};
```

If you now try to make a penguin fly, compilers will reprimand you for your transgression:

```
Penguin p;

p.fly();                           // error!
```

This is very different from the behavior you get if you adopt the approach that generates runtime errors. With that methodology, compilers won't say a word about the call to p.fly. Item 18 explains that good interfaces prevent invalid code from compiling, so you should prefer the design that rejects penguin flight attempts during compilation to the one that detects them only at runtime.

Perhaps you'll concede that your ornithological intuition may be lacking, but you can rely on your mastery of elementary geometry, right? I mean, how complicated can rectangles and squares be?

Well, answer this simple question: should class Square publicly inherit from class Rectangle?

"Duh!" you say, "Of course it should! Everybody knows that a square is a rectangle, but generally not vice versa." True enough, at least in school. But I don't think we're in school anymore.

Consider this code:

```
class Rectangle {
public:
    virtual void setHeight(int newHeight);
    virtual void setWidth(int newWidth);

    virtual int height() const;          // return current values
    virtual int width() const;

    ...
};
void makeBigger(Rectangle& r)            // function to increase r's area
{
    int oldHeight = r.height();

    r.setWidth(r.width() + 10);          // add 10 to r's width

    assert(r.height() == oldHeight);     // assert that r's
}                                        // height is unchanged
```

Clearly, the assertion should never fail. makeBigger only changes r's width. Its height is never modified.

Now consider this code, which uses public inheritance to allow squares to be treated like rectangles:

```
class Square: public Rectangle { ... };

Square s;

...

assert(s.width() == s.height());         // this must be true for all squares

makeBigger(s);                           // by inheritance, s is-a Rectangle,
                                         // so we can increase its area

assert(s.width() == s.height());         // this must still be true
                                         // for all squares
```

It's just as clear that this second assertion should also never fail. By definition, the width of a square is the same as its height.

But now we have a problem. How can we reconcile the following assertions?

- Before calling makeBigger, s's height is the same as its width;

- Inside makeBigger, s's width is changed, but its height is not;

▪ After returning from makeBigger, s's height is again the same as its width. (Note that s is passed to makeBigger by reference, so make-Bigger modifies s itself, not a copy of s.)

Well?

Welcome to the wonderful world of public inheritance, where the instincts you've developed in other fields of study — including mathematics — may not serve you as well as you expect. The fundamental difficulty in this case is that something applicable to a rectangle (its width may be modified independently of its height) is not applicable to a square (its width and height must be the same). But public inheritance asserts that everything that applies to base class objects — *everything!* — also applies to derived class objects. In the case of rectangles and squares (as well as an example involving sets and lists in Item 38), that assertion fails to hold, so using public inheritance to model their relationship is simply incorrect. Compilers will let you do it, but as we've just seen, that's no guarantee the code will behave properly. As every programmer must learn (some more often than others), just because the code compiles doesn't mean it will work.

Don't fret that the software intuition you've developed over the years will fail you as you approach object-oriented design. That knowledge is still valuable, but now that you've added inheritance to your arsenal of design alternatives, you'll have to augment your intuition with new insights to guide you in inheritance's proper application. In time, the notion of having Penguin inherit from Bird or Square inherit from Rectangle will give you the same funny feeling you probably get now when somebody shows you a function several pages long. It's *possibly* the right way to approach things, it's just not very likely.

The is-a relationship is not the only one that can exist between classes. Two other common inter-class relationships are "has-a" and "is-implemented-in-terms-of." These relationships are considered in Items 38 and 39. It's not uncommon for C++ designs to go awry because one of these other important relationships was incorrectly modeled as is-a, so you should make sure that you understand the differences among these relationships and that you know how each is best modeled in C++.

Things to Remember

✦ Public inheritance means "is-a." Everything that applies to base classes must also apply to derived classes, because every derived class object *is* a base class object.

Item 33: Avoid hiding inherited names.

Shakespeare had a thing about names. "What's in a name?" he asked, "A rose by any other name would smell as sweet." The Bard also wrote, "he that filches from me my good name ... makes me poor indeed." Right. Which brings us to inherited names in C++.

The matter actually has nothing to do with inheritance. It has to do with scopes. We all know that in code like this,

```
int x;                          // global variable
void someFunc()
{
    double x;                   // local variable
    std::cin >> x;              // read a new value for local x
}
```

the statement reading into x refers to the local variable x instead of the global variable x, because names in inner scopes hide ("shadow") names in outer scopes. We can visualize the scope situation this way:

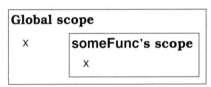

When compilers are in someFunc's scope and they encounter the name x, they look in the local scope to see if there is something with that name. Because there is, they never examine any other scope. In this case, someFunc's x is of type double and the global x is of type int, but that doesn't matter. C++'s name-hiding rules do just that: hide *names*. Whether the names correspond to the same or different types is immaterial. In this case, a double named x hides an int named x.

Enter inheritance. We know that when we're inside a derived class member function and we refer to something in a base class (e.g., a member function, a typedef, or a data member), compilers can find what we're referring to because derived classes inherit the things declared in base classes. The way that actually works is that the scope of a derived class is nested inside its base class's scope. For example:

```
class Base {
private:
  int x;

public:
  virtual void mf1() = 0;
  virtual void mf2();
  void mf3();
  ...
};

class Derived: public Base {
public:
  virtual void mf1();
  void mf4();
  ...
};
```

Base's scope

x (data member)
mf1 (1 function)
mf2 (1 function)
mf3 (1 function)

Derived's scope

mf1 (1 function)
mf4 (1 function)

This example includes a mix of public and private names as well as names of both data members and member functions. The member functions are pure virtual, simple (impure) virtual, and non-virtual. That's to emphasize that we're talking about *names*. The example could also have included names of types, e.g., enums, nested classes, and typedefs. The only thing that matters in this discussion is that they're names. What they're names *of* is irrelevant. The example uses single inheritance, but once you understand what's happening under single inheritance, C++'s behavior under multiple inheritance is easy to anticipate.

Suppose mf4 in the derived class is implemented, in part, like this:

```
void Derived::mf4()
{
  ...
  mf2();
  ...
}
```

When compilers see the use of the name mf2 here, they have to figure out what it refers to. They do that by searching scopes for a declaration of something named mf2. First they look in the local scope (that of mf4), but they find no declaration for anything called mf2. They then search the containing scope, that of the class Derived. They still find nothing named mf2, so they move on to the next containing scope, that of the base class. There they find something named mf2, so the search stops. If there were no mf2 in Base, the search would continue, first to the namespace(s) containing Base, if any, and finally to the global scope.

The process I just described is accurate, but it's not a comprehensive description of how names are found in C++. Our goal isn't to know enough about name lookup to write a compiler, however. It's to know enough to avoid unpleasant surprises, and for that task, we already have plenty of information.

Consider the previous example again, except this time let's overload mf1 and mf3, and let's add a version of mf3 to Derived. (As Item 36 explains, Derived's declaration of mf3 — an inherited non-virtual function — makes this design instantly suspicious, but in the interest of understanding name visibility under inheritance, we'll overlook that.)

```
class Base {
private:
    int x;

public:
    virtual void mf1() = 0;
    virtual void mf1(int);

    virtual void mf2();

    void mf3();
    void mf3(double);
    ...
};

class Derived: public Base {
public:
    virtual void mf1();
    void mf3();
    void mf4();

    ...
};
```

Base's scope

   x (data member)
   mf1 (2 functions)
   mf2 (1 function)
   mf3 (2 functions)

Derived's scope

   mf1 (1 function)
   mf3 (1 function)
   mf4 (1 function)

This code leads to behavior that surprises every C++ programmer the first time they encounter it. The scope-based name hiding rule hasn't changed, so *all* functions named mf1 and mf3 in the base class are hidden by the functions named mf1 and mf3 in the derived class. From the perspective of name lookup, Base::mf1 and Base::mf3 are no longer inherited by Derived!

```
Derived d;
int x;

...

d.mf1();            // fine, calls Derived::mf1
d.mf1(x);           // error! Derived::mf1 hides Base::mf1
```

```
d.mf2();                    // fine, calls Base::mf2
d.mf3();                    // fine, calls Derived::mf3
d.mf3(x);                   // error! Derived::mf3 hides Base::mf3
```

As you can see, this applies even though the functions in the base and derived classes take different parameter types, and it also applies regardless of whether the functions are virtual or non-virtual. In the same way that, at the beginning of this Item, the double x in the function someFunc hides the int x at global scope, here the function mf3 in Derived hides a Base function named mf3 that has a different type.

The rationale behind this behavior is that it prevents you from accidentally inheriting overloads from distant base classes when you create a new derived class in a library or application framework. Unfortunately, you typically *want* to inherit the overloads. In fact, if you're using public inheritance and you don't inherit the overloads, you're violating the is-a relationship between base and derived classes that Item 32 explains is fundamental to public inheritance. That being the case, you'll almost always want to override C++'s default hiding of inherited names.

You do it with *using declarations*:

```
class Base {
private:
  int x;

public:
  virtual void mf1() = 0;
  virtual void mf1(int);

  virtual void mf2();

  void mf3();
  void mf3(double);
  ...
};
```

Base's scope
x (data member)
mf1 (2 functions)
mf2 (1 function)
mf3 (2 functions)

Derived's scope
mf1 (2 functions)
mf3 (2 functions)
mf4 (1 function)

```
class Derived: public Base {
public:
  using Base::mf1;            // make all things in Base named mf1 and mf3
  using Base::mf3;            // visible (and public) in Derived's scope

  virtual void mf1();
  void mf3();
  void mf4();
  ...
};
```

Now inheritance will work as expected:

```
Derived d;
int x;

...

d.mf1();              // still fine, still calls Derived::mf1
d.mf1(x);             // now okay, calls Base::mf1

d.mf2();              // still fine, still calls Base::mf2

d.mf3();              // fine, calls Derived::mf3
d.mf3(x);             // now okay, calls Base::mf3
```

This means that if you inherit from a base class with overloaded functions and you want to redefine or override only some of them, you need to include a using declaration for each name you'd otherwise be hiding. If you don't, some of the names you'd like to inherit will be hidden.

It's conceivable that you sometimes won't want to inherit all the functions from your base classes. Under public inheritance, this should never be the case, because, again, it violates public inheritance's is-a relationship between base and derived classes. (That's why the using declarations above are in the public part of the derived class: names that are public in a base class should also be public in a publicly derived class.) Under private inheritance (see Item 39), however, it can make sense. For example, suppose Derived privately inherits from Base, and the only version of mf1 that Derived wants to inherit is the one taking no parameters. A using declaration won't do the trick here, because a using declaration makes *all* inherited functions with a given name visible in the derived class. No, this is a case for a different technique, namely, a simple forwarding function:

```
class Base {
public:
  virtual void mf1() = 0;
  virtual void mf1(int);

    ...                        // as before
};
class Derived: private Base {
public:
  virtual void mf1()           // forwarding function; implicitly
  { Base::mf1(); }             // inline — see Item 30. (For info
    ...                        // on calling a pure virtual
};                             // function, see Item 34.)

...

Derived d;
int x;

d.mf1();                       // fine, calls Derived::mf1
d.mf1(x);                      // error! Base::mf1() is hidden
```

Another use for inline forwarding functions is to work around ancient compilers that (incorrectly) don't support using declarations to import inherited names into the scope of a derived class.

That's the whole story on inheritance and name hiding, but when inheritance is combined with templates, an entirely different form of the "inherited names are hidden" issue arises. For all the angle-bracket-demarcated details, see Item 43.

Things to Remember

✦ Names in derived classes hide names in base classes. Under public inheritance, this is never desirable.

✦ To make hidden names visible again, employ using declarations or forwarding functions.

Item 34: Differentiate between inheritance of interface and inheritance of implementation.

The seemingly straightforward notion of (public) inheritance turns out, upon closer examination, to be composed of two separable parts: inheritance of function interfaces and inheritance of function implementations. The difference between these two kinds of inheritance corresponds exactly to the difference between function declarations and function definitions discussed in the Introduction to this book.

As a class designer, you sometimes want derived classes to inherit only the interface (declaration) of a member function. Sometimes you want derived classes to inherit both a function's interface and implementation, but you want to allow them to override the implementation they inherit. And sometimes you want derived classes to inherit a function's interface and implementation without allowing them to override anything.

To get a better feel for the differences among these options, consider a class hierarchy for representing geometric shapes in a graphics application:

```
class Shape {
public:
  virtual void draw() const = 0;

  virtual void error(const std::string& msg);

  int objectID() const;

  ...
};

class Rectangle: public Shape { ... };

class Ellipse: public Shape { ... };
```

Shape is an abstract class; its pure virtual function draw marks it as such. As a result, clients cannot create instances of the Shape class, only of classes derived from it. Nonetheless, Shape exerts a strong influence on all classes that (publicly) inherit from it, because

- Member function *interfaces are always inherited*. As explained in Item 32, public inheritance means is-a, so anything that is true of a base class must also be true of its derived classes. Hence, if a function applies to a class, it must also apply to its derived classes.

Three functions are declared in the Shape class. The first, draw, draws the current object on an implicit display. The second, error, is called when an error needs to be reported. The third, objectID, returns a unique integer identifier for the current object. Each function is declared in a different way: draw is a pure virtual function; error is a simple (impure?) virtual function; and objectID is a non-virtual function. What are the implications of these different declarations?

Consider first the pure virtual function draw:

```
class Shape {
public:
    virtual void draw() const = 0;
    ...
};
```

The two most salient features of pure virtual functions are that they *must* be redeclared by any concrete class that inherits them, and they typically have no definition in abstract classes. Put these two characteristics together, and you realize that

- The purpose of declaring a pure virtual function is to have derived classes inherit a function *interface only*.

This makes perfect sense for the Shape::draw function, because it is a reasonable demand that all Shape objects must be drawable, but the Shape class can provide no reasonable default implementation for that function. The algorithm for drawing an ellipse is very different from the algorithm for drawing a rectangle, for example. The declaration of Shape::draw says to designers of concrete derived classes, "You must provide a draw function, but I have no idea how you're going to implement it."

Incidentally, it *is* possible to provide a definition for a pure virtual function. That is, you could provide an implementation for Shape::draw, and C++ wouldn't complain, but the only way to call it would be to qualify the call with the class name:

```
Shape *ps = new Shape;              // error! Shape is abstract

Shape *ps1 = new Rectangle;         // fine
ps1->draw();                        // calls Rectangle::draw

Shape *ps2 = new Ellipse;           // fine
ps2->draw();                        // calls Ellipse::draw

ps1->Shape::draw();                 // calls Shape::draw

ps2->Shape::draw();                 // calls Shape::draw
```

Aside from helping you impress fellow programmers at cocktail parties, knowledge of this feature is generally of limited utility. As you'll see below, however, it can be employed as a mechanism for providing a safer-than-usual default implementation for simple (impure) virtual functions.

The story behind simple virtual functions is a bit different from that behind pure virtuals. As usual, derived classes inherit the interface of the function, but simple virtual functions provide an implementation that derived classes may override. If you think about this for a minute, you'll realize that

- The purpose of declaring a simple virtual function is to have derived classes inherit a function *interface as well as a default implementation.*

Consider the case of Shape::error:

```
class Shape {
public:
    virtual void error(const std::string& msg);
    ...
};
```

The interface says that every class must support a function to be called when an error is encountered, but each class is free to handle errors in whatever way it sees fit. If a class doesn't want to do anything special, it can just fall back on the default error handling provided in the Shape class. That is, the declaration of Shape::error says to designers of derived classes, "You've got to support an error function, but if you don't want to write your own, you can fall back on the default version in the Shape class."

It turns out that it can be dangerous to allow simple virtual functions to specify both a function interface and a default implementation. To see why, consider a hierarchy of airplanes for XYZ Airlines. XYZ has only two kinds of planes, the Model A and the Model B, and both are flown in exactly the same way. Hence, XYZ designs the following hierarchy:

```
class Airport { ... };                          // represents airports

class Airplane {
public:
    virtual void fly(const Airport& destination);

    ...

};

void Airplane::fly(const Airport& destination)
{
    default code for flying an airplane to the given destination
}

class ModelA: public Airplane { ... };

class ModelB: public Airplane { ... };
```

To express that all planes have to support a fly function, and in recognition of the fact that different models of plane could, in principle, require different implementations for fly, Airplane::fly is declared virtual. However, in order to avoid writing identical code in the ModelA and ModelB classes, the default flying behavior is provided as the body of Airplane::fly, which both ModelA and ModelB inherit.

This is a classic object-oriented design. Two classes share a common feature (the way they implement fly), so the common feature is moved into a base class, and the feature is inherited by the two classes. This design makes common features explicit, avoids code duplication, facilitates future enhancements, and eases long-term maintenance — all the things for which object-oriented technology is so highly touted. XYZ Airlines should be proud.

Now suppose that XYZ, its fortunes on the rise, decides to acquire a new type of airplane, the Model C. The Model C differs in some ways from the Model A and the Model B. In particular, it is flown differently.

XYZ's programmers add the class for Model C to the hierarchy, but in their haste to get the new model into service, they forget to redefine the fly function:

```
class ModelC: public Airplane {
                                    // no fly function is declared
    ...
};
```

In their code, then, they have something akin to the following:

```
Airport PDX(...);                   // PDX is the airport near my home

Airplane *pa = new ModelC;

...

pa->fly(PDX);                       // calls Airplane::fly!
```

This is a disaster: an attempt is being made to fly a ModelC object as if it were a ModelA or a ModelB. That's not the kind of behavior that inspires confidence in the traveling public.

The problem here is not that Airplane::fly has default behavior, but that ModelC was allowed to inherit that behavior without explicitly saying that it wanted to. Fortunately, it's easy to offer default behavior to derived classes but not give it to them unless they ask for it. The trick is to sever the connection between the *interface* of the virtual function and its default *implementation*. Here's one way to do it:

```
class Airplane {
public:
  virtual void fly(const Airport& destination) = 0;

  ...

protected:
  void defaultFly(const Airport& destination);
};

void Airplane::defaultFly(const Airport& destination)
{
    default code for flying an airplane to the given destination
}
```

Notice how Airplane::fly has been turned into a *pure* virtual function. That provides the interface for flying. The default implementation is also present in the Airplane class, but now it's in the form of an independent function, defaultFly. Classes like ModelA and ModelB that want to use the default behavior simply make an inline call to defaultFly inside their body of fly (but see Item 30 for information on the interaction of inlining and virtual functions):

```
class ModelA: public Airplane {
public:
  virtual void fly(const Airport& destination)
  { defaultFly(destination); }

  ...

};

class ModelB: public Airplane {
public:
  virtual void fly(const Airport& destination)
  { defaultFly(destination); }

  ...

};
```

For the ModelC class, there is no possibility of accidentally inheriting the incorrect implementation of fly, because the pure virtual in Airplane forces ModelC to provide its own version of fly.

```
class ModelC: public Airplane {
public:
  virtual void fly(const Airport& destination);

  ...

};

void ModelC::fly(const Airport& destination)
{
  code for flying a ModelC airplane to the given destination
}
```

This scheme isn't foolproof (programmers can still copy-and-paste themselves into trouble), but it's more reliable than the original design. As for Airplane::defaultFly, it's protected because it's truly an implementation detail of Airplane and its derived classes. Clients using airplanes should care only that they can be flown, not how the flying is implemented.

It's also important that Airplane::defaultFly is a *non-virtual* function. This is because no derived class should redefine this function, a truth to which Item 36 is devoted. If defaultFly were virtual, you'd have a circular problem: what if some derived class forgets to redefine defaultFly when it's supposed to?

Some people object to the idea of having separate functions for providing interface and default implementation, such as fly and defaultFly above. For one thing, they note, it pollutes the class namespace with a proliferation of closely related function names. Yet they still agree that interface and default implementation should be separated. How do they resolve this seeming contradiction? By taking advantage of the fact that pure virtual functions must be redeclared in concrete derived classes, but they may also have implementations of their own. Here's how the Airplane hierarchy could take advantage of the ability to define a pure virtual function:

```
class Airplane {
public:
  virtual void fly(const Airport& destination) = 0;

  ...

};
```

```
void Airplane::fly(const Airport& destination)        // an implementation of
{                                                     // a pure virtual function
    default code for flying an airplane to
    the given destination
}
class ModelA: public Airplane {
public:
    virtual void fly(const Airport& destination)
    { Airplane::fly(destination); }

    ...

};
class ModelB: public Airplane {
public:
    virtual void fly(const Airport& destination)
    { Airplane::fly(destination); }

    ...

};
class ModelC: public Airplane {
public:
    virtual void fly(const Airport& destination);

    ...

};
void ModelC::fly(const Airport& destination)
{
    code for flying a ModelC airplane to the given destination
}
```

This is almost exactly the same design as before, except that the body of the pure virtual function Airplane::fly takes the place of the independent function Airplane::defaultFly. In essence, fly has been broken into its two fundamental components. Its declaration specifies its interface (which derived classes *must* use), while its definition specifies its default behavior (which derived classes *may* use, but only if they explicitly request it). In merging fly and defaultFly, however, you've lost the ability to give the two functions different protection levels: the code that used to be protected (by being in defaultFly) is now public (because it's in fly).

Finally, we come to Shape's non-virtual function, objectID:

```
class Shape {
public:
    int objectID() const;
    ...
};
```

When a member function is non-virtual, it's not supposed to behave differently in derived classes. In fact, a non-virtual member function specifies an *invariant over specialization*, because it identifies behavior that is not supposed to change, no matter how specialized a derived class becomes. As such,

- The purpose of declaring a non-virtual function is to have derived classes inherit a function *interface as well as a mandatory implementation.*

You can think of the declaration for Shape::objectID as saying, "Every Shape object has a function that yields an object identifier, and that object identifier is always computed the same way. That way is determined by the definition of Shape::objectID, and no derived class should try to change how it's done." Because a non-virtual function identifies an *invariant* over specialization, it should never be redefined in a derived class, a point that is discussed in detail in Item 36.

The differences in declarations for pure virtual, simple virtual, and non-virtual functions allow you to specify with precision what you want derived classes to inherit: interface only, interface and a default implementation, or interface and a mandatory implementation, respectively. Because these different types of declarations mean fundamentally different things, you must choose carefully among them when you declare your member functions. If you do, you should avoid the two most common mistakes made by inexperienced class designers.

The first mistake is to declare all functions non-virtual. That leaves no room for specialization in derived classes; non-virtual destructors are particularly problematic (see Item 7). Of course, it's perfectly reasonable to design a class that is not intended to be used as a base class. In that case, a set of exclusively non-virtual member functions is appropriate. Too often, however, such classes are declared either out of ignorance of the differences between virtual and non-virtual functions or as a result of an unsubstantiated concern over the performance cost of virtual functions. The fact of the matter is that almost any class that's to be used as a base class will have virtual functions (again, see Item 7).

If you're concerned about the cost of virtual functions, allow me to bring up the empirically-based rule of 80-20 (see also Item 30), which states that in a typical program, 80% of the runtime will be spent executing just 20% of the code. This rule is important, because it means that, on average, 80% of your function calls can be virtual without having the slightest detectable impact on your program's overall performance. Before you go gray worrying about whether you can afford the cost of a virtual function, take the simple precaution of making sure that you're focusing on the 20% of your program where the decision might really make a difference.

The other common problem is to declare *all* member functions virtual. Sometimes this is the right thing to do — witness Item 31's Interface classes. However, it can also be a sign of a class designer who lacks the backbone to take a stand. Some functions should *not* be redefinable in derived classes, and whenever that's the case, you've got to say so by making those functions non-virtual. It serves no one to pretend that your class can be all things to all people if they'll just take the time to redefine all your functions. If you have an invariant over specialization, don't be afraid to say so!

Things to Remember

✦ Inheritance of interface is different from inheritance of implementation. Under public inheritance, derived classes always inherit base class interfaces.

✦ Pure virtual functions specify inheritance of interface only.

✦ Simple (impure) virtual functions specify inheritance of interface plus inheritance of a default implementation.

✦ Non-virtual functions specify inheritance of interface plus inheritance of a mandatory implementation.

Item 35: Consider alternatives to virtual functions.

So you're working on a video game, and you're designing a hierarchy for characters in the game. Your game being of the slash-and-burn variety, it's not uncommon for characters to be injured or otherwise in a reduced state of health. You therefore decide to offer a member function, healthValue, that returns an integer indicating how healthy the character is. Because different characters may calculate their health in different ways, declaring healthValue virtual seems the obvious way to design things:

```
class GameCharacter {
public:
    virtual int healthValue() const;      // return character's health rating;
    ...                                    // derived classes may redefine this
};
```

The fact that healthValue isn't declared pure virtual suggests that there is a default algorithm for calculating health (see Item 34).

This is, indeed, the obvious way to design things, and in some sense, that's its weakness. Because this design is so obvious, you may not give adequate consideration to its alternatives. In the interest of helping you escape the ruts in the road of object-oriented design, let's consider some other ways to approach this problem.

The Template Method Pattern via the Non-Virtual Interface Idiom

We'll begin with an interesting school of thought that argues that virtual functions should almost always be private. Adherents to this school would suggest that a better design would retain healthValue as a public member function but make it non-virtual and have it call a private virtual function to do the real work, say, doHealthValue:

```cpp
class GameCharacter {
public:
  int healthValue() const        // derived classes do not redefine
  {                              // this — see Item 36

    ...                         // do "before" stuff — see below

    int retVal = doHealthValue();   // do the real work

    ...                         // do "after" stuff — see below

    return retVal;
  }
  ...
private:
  virtual int doHealthValue() const    // derived classes may redefine this
  {
    ...                         // default algorithm for calculating
  }                            // character's health
};
```

In this code (and for the rest of this Item), I'm showing the bodies of member functions in class definitions. As Item 30 explains, that implicitly declares them inline. I'm showing the code this way only to make it easier to see what is going on. The designs I'm describing are independent of inlining decisions, so don't think it's meaningful that the member functions are defined inside classes. It's not.

This basic design — having clients call private virtual functions indirectly through public non-virtual member functions — is known as the *non-virtual interface (NVI) idiom*. It's a particular manifestation of the more general design pattern called Template Method (a pattern that, unfortunately, has nothing to do with C++ templates). I call the non-virtual function (e.g., healthValue) the virtual function's *wrapper*.

An advantage of the NVI idiom is suggested by the "do 'before' stuff" and "do 'after' stuff" comments in the code. Those comments identify code segments guaranteed to be called before and after the virtual function that does the real work. This means that the wrapper ensures that before a virtual function is called, the proper context is set up, and after the call is over, the context is cleaned up. For example, the "before" stuff could include locking a mutex, making a log entry, verifying that class invariants and function preconditions are satisfied, etc. The "after" stuff could include unlocking a mutex, verifying function postconditions, reverifying class invariants, etc. There's not really any good way to do that if you let clients call virtual functions directly.

It may have crossed your mind that the NVI idiom involves derived classes redefining private virtual functions — redefining functions they can't call! There's no design contradiction here. Redefining a virtual function specifies *how* something is to be done. Calling a virtual function specifies *when* it will be done. These concerns are independent. The NVI idiom allows derived classes to redefine a virtual function, thus giving them control over *how* functionality is implemented, but the base class reserves for itself the right to say *when* the function will be called. It may seem odd at first, but C++'s rule that derived classes may redefine private inherited virtual functions is perfectly sensible.

Under the NVI idiom, it's not strictly necessary that the virtual functions be private. In some class hierarchies, derived class implementations of a virtual function are expected to invoke their base class counterparts (e.g., the example on page 120), and for such calls to be legal, the virtuals must be protected, not private. Sometimes a virtual function even has to be public (e.g., destructors in polymorphic base classes — see Item 7), but then the NVI idiom can't really be applied.

The Strategy Pattern via Function Pointers

The NVI idiom is an interesting alternative to public virtual functions, but from a design point of view, it's little more than window dressing. After all, we're still using virtual functions to calculate each character's health. A more dramatic design assertion would be to say that calculating a character's health is independent of the character's type — that such calculations need not be part of the character at all. For example, we could require that each character's constructor be passed a pointer to a health calculation function, and we could call that function to do the actual calculation:

```
class GameCharacter;                              // forward declaration
// function for the default health calculation algorithm
int defaultHealthCalc(const GameCharacter& gc);

class GameCharacter {
public:
    typedef int (*HealthCalcFunc)(const GameCharacter&);

    explicit GameCharacter(HealthCalcFunc hcf = defaultHealthCalc)
    : healthFunc(hcf)
    {}

    int healthValue() const
    { return healthFunc(*this); }

    ...

private:
    HealthCalcFunc healthFunc;
};
```

This approach is a simple application of another common design pattern, Strategy. Compared to approaches based on virtual functions in the GameCharacter hierarchy, it offers some interesting flexibility:

- Different instances of the same character type can have different health calculation functions. For example:

```
class EvilBadGuy: public GameCharacter {
public:
    explicit EvilBadGuy(HealthCalcFunc hcf = defaultHealthCalc)
    : GameCharacter(hcf)
    { ... }

    ...

};
int loseHealthQuickly(const GameCharacter&);    // health calculation
int loseHealthSlowly(const GameCharacter&);     // funcs with different
                                                // behavior

EvilBadGuy ebg1(loseHealthQuickly);             // same-type charac-
EvilBadGuy ebg2(loseHealthSlowly);              // ters with different
                                                // health-related
                                                // behavior
```

- Health calculation functions for a particular character may be changed at runtime. For example, GameCharacter might offer a member function, setHealthCalculator, that allowed replacement of the current health calculation function.

On the other hand, the fact that the health calculation function is no longer a member function of the GameCharacter hierarchy means that it has no special access to the internal parts of the object whose health it's calculating. For example, defaultHealthCalc has no access to the non-public parts of EvilBadGuy. If a character's health can be calculated based purely on information available through the character's public interface, this is not a problem, but if accurate health calculation requires non-public information, it is. In fact, it's a potential issue anytime you replace functionality inside a class (e.g., via a member function) with equivalent functionality outside the class (e.g., via a non-member non-friend function or via a non-friend member function of another class). This issue will persist for the remainder of this Item, because all the other design alternatives we're going to consider involve the use of functions outside the GameCharacter hierarchy.

As a general rule, the only way to resolve the need for non-member functions to have access to non-public parts of a class is to weaken the class's encapsulation. For example, the class might declare the non-member functions to be friends, or it might offer public accessor functions for parts of its implementation it would otherwise prefer to keep hidden. Whether the advantages of using a function pointer instead of a virtual function (e.g., the ability to have per-object health calculation functions and the ability to change such functions at run-time) offset the possible need to decrease GameCharacter's encapsulation is something you must decide on a design-by-design basis.

The Strategy Pattern via tr1::function

Once you accustom yourself to templates and their use of implicit interfaces (see Item 41), the function-pointer-based approach looks rather rigid. Why must the health calculator be a function instead of simply something that *acts* like a function (e.g., a function object)? If it must be a function, why can't it be a member function? And why must it return an int instead of any type *convertible* to an int?

These constraints evaporate if we replace the use of a function pointer (such as healthFunc) with an object of type tr1::function. As Item 54 explains, such objects may hold *any callable entity* (i.e., function pointer, function object, or member function pointer) whose signature is compatible with what is expected. Here's the design we just saw, this time using tr1::function:

```
class GameCharacter;                                    // as before
int defaultHealthCalc(const GameCharacter& gc);         // as before

class GameCharacter {
public:
    // HealthCalcFunc is any callable entity that can be called with
    // anything compatible with a GameCharacter and that returns anything
    // compatible with an int; see below for details
    typedef std::tr1::function<int (const GameCharacter&)> HealthCalcFunc;
```

```
explicit GameCharacter(HealthCalcFunc hcf = defaultHealthCalc)
: healthFunc(hcf)
{}

int healthValue() const
{ return healthFunc(*this); }

...

private:
  HealthCalcFunc healthFunc;
};
```

As you can see, HealthCalcFunc is a typedef for a tr1::function instantiation. That means it acts like a generalized function pointer type. Look closely at what HealthCalcFunc is a typedef for:

```
std::tr1::function<int (const GameCharacter&)>
```

Here I've highlighted the "target signature" of this tr1::function instantiation. That target signature is "function taking a const GameCharacter& and returning an int." An object of this tr1::function type (i.e., of type HealthCalcFunc) may hold any callable entity compatible with the target signature. To be compatible means that const GameCharacter& either is or can be converted to the type of the entity's parameter, and the entity's return type either is or can be implicitly converted to int.

Compared to the last design we saw (where GameCharacter held a pointer to a function), this design is almost the same. The only difference is that GameCharacter now holds a tr1::function object — a *generalized* pointer to a function. This change is so small, I'd call it inconsequential, except that a consequence is that clients now have staggeringly more flexibility in specifying health calculation functions:

```
short calcHealth(const GameCharacter&);          // health calculation
                                                 // function; note
                                                 // non-int return type

struct HealthCalculator {                        // class for health
  int operator()(const GameCharacter&) const     // calculation function
  { ... }                                        // objects
};

class GameLevel {
public:
  float health(const GameCharacter&) const;      // health calculation
  ...                                            // mem function; note
};                                               // non-int return type


class EvilBadGuy: public GameCharacter {         // as before

  ...
};
```

```
class EyeCandyCharacter: public GameCharacter {    // another character
    ...                                            // type; assume same
};                                                 // constructor as
                                                   // EvilBadGuy


EvilBadGuy ebg1(calcHealth);                        // character using a
                                                    // health calculation
                                                    // function

EyeCandyCharacter ecc1(HealthCalculator());         // character using a
                                                    // health calculation
                                                    // function object

GameLevel currentLevel;
...

EvilBadGuy ebg2(                                    // character using a
    std::tr1::bind(&GameLevel::health,              // health calculation
                    currentLevel,                   // member function;
                    _1)                             // see below for details
);
```

Personally, I find what tr1::function lets you do so amazing, it makes me tingle all over. If you're not tingling, it may be because you're staring at the definition of ebg2 and wondering what's going on with the call to tr1::bind. Kindly allow me to explain.

We want to say that to calculate ebg2's health rating, the health member function in the GameLevel class should be used. Now, GameLevel::health is a function that is declared to take one parameter (a reference to a GameCharacter), but it really takes two, because it also gets an implicit GameLevel parameter — the one this points to. Health calculation functions for GameCharacters, however, take a single parameter: the GameCharacter whose health is to be calculated. If we're to use GameLevel::health for ebg2's health calculation, we have to somehow "adapt" it so that instead of taking two parameters (a GameCharacter and a GameLevel), it takes only one (a GameCharacter). In this example, we always want to use currentLevel as the GameLevel object for ebg2's health calculation, so we "bind" currentLevel as the GameLevel object to be used each time GameLevel::health is called to calculate ebg2's health. That's what the tr1::bind call does: it specifies that ebg2's health calculation function should always use currentLevel as the GameLevel object.

I'm skipping over a host of details regarding the call to tr1::bind, because such details wouldn't be terribly illuminating, and they'd distract from the fundamental point I want to make: by using tr1::function instead of a function pointer, we're allowing clients to use *any compatible callable entity* when calculating a character's health. Is that cool or what?

The "Classic" Strategy Pattern

If you're more into design patterns than C++ coolness, a more conventional approach to Strategy would be to make the health-calculation function a virtual member function of a separate health-calculation hierarchy. The resulting hierarchy design would look like this:

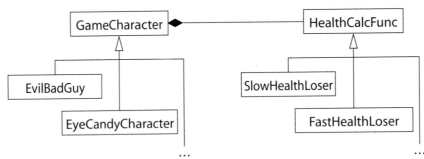

If you're not up on your UML notation, this just says that GameCharacter is the root of an inheritance hierarchy where EvilBadGuy and EyeCandyCharacter are derived classes; HealthCalcFunc is the root of an inheritance hierarchy with derived classes SlowHealthLoser and FastHealthLoser; and each object of type GameCharacter contains a pointer to an object from the HealthCalcFunc hierarchy.

Here's the corresponding code skeleton:

```
class GameCharacter;                          // forward declaration

class HealthCalcFunc {
public:
    ...
    virtual int calc(const GameCharacter& gc) const
    { ... }
    ...
};

HealthCalcFunc defaultHealthCalc;

class GameCharacter {
public:
    explicit GameCharacter(HealthCalcFunc *phcf = &defaultHealthCalc)
    : pHealthCalc(phcf)
    {}

    int healthValue() const
    { return pHealthCalc->calc(*this); }

    ...

private:
    HealthCalcFunc *pHealthCalc;
};
```

This approach has the appeal of being quickly recognizable to people familiar with the "standard" Strategy pattern implementation, plus it offers the possibility that an existing health calculation algorithm can be tweaked by adding a derived class to the HealthCalcFunc hierarchy.

Summary

The fundamental advice of this Item is to consider alternatives to virtual functions when searching for a design for the problem you're trying to solve. Here's a quick recap of the alternatives we examined:

- Use the **non-virtual interface idiom** (NVI idiom), a form of the Template Method design pattern that wraps public non-virtual member functions around less accessible virtual functions.

- Replace virtual functions with **function pointer data members**, a stripped-down manifestation of the Strategy design pattern.

- Replace virtual functions with **tr1::function data members**, thus allowing use of any callable entity with a signature compatible with what you need. This, too, is a form of the Strategy design pattern.

- Replace virtual functions in one hierarchy with **virtual functions in another hierarchy**. This is the conventional implementation of the Strategy design pattern.

This isn't an exhaustive list of design alternatives to virtual functions, but it should be enough to convince you that there *are* alternatives. Furthermore, their comparative advantages and disadvantages should make clear that you *should* consider them.

To avoid getting stuck in the ruts of the road of object-oriented design, give the wheel a good jerk from time to time. There are lots of other roads. It's worth taking the time to investigate them.

Things to Remember

- Alternatives to virtual functions include the NVI idiom and various forms of the Strategy design pattern. The NVI idiom is itself an example of the Template Method design pattern.

- A disadvantage of moving functionality from a member function to a function outside the class is that the non-member function lacks access to the class's non-public members.

- tr1::function objects act like generalized function pointers. Such objects support all callable entities compatible with a given target signature.

Item 36: Never redefine an inherited non-virtual function.

Suppose I tell you that a class D is publicly derived from a class B and that there is a public member function mf defined in class B. The parameters and return type of mf are unimportant, so let's just assume they're both void. In other words, I say this:

```
class B {
public:
  void mf();

  ...
};

class D: public B { ... };
```

Even without knowing anything about B, D, or mf, given an object x of type D,

```
D x;                              // x is an object of type D
```

you would probably be quite surprised if this,

```
B *pB = &x;                       // get pointer to x

pB->mf();                         // call mf through pointer
```

behaved differently from this:

```
D *pD = &x;                       // get pointer to x

pD->mf();                         // call mf through pointer
```

That's because in both cases you're invoking the member function mf on the object x. Because it's the same function and the same object in both cases, it should behave the same way, right?

Right, it should. But it might not. In particular, it won't if mf is non-virtual and D has defined its own version of mf:

```
class D: public B {
public:
  void mf();                      // hides B::mf; see Item 33

  ...
};

pB->mf();                         // calls B::mf

pD->mf();                         // calls D::mf
```

The reason for this two-faced behavior is that *non-virtual* functions like B::mf and D::mf are statically bound (see Item 37). That means that because pB is declared to be of type pointer-to-B, non-virtual functions invoked through pB will *always* be those defined for class B, even if pB points to an object of a class derived from B, as it does in this example.

Virtual functions, on the other hand, are dynamically bound (again, see Item 37), so they don't suffer from this problem. If mf were a virtual function, a call to mf through either pB or pD would result in an invocation of D::mf, because what pB and pD *really* point to is an object of type D.

If you are writing class D and you redefine a non-virtual function mf that you inherit from class B, D objects will likely exhibit inconsistent behavior. In particular, any given D object may act like either a B or a D when mf is called, and the determining factor will have nothing to do with the object itself, but with the declared type of the pointer that points to it. References exhibit the same baffling behavior as do pointers.

But that's just a pragmatic argument. What you really want, I know, is some kind of theoretical justification for not redefining inherited non-virtual functions. I am pleased to oblige.

Item 32 explains that public inheritance means is-a, and Item 34 describes why declaring a non-virtual function in a class establishes an invariant over specialization for that class. If you apply these observations to the classes B and D and to the non-virtual member function B::mf, then

- Everything that applies to B objects also applies to D objects, because every D object is-a B object;

- Classes derived from B must inherit both the interface *and* the implementation of mf, because mf is non-virtual in B.

Now, if D redefines mf, there is a contradiction in your design. If D *really* needs to implement mf differently from B, and if every B object — no matter how specialized — *really* has to use the B implementation for mf, then it's simply not true that every D is-a B. In that case, D shouldn't publicly inherit from B. On the other hand, if D *really* has to publicly inherit from B, and if D *really* needs to implement mf differently from B, then it's just not true that mf reflects an invariant over specialization for B. In that case, mf should be virtual. Finally, if every D *really* is-a B, and if mf really corresponds to an invariant over specialization for B, then D can't honestly need to redefine mf, and it shouldn't try to.

Regardless of which argument applies, something has to give, and under no conditions is it the prohibition on redefining an inherited non-virtual function.

If reading this Item gives you a sense of *déjà vu*, it's probably because you've already read Item 7, which explains why destructors in polymorphic base classes should be virtual. If you violate that guideline (i.e., if you declare a non-virtual destructor in a polymorphic base class), you'll also be violating this guideline, because derived classes would invariably redefine an inherited non-virtual function: the base class's destructor. This would be true even for derived classes that declare no destructor, because, as Item 5 explains, the destructor is one of the member functions that compilers generate for you if you don't declare one yourself. In essence, Item 7 is nothing more than a special case of this Item, though it's important enough to merit calling out on its own.

Things to Remember

✦ Never redefine an inherited non-virtual function.

Item 37: Never redefine a function's inherited default parameter value.

Let's simplify this discussion right from the start. There are only two kinds of functions you can inherit: virtual and non-virtual. However, it's always a mistake to redefine an inherited non-virtual function (see Item 36), so we can safely limit our discussion here to the situation in which you inherit a *virtual* function with a default parameter value.

That being the case, the justification for this Item becomes quite straightforward: virtual functions are dynamically bound, but default parameter values are statically bound.

What's that? You say the difference between static and dynamic binding has slipped your already overburdened mind? (For the record, static binding is also known as *early binding*, and dynamic binding is also known as *late binding*.) Let's review, then.

An object's *static type* is the type you declare it to have in the program text. Consider this class hierarchy:

```
// a class for geometric shapes
class Shape {
public:
    enum ShapeColor { Red, Green, Blue };

    // all shapes must offer a function to draw themselves
    virtual void draw(ShapeColor color = Red) const = 0;
    ...
};
```

```
class Rectangle: public Shape {
public:
    // notice the different default parameter value — bad!
    virtual void draw(ShapeColor color = Green) const;
    ...
};
class Circle: public Shape {
public:
    virtual void draw(ShapeColor color) const;
    ...
};
```

Graphically, it looks like this:

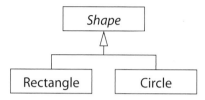

Now consider these pointers:

```
Shape *ps;                          // static type = Shape*
Shape *pc = new Circle;             // static type = Shape*
Shape *pr = new Rectangle;          // static type = Shape*
```

In this example, ps, pc, and pr are all declared to be of type pointer-to-Shape, so they all have that as their static type. Notice that it makes absolutely no difference what they're *really* pointing to — their static type is Shape* regardless.

An object's *dynamic type* is determined by the type of the object to which it currently refers. That is, its dynamic type indicates how it will behave. In the example above, pc's dynamic type is Circle*, and pr's dynamic type is Rectangle*. As for ps, it doesn't really have a dynamic type, because it doesn't refer to any object (yet).

Dynamic types, as their name suggests, can change as a program runs, typically through assignments:

```
ps = pc;                            // ps's dynamic type is
                                    // now Circle*

ps = pr;                            // ps's dynamic type is
                                    // now Rectangle*
```

Virtual functions are *dynamically bound*, meaning that the particular function called is determined by the dynamic type of the object through which it's invoked:

```
pc->draw(Shape::Red);              // calls Circle::draw(Shape::Red)
pr->draw(Shape::Red);              // calls Rectangle::draw(Shape::Red)
```

This is all old hat, I know; you surely understand virtual functions. The twist comes in when you consider virtual functions with default parameter values, because, as I said above, virtual functions are dynamically bound, but default parameters are statically bound. That means you may end up invoking a virtual function defined in a *derived class* but using a default parameter value from a *base class*:

```
pr->draw();                        // calls Rectangle::draw(Shape::Red)!
```

In this case, pr's dynamic type is Rectangle*, so the Rectangle virtual function is called, just as you would expect. In Rectangle::draw, the default parameter value is Green. Because pr's static type is Shape*, however, the default parameter value for this function call is taken from the Shape class, not the Rectangle class! The result is a call consisting of a strange and almost certainly unanticipated combination of the declarations for draw in both the Shape and Rectangle classes.

The fact that ps, pc, and pr are pointers is of no consequence in this matter. Were they references, the problem would persist. The only important things are that draw is a virtual function, and one of its default parameter values is redefined in a derived class.

Why does C++ insist on acting in this perverse manner? The answer has to do with runtime efficiency. If default parameter values were dynamically bound, compilers would have to come up with a way to determine the appropriate default value(s) for parameters of virtual functions at runtime, which would be slower and more complicated than the current mechanism of determining them during compilation. The decision was made to err on the side of speed and simplicity of implementation, and the result is that you now enjoy execution behavior that is efficient, but, if you fail to heed the advice of this Item, confusing.

That's all well and good, but look what happens if you try to follow this rule and also offer default parameter values to users of both base and derived classes:

```
class Shape {
public:
    enum ShapeColor { Red, Green, Blue };

    virtual void draw(ShapeColor color = Red) const = 0;

    ...
};
```

```
class Rectangle: public Shape {
public:
  virtual void draw(ShapeColor color = Red) const;
  ...
};
```

Uh oh, code duplication. Worse yet, code duplication with dependencies: if the default parameter value is changed in Shape, all derived classes that repeat it must also be changed. Otherwise they'll end up redefining an inherited default parameter value. What to do?

When you're having trouble making a virtual function behave the way you'd like, it's wise to consider alternative designs, and Item 35 is filled with alternatives to virtual functions. One of the alternatives is the *non-virtual interface idiom* (NVI idiom): having a public non-virtual function in a base class call a private virtual function that derived classes may redefine. Here, we have the non-virtual function specify the default parameter, while the virtual function does the actual work:

```
class Shape {
public:
  enum ShapeColor { Red, Green, Blue };

  void draw(ShapeColor color = Red) const        // now non-virtual
  {
    doDraw(color);                                // calls a virtual
  }

  ...

private:
  virtual void doDraw(ShapeColor color) const = 0;    // the actual work is
};                                                      // done in this func

class Rectangle: public Shape {
public:

  ...

private:
  virtual void doDraw(ShapeColor color) const;        // note lack of a
  ...                                                  // default param val.
};
```

Because non-virtual functions should never be redefined by derived classes (see Item 36), this design makes clear that the default value for draw's color parameter should always be Red.

Things to Remember

✦ Never redefine an inherited default parameter value, because default parameter values are statically bound, while virtual functions — the only functions you should be redefining — are dynamically bound.

Item 38: Model "has-a" or "is-implemented-in-terms-of" through composition.

Composition is the relationship between types that arises when objects of one type contain objects of another type. For example:

```
class Address { ... };                    // where someone lives

class PhoneNumber { ... };

class Person {
public:

  ...

private:
  std::string name;                       // composed object
  Address address;                        // ditto
  PhoneNumber voiceNumber;                // ditto
  PhoneNumber faxNumber;                  // ditto
};
```

In this example, Person objects are composed of string, Address, and PhoneNumber objects. Among programmers, the term *composition* has lots of synonyms. It's also known as *layering, containment, aggregation,* and *embedding.*

Item 32 explains that public inheritance means "is-a." Composition has a meaning, too. Actually, it has two meanings. Composition means either "has-a" or "is-implemented-in-terms-of." That's because you are dealing with two different domains in your software. Some objects in your programs correspond to things in the world you are modeling, e.g., people, vehicles, video frames, etc. Such objects are part of the *application domain.* Other objects are purely implementation artifacts, e.g., buffers, mutexes, search trees, etc. These kinds of objects correspond to your software's *implementation domain.* When composition occurs between objects in the application domain, it expresses a has-a relationship. When it occurs in the implementation domain, it expresses an is-implemented-in-terms-of relationship.

The Person class above demonstrates the has-a relationship. A Person object has a name, an address, and voice and fax telephone numbers. You wouldn't say that a person *is* a name or that a person *is* an address. You would say that a person *has* a name and *has* an address. Most people have little difficulty with this distinction, so confusion between the roles of is-a and has-a is relatively rare.

Somewhat more troublesome is the difference between is-a and is-implemented-in-terms-of. For example, suppose you need a template for classes representing fairly small sets of objects, i.e., collections without duplicates. Because reuse is a wonderful thing, your first instinct is to employ the standard library's set template. Why write a new template when you can use one that's already been written?

Unfortunately, set implementations typically incur an overhead of three pointers per element. This is because sets are usually implemented as balanced search trees, something that allows them to guarantee logarithmic-time lookups, insertions, and erasures. When speed is more important than space, this is a reasonable design, but it turns out that for your application, space is more important than speed. The standard library's set thus offers the wrong trade-off for you. It seems you'll need to write your own template after all.

Still, reuse *is* a wonderful thing. Being the data structure maven you are, you know that of the many choices for implementing sets, one is to use linked lists. You also know that the standard C++ library has a list template, so you decide to (re)use it.

In particular, you decide to have your nascent Set template inherit from list. That is, Set<T> will inherit from list<T>. After all, in your implementation, a Set object will in fact *be* a list object. You thus declare your Set template like this:

```
template<typename T>                    // the wrong way to use list for Set
class Set: public std::list<T> { ... };
```

Everything may seem fine at this point, but in fact there is something quite wrong. As Item 32 explains, if D is-a B, everything true of B is also true of D. However, a list object may contain duplicates, so if the value 3051 is inserted into a list<int> twice, that list will contain two copies of 3051. In contrast, a Set may not contain duplicates, so if the value 3051 is inserted into a Set<int> twice, the set contains only one copy of the value. It is thus untrue that a Set is-a list, because some of the things that are true for list objects are not true for Set objects.

Because the relationship between these two classes isn't is-a, public inheritance is the wrong way to model that relationship. The right way is to realize that a Set object can be *implemented in terms of* a list object:

```
template<class T>                       // the right way to use list for Set
class Set {
public:
    bool member(const T& item) const;

    void insert(const T& item);
    void remove(const T& item);

    std::size_t size() const;

private:
    std::list<T> rep;                   // representation for Set data
};
```

Set's member functions can lean heavily on functionality already offered by list and other parts of the standard library, so the implementation is straightforward, as long as you're familiar with the basics of programming with the STL:

```
template<typename T>
bool Set<T>::member(const T& item) const
{
    return std::find(rep.begin(), rep.end(), item) != rep.end();
}

template<typename T>
void Set<T>::insert(const T& item)
{
    if (!member(item)) rep.push_back(item);
}

template<typename T>
void Set<T>::remove(const T& item)
{
    typename std::list<T>::iterator it =        // see Item 42 for info on
        std::find(rep.begin(), rep.end(), item);  // "typename" here

    if (it != rep.end()) rep.erase(it);
}

template<typename T>
std::size_t Set<T>::size() const
{
    return rep.size();
}
```

These functions are simple enough that they make reasonable candidates for inlining, though I know you'd want to review the discussion in Item 30 before making any firm inlining decisions.

One can argue that Set's interface would be more in accord with Item 18's admonition to design interfaces that are easy to use correctly and hard to use incorrectly if it followed the STL container conventions, but following those conventions here would require adding a lot of stuff to Set that would obscure the relationship between it and list. Since that relationship is the point of this Item, we'll trade STL compatibility for pedagogical clarity. Besides, nits about Set's interface shouldn't overshadow what's indisputably right about Set: the relationship between it and list. That relationship is not is-a (though it initially looked like it might be), it's is-implemented-in-terms-of.

Things to Remember

✦ Composition has meanings completely different from that of public inheritance.

✦ In the application domain, composition means has-a. In the implementation domain, it means is-implemented-in-terms-of.

Item 39: Use private inheritance judiciously.

Item 32 demonstrates that C++ treats public inheritance as an is-a relationship. It does this by showing that compilers, when given a hierarchy in which a class Student publicly inherits from a class Person, implicitly convert Students to Persons when that is necessary for a function call to succeed. It's worth repeating a portion of that example using private inheritance instead of public inheritance:

```
class Person { ... };

class Student: private Person { ... };    // inheritance is now private

void eat(const Person& p);                // anyone can eat

void study(const Student& s);             // only students study

Person p;                                 // p is a Person
Student s;                                // s is a Student

eat(p);                                   // fine, p is a Person

eat(s);                                   // error! a Student isn't a Person
```

Clearly, private inheritance doesn't mean is-a. What does it mean then?

"Whoa!" you say. "Before we get to the meaning, let's cover the behavior. How does private inheritance behave?" Well, the first rule governing private inheritance you've just seen in action: in contrast to public inheritance, compilers will generally *not* convert a derived class object (such as Student) into a base class object (such as Person) if the inheritance relationship between the classes is private. That's why the call to eat fails for the object s. The second rule is that members inherited from a private base class become private members of the derived class, even if they were protected or public in the base class.

So much for behavior. That brings us to meaning. Private inheritance means is-implemented-in-terms-of. If you make a class D privately inherit from a class B, you do so because you are interested in taking advantage of some of the features available in class B, not because there is any conceptual relationship between objects of types B and D. As such, private inheritance is purely an implementation technique. (That's why everything you inherit from a private base class becomes private in your class: it's all just implementation detail.) Using the terms introduced in Item 34, private inheritance means that implementation *only* should be inherited; interface should be ignored. If D privately inherits from B, it means that D objects are implemented in terms of B objects, nothing more. Private inheritance means nothing during software *design*, only during software *implementation*.

The fact that private inheritance means is-implemented-in-terms-of is a little disturbing, because Item 38 points out that composition can mean the same thing. How are you supposed to choose between them? The answer is simple: use composition whenever you can, and use private inheritance whenever you must. When must you? Primarily when protected members and/or virtual functions enter the picture, though there's also an edge case where space concerns can tip the scales toward private inheritance. We'll worry about the edge case later. After all, it's an edge case.

Suppose we're working on an application involving Widgets, and we decide we need to better understand how Widgets are being used. For example, not only do we want to know things like how often Widget member functions are called, we also want to know how the call ratios change over time. Programs with distinct phases of execution can have different behavioral profiles during the different phases. For example, the functions used during the parsing phase of a compiler are largely different from the functions used during optimization and code generation.

We decide to modify the Widget class to keep track of how many times each member function is called. At runtime, we'll periodically examine that information, possibly along with the values of each Widget and whatever other data we deem useful. To make this work, we'll need to set up a timer of some kind so that we'll know when it's time to collect the usage statistics.

Preferring to reuse existing code over writing new code, we rummage around in our utility toolkit and are pleased to find the following class:

```
class Timer {
public:
  explicit Timer(int tickFrequency);

  virtual void onTick() const;        // automatically called for each tick

  ...
};
```

This is just what we're looking for. A Timer object can be configured to tick with whatever frequency we need, and on each tick, it calls a virtual function. We can redefine that virtual function so that it examines the current state of the Widget world. Perfect!

In order for Widget to redefine a virtual function in Timer, Widget must inherit from Timer. But public inheritance is inappropriate in this case. It's not true that a Widget is-a Timer. Widget clients shouldn't be able to call onTick on a Widget, because that's not part of the conceptual Widget interface. Allowing such a function call would make it easy for clients to use the Widget interface incorrectly, a clear violation of Item 18's advice to make interfaces easy to use correctly and hard to use incorrectly. Public inheritance is not a valid option here.

We thus inherit privately:

```
class Widget: private Timer {
private:
  virtual void onTick() const;          // look at Widget usage data, etc.
  ...
};
```

By virtue of private inheritance, Timer's public onTick function becomes private in Widget, and we keep it there when we redeclare it. Again, putting onTick in the public interface would mislead clients into thinking they could call it, and that would violate Item 18.

This is a nice design, but it's worth noting that private inheritance isn't strictly necessary. If we were determined to use composition instead, we could. We'd just declare a private nested class inside Widget that would publicly inherit from Timer, redefine onTick there, and put an object of that type inside Widget. Here's a sketch of the approach:

```
class Widget {
private:
  class WidgetTimer: public Timer {
  public:
    virtual void onTick() const;
    ...
  };
  WidgetTimer timer;
  ...
};
```

This design is more complicated than the one using only private inheritance, because it involves both (public) inheritance and composition, as well as the introduction of a new class (WidgetTimer). To be honest, I show it primarily to remind you that there is more than one way to approach a design problem, and it's worth training yourself to consider multiple approaches (see also Item 35). Nevertheless, I can think of two reasons why you might prefer public inheritance plus composition over private inheritance.

First, you might want to design Widget to allow for derived classes, but you might also want to prevent derived classes from redefining onTick. If Widget inherits from Timer, that's not possible, not even if the inheritance is private. (Recall from Item 35 that derived classes may redefine virtual functions even if they are not permitted to call them.) But if WidgetTimer is private in Widget and inherits from Timer, Widget's derived classes have no access to WidgetTimer, hence can't inherit from it or redefine its virtual functions. If you've programmed in Java or C# and miss the ability to prevent derived classes from redefining virtual functions (i.e., Java's final methods and C#'s sealed ones), now you have an idea how to approximate that behavior in C++.

Second, you might want to minimize Widget's compilation dependencies. If Widget inherits from Timer, Timer's definition must be available when Widget is compiled, so the file defining Widget probably has to #include Timer.h. On the other hand, if WidgetTimer is moved out of Widget and Widget contains only a pointer to a WidgetTimer, Widget can get by with a simple declaration for the WidgetTimer class; it need not #include anything to do with Timer. For large systems, such decouplings can be important. (For details on minimizing compilation dependencies, consult Item 31.)

I remarked earlier that private inheritance is useful primarily when a would-be derived class wants access to the protected parts of a would-be base class or would like to redefine one or more of its virtual functions, but the conceptual relationship between the classes is is-implemented-in-terms-of instead of is-a. However, I also said that there was an edge case involving space optimization that could nudge you to prefer private inheritance over composition.

The edge case is edgy indeed: it applies only when you're dealing with a class that has no data in it. Such classes have no non-static data members; no virtual functions (because the existence of such functions adds a vptr to each object — see Item 7); and no virtual base classes (because such base classes also incur a size overhead — see Item 40). Conceptually, objects of such *empty classes* should use no space, because there is no per-object data to be stored. However, there are technical reasons for C++ decreeing that freestanding objects must have non-zero size, so if you do this,

```
class Empty {};                        // has no data, so objects should
                                       // use no memory

class HoldsAnInt {                     // should need only space for an int
private:
  int x;
  Empty e;                             // should require no memory
};
```

you'll find that sizeof(HoldsAnInt) > sizeof(int); an Empty data member requires memory. With most compilers, sizeof(Empty) is 1, because

C++'s edict against zero-size freestanding objects is typically satisfied by the silent insertion of a char into "empty" objects. However, alignment requirements (see Item 50) may cause compilers to add padding to classes like HoldsAnInt, so it's likely that HoldsAnInt objects wouldn't gain just the size of a char, they would actually enlarge enough to hold a second int. (On all the compilers I tested, that's exactly what happened.)

But perhaps you've noticed that I've been careful to say that "freestanding" objects mustn't have zero size. This constraint doesn't apply to base class parts of derived class objects, because they're not freestanding. If you *inherit* from Empty instead of containing an object of that type,

```
class HoldsAnInt: private Empty {
private:
  int x;
};
```

you're almost sure to find that sizeof(HoldsAnInt) == sizeof(int). This is known as the *empty base optimization* (EBO), and it's implemented by all the compilers I tested. If you're a library developer whose clients care about space, the EBO is worth knowing about. Also worth knowing is that the EBO is generally viable only under single inheritance. The rules governing C++ object layout generally mean that the EBO can't be applied to derived classes that have more than one base.

In practice, "empty" classes aren't truly empty. Though they never have non-static data members, they often contain typedefs, enums, static data members, or non-virtual functions. The STL has many technically empty classes that contain useful members (usually typedefs), including the base classes unary_function and binary_function, from which classes for user-defined function objects typically inherit. Thanks to widespread implementation of the EBO, such inheritance rarely increases the size of the inheriting classes.

Still, let's get back to basics. Most classes aren't empty, so the EBO is rarely a legitimate justification for private inheritance. Furthermore, most inheritance corresponds to is-a, and that's a job for public inheritance, not private. Both composition and private inheritance mean is-implemented-in-terms-of, but composition is easier to understand, so you should use it whenever you can.

Private inheritance is most likely to be a legitimate design strategy when you're dealing with two classes not related by is-a where one either needs access to the protected members of another or needs to redefine one or more of its virtual functions. Even in that case, we've seen that a mixture of public inheritance and containment can often yield the behavior you want, albeit with greater design complexity. Using private inheritance *judiciously* means employing it when, having considered all the alternatives, it's the best way to express the relationship between two classes in your software.

Things to Remember

✦ Private inheritance means is-implemented-in-terms of. It's usually inferior to composition, but it makes sense when a derived class needs access to protected base class members or needs to redefine inherited virtual functions.

✦ Unlike composition, private inheritance can enable the empty base optimization. This can be important for library developers who strive to minimize object sizes.

Item 40: Use multiple inheritance judiciously.

When it comes to multiple inheritance (MI), the C++ community largely breaks into two basic camps. One camp believes that if single inheritance (SI) is good, multiple inheritance must be better. The other camp argues that single inheritance is good, but multiple inheritance isn't worth the trouble. In this Item, our primary goal is to understand both perspectives on the MI question.

One of the first things to recognize is that when MI enters the design-scape, it becomes possible to inherit the same name (e.g., function, typedef, etc.) from more than one base class. That leads to new opportunities for ambiguity. For example:

```
class BorrowableItem {         // something a library lets you borrow
public:
  void checkOut();             // check the item out from the library
  ...
};

class ElectronicGadget {
private:
  bool checkOut() const;       // perform self-test, return whether
  ...                          // test succeeds
};

class MP3Player:               // note MI here
  public BorrowableItem,       // (some libraries loan MP3 players)
  public ElectronicGadget
{ ... };                       // class definition is unimportant

MP3Player mp;

mp.checkOut();                 // ambiguous! which checkOut?
```

Note that in this example, the call to checkOut is ambiguous, even though only one of the two functions is accessible. (checkOut is public in BorrowableItem but private in ElectronicGadget.) That's in accord with the C++ rules for resolving calls to overloaded functions: before seeing whether a function is accessible, C++ first identifies the function that's the best match for the call. It checks accessibility only after finding the best-match function. In this case, both checkOuts are equally good matches, so there's no best match. The accessibility of ElectronicGadget::checkOut is therefore never examined.

To resolve the ambiguity, you must specify which base class's function to call:

```
    mp.BorrowableItem::checkOut();                    // ah, that checkOut...
```

You could try to explicitly call ElectronicGadget::checkOut, too, of course, but then the ambiguity error would be replaced with a "you're trying to call a private member function" error.

Multiple inheritance just means inheriting from more than one base class, but it is not uncommon for MI to be found in hierarchies that have higher-level base classes, too. That can lead to what is sometimes known as the "deadly MI diamond":

```
class File { ... };

class InputFile: public File { ... };

class OutputFile: public File { ... };

class IOFile: public InputFile,
              public OutputFile
{ ... };
```

Any time you have an inheritance hierarchy with more than one path between a base class and a derived class (such as between File and IOFile above, which has paths through both InputFile and OutputFile), you must confront the question of whether you want the data members in the base class to be replicated for each of the paths. For example, suppose that the File class has a data member, fileName. How many copies of this field should IOFile have? On the one hand, it inherits a copy from each of its base classes, so that suggests that IOFile should have two fileName data members. On the other hand, simple logic says that an IOFile object has only one file name, so the fileName field it inherits through its two base classes should not be replicated.

C++ takes no position on this debate. It happily supports both options, though its default is to perform the replication. If that's not what you want, you must make the class with the data (i.e., File) a *vir-*

tual base class. To do that, you have all classes that immediately inherit from it use *virtual inheritance*:

```
class File { ... };
class InputFile: virtual public File { ... };
class OutputFile: virtual public File { ... };
class IOFile: public InputFile,
              public OutputFile
       { ... };
```

The standard C++ library contains an MI hierarchy just like this one, except the classes are class templates, and the names are basic_ios, basic_istream, basic_ostream, and basic_iostream instead of File, InputFile, OutputFile, and IOFile.

From the viewpoint of correct behavior, public inheritance should always be virtual. If that were the only point of view, the rule would be simple: anytime you use public inheritance, use *virtual* public inheritance. Alas, correctness is not the only perspective. Avoiding the replication of inherited fields requires some behind-the-scenes legerdemain on the part of compilers, and the result is that objects created from classes using virtual inheritance are generally larger than they would be without virtual inheritance. Access to data members in virtual base classes is also slower than to those in non-virtual base classes. The details vary from compiler to compiler, but the basic thrust is clear: virtual inheritance costs.

It costs in other ways, too. The rules governing the initialization of virtual base classes are more complicated and less intuitive than are those for non-virtual bases. The responsibility for initializing a virtual base is borne by the *most derived class* in the hierarchy. Implications of this rule include (1) classes derived from virtual bases that require initialization must be aware of their virtual bases, no matter how far distant the bases are, and (2) when a new derived class is added to the hierarchy, it must assume initialization responsibilities for its virtual bases (both direct and indirect).

My advice on virtual base classes (i.e., on virtual inheritance) is simple. First, don't use virtual bases unless you need to. By default, use non-virtual inheritance. Second, if you must use virtual base classes, try to avoid putting data in them. That way you won't have to worry about oddities in the initialization (and, as it turns out, assignment) rules for such classes. It's worth noting that Interfaces in Java and .NET, which are in many ways comparable to virtual base classes in C++, are not allowed to contain any data.

Let us now turn to the following C++ Interface class (see Item 31) for modeling persons:

```
class IPerson {
public:
  virtual ~IPerson();

  virtual std::string name() const = 0;
  virtual std::string birthDate() const = 0;
};
```

IPerson clients must program in terms of IPerson pointers and references, because abstract classes cannot be instantiated. To create objects that can be manipulated as IPerson objects, clients of IPerson use factory functions (again, see Item 31) to instantiate concrete classes derived from IPerson:

```
// factory function to create a Person object from a unique database ID;
// see Item 18 for why the return type isn't a raw pointer
std::tr1::shared_ptr<IPerson> makePerson(DatabaseID personIdentifier);

// function to get a database ID from the user
DatabaseID askUserForDatabaseID();


DatabaseID id(askUserForDatabaseID());
std::tr1::shared_ptr<IPerson> pp(makePerson(id));    // create an object
                                                     // supporting the
                                                     // IPerson interface

...                                                  // manipulate *pp via
                                                     // IPerson's member
                                                     // functions
```

But how does makePerson create the objects to which it returns pointers? Clearly, there must be some concrete class derived from IPerson that makePerson can instantiate.

Suppose this class is called CPerson. As a concrete class, CPerson must provide implementations for the pure virtual functions it inherits from IPerson. It could write these from scratch, but it would be better to take advantage of existing components that do most or all of what's necessary. For example, suppose an old database-specific class PersonInfo offers the essence of what CPerson needs:

```
class PersonInfo {
public:
  explicit PersonInfo(DatabaseID pid);
  virtual ~PersonInfo();

  virtual const char * theName() const;
  virtual const char * theBirthDate() const;
  ...
private:
  virtual const char * valueDelimOpen() const;     // see
  virtual const char * valueDelimClose() const;    // below
  ...
};
```

You can tell this is an old class, because the member functions return const char*s instead of string objects. Still, if the shoe fits, why not wear it? The names of this class's member functions suggest that the result is likely to be pretty comfortable.

You come to discover that PersonInfo was designed to facilitate printing database fields in various formats, with the beginning and end of each field value delimited by special strings. By default, the opening and closing delimiters for field values are square brackets, so the field value "Ring-tailed Lemur" would be formatted this way:

[Ring-tailed Lemur]

In recognition of the fact that square brackets are not universally desired by clients of PersonInfo, the virtual functions valueDelimOpen and valueDelimClose allow derived classes to specify their own opening and closing delimiter strings. The implementations of PersonInfo's member functions call these virtual functions to add the appropriate delimiters to the values they return. Using PersonInfo::theName as an example, the code looks like this:

```
const char * PersonInfo::valueDelimOpen() const
{
    return "[";                          // default opening delimiter
}
const char * PersonInfo::valueDelimClose() const
{
    return "]";                          // default closing delimiter
}
const char * PersonInfo::theName() const
{
    // reserve buffer for return value; because this is
    // static, it's automatically initialized to all zeros
    static char value[Max_Formatted_Field_Value_Length];

    // write opening delimiter
    std::strcpy(value, valueDelimOpen());

    append to the string in value this object's name field (being careful
    to avoid buffer overruns!)

    // write closing delimiter
    std::strcat(value, valueDelimClose());

    return value;
}
```

One might question the antiquated design of PersonInfo::theName (especially the use of a fixed-size static buffer, something that's rife for both overrun and threading problems — see also Item 21), but set such questions aside and focus instead on this: theName calls valueDelim-Open to generate the opening delimiter of the string it will return, then it generates the name value itself, then it calls valueDelimClose.

Because valueDelimOpen and valueDelimClose are virtual functions, the result returned by theName is dependent not only on PersonInfo but also on the classes derived from PersonInfo.

As the implementer of CPerson, that's good news, because while perusing the fine print in the IPerson documentation, you discover that name and birthDate are required to return unadorned values, i.e., no delimiters are allowed. That is, if a person is named Homer, a call to that person's name function should return "Homer", not "[Homer]".

The relationship between CPerson and PersonInfo is that PersonInfo happens to have some functions that would make CPerson easier to implement. That's all. Their relationship is thus is-implemented-in-terms-of, and we know that can be represented in two ways: via composition (see Item 38) and via private inheritance (see Item 39). Item 39 points out that composition is the generally preferred approach, but inheritance is necessary if virtual functions are to be redefined. In this case, CPerson needs to redefine valueDelimOpen and valueDelimClose, so simple composition won't do. The most straightforward solution is to have CPerson privately inherit from PersonInfo, though Item 39 explains that with a bit more work, CPerson could also use a combination of composition and inheritance to effectively redefine PersonInfo's virtuals. Here, we'll use private inheritance.

But CPerson must also implement the IPerson interface, and that calls for public inheritance. This leads to one reasonable application of multiple inheritance: combine public inheritance of an interface with private inheritance of an implementation:

```
class IPerson {                          // this class specifies the
public:                                  // interface to be implemented
    virtual ~IPerson();

    virtual std::string name() const = 0;
    virtual std::string birthDate() const = 0;
};
class DatabaseID { ... };                // used below; details are
                                         // unimportant

class PersonInfo {                       // this class has functions
public:                                  // useful in implementing
    explicit PersonInfo(DatabaseID pid); // the IPerson interface
    virtual ~PersonInfo();

    virtual const char * theName() const;
    virtual const char * theBirthDate() const;

    virtual const char * valueDelimOpen() const;
    virtual const char * valueDelimClose() const;
    ...
};
```

```
class CPerson: public IPerson, private PersonInfo {        // note use of MI
public:
    explicit CPerson(DatabaseID pid): PersonInfo(pid) {}

    virtual std::string name() const                      // implementations
    { return PersonInfo::theName(); }                     // of the required
                                                          // IPerson member
    virtual std::string birthDate() const                 // functions
    { return PersonInfo::theBirthDate(); }

private:                                                   // redefinitions of
    const char * valueDelimOpen() const { return ""; }    // inherited virtual
    const char * valueDelimClose() const { return ""; }   // delimiter
};                                                         // functions
```

In UML, the design looks like this:

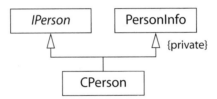

This example demonstrates that MI can be both useful and comprehensible.

At the end of the day, multiple inheritance is just another tool in the object-oriented toolbox. Compared to single inheritance, it's typically more complicated to use and more complicated to understand, so if you've got an SI design that's more or less equivalent to an MI design, the SI design is almost certainly preferable. If the only design you can come up with involves MI, you should think a little harder — there's almost certainly *some* way to make SI work. At the same time, MI is sometimes the clearest, most maintainable, most reasonable way to get the job done. When that's the case, don't be afraid to use it. Just be sure to use it judiciously.

Things to Remember

✦ Multiple inheritance is more complex than single inheritance. It can lead to new ambiguity issues and to the need for virtual inheritance.

✦ Virtual inheritance imposes costs in size, speed, and complexity of initialization and assignment. It's most practical when virtual base classes have no data.

✦ Multiple inheritance does have legitimate uses. One scenario involves combining public inheritance from an Interface class with private inheritance from a class that helps with implementation.

Templates and Generic Programming

The initial motivation for C++ templates was straightforward: to make it possible to create type-safe containers like vector, list, and map. The more people worked with templates, however, the wider the variety of things they found they could do with them. Containers were good, but generic programming — the ability to write code that is independent of the types of objects being manipulated — was even better. STL algorithms like for_each, find, and merge are examples of such programming. Ultimately, it was discovered that the C++ template mechanism is itself Turing-complete: it can be used to compute any computable value. That led to template metaprogramming: the creation of programs that execute inside C++ compilers and that stop running when compilation is complete. These days, containers are but a small part of the C++ template pie. Despite the breadth of template applications, however, a set of core ideas underlie all template-based programming. Those ideas are the focus of this chapter.

This chapter won't make you an expert template programmer, but it will make you a better one. It will also give you information you need to expand your template-programming boundaries as far as you desire.

Item 41: Understand implicit interfaces and compile-time polymorphism.

The world of object-oriented programming revolves around *explicit* interfaces and *runtime* polymorphism. For example, given this (meaningless) class,

```
class Widget {
public:
  Widget();
  virtual ~Widget();
```

```
virtual std::size_t size() const;
virtual void normalize();
void swap(Widget& other);                       // see Item 25

...
};
```

and this (equally meaningless) function,

```
void doProcessing(Widget& w)
{
  if (w.size() > 10 && w != someNastyWidget) {
    Widget temp(w);
    temp.normalize();
    temp.swap(w);
  }
}
```

we can say this about w in doProcessing:

- Because w is declared to be of type Widget, w must support the Widget interface. We can look up this interface in the source code (e.g., the .h file for Widget) to see exactly what it looks like, so I call this an *explicit interface* — one explicitly visible in the source code.

- Because some of Widget's member functions are virtual, w's calls to those functions will exhibit *runtime polymorphism*: the specific function to call will be determined at runtime based on w's dynamic type (see Item 37).

The world of templates and generic programming is fundamentally different. In that world, explicit interfaces and runtime polymorphism continue to exist, but they're less important. Instead, *implicit interfaces* and *compile-time polymorphism* move to the fore. To see how this is the case, look what happens when we turn doProcessing from a function into a function template:

```
template<typename T>
void doProcessing(T& w)
{
  if (w.size() > 10 && w != someNastyWidget) {
    T temp(w);
    temp.normalize();
    temp.swap(w);
  }
}
```

Now what can we say about w in doProcessing?

- The interface that w must support is determined by the operations performed on w in the template. In this example, it appears that w's type (T) must support the size, normalize, and swap member functions; copy construction (to create temp); and comparison for inequality (for comparison with someNastyWidget). We'll soon see that this isn't quite accurate, but it's true enough for now. What's important is that the set of expressions that must be valid in order for the template to compile is the *implicit interface* that T must support.

- The calls to functions involving w such as operator> and operator!= may involve instantiating templates to make these calls succeed. Such instantiation occurs during compilation. Because instantiating function templates with different template parameters leads to different functions being called, this is known as *compile-time polymorphism*.

Even if you've never used templates, you should be familiar with the difference between runtime and compile-time polymorphism, because it's similar to the difference between the process of determining which of a set of overloaded functions should be called (which takes place during compilation) and dynamic binding of virtual function calls (which takes place at runtime). The difference between explicit and implicit interfaces is new to templates, however, and it bears closer examination.

An explicit interface typically consists of function signatures, i.e., function names, parameter types, return types, etc. The Widget class public interface, for example,

```
class Widget {
public:
  Widget();
  virtual ~Widget();

  virtual std::size_t size() const;
  virtual void normalize();
  void swap(Widget& other);
};
```

consists of a constructor, a destructor, and the functions size, normalize, and swap, along with the parameter types, return types, and constnesses of these functions. (It also includes the compiler-generated copy constructor and copy assignment operator — see Item 5.) It could also include typedefs and, if you were so bold as to violate Item 22's advice to make data members private, data members, though in this case, it does not.

An implicit interface is quite different. It is not based on function signatures. Rather, it consists of valid *expressions*. Look again at the conditional at the beginning of the doProcessing template:

```
template<typename T>
void doProcessing(T& w)
{
    if (w.size() > 10 && w != someNastyWidget) {
    ...
```

The implicit interface for T (w's type) appears to have these constraints:

- It must offer a member function named size that returns an integral value.

- It must support an operator!= function that compares two objects of type T. (Here, we assume that someNastyWidget is of type T.)

Thanks to the possibility of operator overloading, neither of these constraints need be satisfied. Yes, T must support a size member function, though it's worth mentioning that the function might be inherited from a base class. But this member function need not return an integral type. It need not even return a numeric type. For that matter, it need not even return a type for which operator> is defined! All it needs to do is return an object of some type X such that there is an operator> that can be called with an object of type X and an int (because 10 is of type int). The operator> need not take a parameter of type X, because it could take a parameter of type Y, and that would be okay as long as there were an implicit conversion from objects of type X to objects of type Y!

Similarly, there is no requirement that T support operator!=, because it would be just as acceptable for operator!= to take one object of type X and one object of type Y. As long as T can be converted to X and some-NastyWidget's type can be converted to Y, the call to operator!= would be valid.

(As an aside, this analysis doesn't take into account the possibility that operator&& could be overloaded, thus changing the meaning of the above expression from a conjunction to something potentially quite different.)

Most people's heads hurt when they first start thinking about implicit interfaces this way, but there's really no need for aspirin. Implicit interfaces are simply made up of a set of valid expressions. The expressions themselves may look complicated, but the constraints they impose are generally straightforward. For example, given the conditional,

```
    if (w.size() > 10 && w != someNastyWidget) ...
```

it's hard to say much about the constraints on the functions size, operator>, operator&&, or operator!=, but it's easy to identify the constraint on the expression as a whole. The conditional part of an if statement must be a boolean expression, so regardless of the exact types involved, whatever "w.size() > 10 && w != someNastyWidget" yields, it must be compatible with bool. This is part of the implicit interface the template doProcessing imposes on its type parameter T. The rest of the interface required by doProcessing is that calls to the copy constructor, to normalize, and to swap must be valid for objects of type T.

The implicit interfaces imposed on a template's parameters are just as real as the explicit interfaces imposed on a class's objects, and both are checked during compilation. Just as you can't use an object in a way contradictory to the explicit interface its class offers (the code won't compile), you can't try to use an object in a template unless that object supports the implicit interface the template requires (again, the code won't compile).

Things to Remember

✦ Both classes and templates support interfaces and polymorphism.

✦ For classes, interfaces are explicit and centered on function signatures. Polymorphism occurs at runtime through virtual functions.

✦ For template parameters, interfaces are implicit and based on valid expressions. Polymorphism occurs during compilation through template instantiation and function overloading resolution.

Item 42: Understand the two meanings of typename.

Question: what is the difference between class and typename in the following template declarations?

```
template<class T> class Widget;          // uses "class"
template<typename T> class Widget;       // uses "typename"
```

Answer: nothing. When declaring a template type parameter, class and typename mean exactly the same thing. Some programmers prefer class all the time, because it's easier to type. Others (including me) prefer typename, because it suggests that the parameter need not be a class type. A few developers employ typename when any type is allowed and reserve class for when only user-defined types are acceptable. But from C++'s point of view, class and typename mean exactly the same thing when declaring a template parameter.

C++ doesn't always view class and typename as equivalent, however. Sometimes you must use typename. To understand when, we have to talk about two kinds of names you can refer to in a template.

Suppose we have a template for a function that takes an STL-compatible container holding objects that can be assigned to ints. Further suppose that this function simply prints the value of its second element. It's a silly function implemented in a silly way, and as I've written it below, it shouldn't even compile, but please overlook those things — there's a method to my madness:

```
template<typename C>               // print 2nd element in
void print2nd(const C& container)  // container;
{                                  // this is not valid C++!
  if (container.size() >= 2) {
    C::const_iterator iter(container.begin());  // get iterator to 1st element
    ++iter;                        // move iter to 2nd element
    int value = *iter;             // copy that element to an int
    std::cout << value;            // print the int
  }
}
```

I've highlighted the two local variables in this function, iter and value. The type of iter is C::const_iterator, a type that depends on the template parameter C. Names in a template that are dependent on a template parameter are called *dependent names*. When a dependent name is nested inside a class, I call it a *nested dependent name*. C::const_iterator is a nested dependent name. In fact, it's a *nested dependent type name*, i.e., a nested dependent name that refers to a type.

The other local variable in print2nd, value, has type int. int is a name that does not depend on any template parameter. Such names are known as *non-dependent names*, (I have no idea why they're not called independent names. If, like me, you find the term "non-dependent" an abomination, you have my sympathies, but "non-dependent" is the term for these kinds of names, so, like me, roll your eyes and resign yourself to it.)

Nested dependent names can lead to parsing difficulties. For example, suppose we made print2nd even sillier by starting it this way:

```
template<typename C>
void print2nd(const C& container)
{
  C::const_iterator * x;
  ...
}
```

This looks like we're declaring x as a local variable that's a pointer to a C::const_iterator. But it looks that way only because we "know" that C::const_iterator is a type. But what if C::const_iterator weren't a type? What if C had a static data member that happened to be named const_iterator, and what if x happened to be the name of a global variable? In that case, the code above wouldn't declare a local variable, it would be a multiplication of C::const_iterator by x! Sure, that sounds crazy, but it's *possible*, and people who write C++ parsers have to worry about all possible inputs, even the crazy ones.

Until C is known, there's no way to know whether C::const_iterator is a type or isn't, and when the template print2nd is parsed, C isn't known. C++ has a rule to resolve this ambiguity: if the parser encounters a nested dependent name in a template, it assumes that the name is *not* a type unless you tell it otherwise. By default, nested dependent names are *not* types. (There is an exception to this rule that I'll get to in a moment.)

With that in mind, look again at the beginning of print2nd:

```
template<typename C>
void print2nd(const C& container)
{
   if (container.size() >= 2) {
      C::const_iterator iter(container.begin());      // this name is assumed to
      ...                                             // not be a type
```

Now it should be clear why this isn't valid C++. The declaration of iter makes sense only if C::const_iterator is a type, but we haven't told C++ that it is, and C++ assumes that it's not. To rectify the situation, we have to tell C++ that C::const_iterator is a type. We do that by putting typename immediately in front of it:

```
template<typename C>                                 // this is valid C++
void print2nd(const C& container)
{
   if (container.size() >= 2) {
      typename C::const_iterator iter(container.begin());

      ...

   }
}
```

The general rule is simple: anytime you refer to a nested dependent type name in a template, you must immediately precede it by the word typename. (Again, I'll describe an exception shortly.)

typename should be used to identify only nested dependent type names; other names shouldn't have it. For example, here's a function template that takes both a container and an iterator into that container:

```
template<typename C>                 // typename allowed (as is "class")
void f(const C& container,           // typename not allowed
       typename C::iterator iter);   // typename required
```

C is not a nested dependent type name (it's not nested inside anything dependent on a template parameter), so it must not be preceded by typename when declaring container, but C::iterator is a nested dependent type name, so it's required to be preceded by typename.

The exception to the "typename must precede nested dependent type names" rule is that typename must not precede nested dependent type names in a list of base classes or as a base class identifier in a member initialization list. For example:

```
template<typename T>
class Derived: public Base<T>::Nested {   // base class list: typename not
public:                                    // allowed
    explicit Derived(int x)
     : Base<T>::Nested(x)                  // base class identifier in mem.
    {                                      // init. list: typename not allowed

        typename Base<T>::Nested temp;     // use of nested dependent type
        ...                                // name not in a base class list or
    }                                      // as a base class identifier in a
    ...                                    // mem. init. list: typename required
};
```

Such inconsistency is irksome, but once you have a bit of experience under your belt, you'll barely notice it.

Let's look at one last typename example, because it's representative of something you're going to see in real code. Suppose we're writing a function template that takes an iterator, and we want to make a local copy, temp, of the object the iterator points to. We can do it like this:

```
template<typename IterT>
void workWithIterator(IterT iter)
{
    typename std::iterator_traits<IterT>::value_type temp(*iter);
    ...
}
```

Don't let the std::iterator_traits<IterT>::value_type startle you. That's just a use of a standard traits class (see Item 47), the C++ way of saying "the type of thing pointed to by objects of type IterT." The statement declares a local variable (temp) of the same type as what IterT objects point to, and it initializes temp with the object that iter points to. If IterT is vector<int>::iterator, temp is of type int. If IterT is list<string>::iterator, temp is of type string. Because std::iterator_traits<IterT>::value_type is a nested dependent type name (value_type is nested inside iterator_traits<IterT>, and IterT is a template parameter), we must precede it by typename.

If you think reading std::iterator_traits<IterT>::value_type is unpleasant, imagine what it's like to type it. If you're like most programmers, the thought of typing it more than once is ghastly, so you'll want to create a typedef. For traits member names like value_type (again, see Item 47 for information on traits), a common convention is for the typedef name to be the same as the traits member name, so such a local typedef is often defined like this:

```
template<typename IterT>
void workWithIterator(IterT iter)
{
  typedef typename std::iterator_traits<IterT>::value_type value_type;

  value_type temp(*iter);

  ...
}
```

Many programmers find the "typedef typename" juxtaposition initially jarring, but it's a logical fallout from the rules for referring to nested dependent type names. You'll get used to it fairly quickly. After all, you have strong motivation. How many times do you want to type typename std::iterator_traits<IterT>::value_type?

As a closing note, I should mention that enforcement of the rules surrounding typename varies from compiler to compiler. Some compilers accept code where typename is required but missing; some accept code where typename is present but not allowed; and a few (usually older ones) reject typename where it's present and required. This means that the interaction of typename and nested dependent type names can lead to some mild portability headaches.

Things to Remember

✦ When declaring template parameters, class and typename are interchangeable.

✦ Use typename to identify nested dependent type names, except in base class lists or as a base class identifier in a member initialization list.

Item 43: Know how to access names in templatized base classes.

Suppose we need to write an application that can send messages to several different companies. Messages can be sent in either encrypted or cleartext (unencrypted) form. If we have enough information during compilation to determine which messages will go to which companies, we can employ a template-based solution:

```
class CompanyA {
public:

    ...
    void sendCleartext(const std::string& msg);
    void sendEncrypted(const std::string& msg);
    ...
};
class CompanyB {
public:

    ...
    void sendCleartext(const std::string& msg);
    void sendEncrypted(const std::string& msg);
    ...
};
    ...                                 // classes for other companies

class MsgInfo { ... };                  // class for holding information
                                        // used to create a message

template<typename Company>
class MsgSender {
public:
    ...                                 // ctors, dtor, etc.

    void sendClear(const MsgInfo& info)
    {
      std::string msg;
      create msg from info;

      Company c;
      c.sendCleartext(msg);
    }

    void sendSecret(const MsgInfo& info)   // similar to sendClear, except
    { ... }                                // calls c.sendEncrypted
};
```

This will work fine, but suppose we sometimes want to log some information each time we send a message. A derived class can easily add that capability, and this seems like a reasonable way to do it:

```
template<typename Company>
class LoggingMsgSender: public MsgSender<Company> {
public:
    ...                                        // ctors, dtor, etc.
    void sendClearMsg(const MsgInfo& info)
    {
      write "before sending" info to the log;

      sendClear(info);                          // call base class function;
                                                // this code will not compile!

      write "after sending" info to the log;
    }
    ...
};
```

Note how the message-sending function in the derived class has a different name (sendClearMsg) from the one in its base class (there, it's called sendClear). That's good design, because it side-steps the issue of hiding inherited names (see Item 33) as well as the problems inherent in redefining an inherited non-virtual function (see Item 36). But the code above won't compile, at least not with conformant compilers. Such compilers will complain that sendClear doesn't exist. We can see that sendClear is in the base class, but compilers won't look for it there. We need to understand why.

The problem is that when compilers encounter the definition for the class template LoggingMsgSender, they don't know what class it inherits from. Sure, it's MsgSender<Company>, but Company is a template parameter, one that won't be known until later (when LoggingMsgSender is instantiated). Without knowing what Company is, there's no way to know what the class MsgSender<Company> looks like. In particular, there's no way to know if it has a sendClear function.

To make the problem concrete, suppose we have a class CompanyZ that insists on encrypted communications:

```
class CompanyZ {                          // this class offers no
public:                                   // sendCleartext function
    ...
    void sendEncrypted(const std::string& msg);
    ...
};
```

The general MsgSender template is inappropriate for CompanyZ, because that template offers a sendClear function that makes no sense for CompanyZ objects. To rectify that problem, we can create a specialized version of MsgSender for CompanyZ:

```
template<>                                // a total specialization of
class MsgSender<CompanyZ> {               // MsgSender; the same as the
public:                                   // general template, except
    ...                                   // sendClear is omitted
    void sendSecret(const MsgInfo& info)
    { ... }
};
```

Note the "template <>" syntax at the beginning of this class definition. It signifies that this is neither a template nor a standalone class. Rather, it's a specialized version of the MsgSender template to be used when the template argument is CompanyZ. This is known as a *total template specialization*: the template MsgSender is specialized for the type CompanyZ, and the specialization is *total* — once the type parameter has been defined to be CompanyZ, no other aspect of the template's parameters can vary.

Given that MsgSender has been specialized for CompanyZ, consider again the derived class LoggingMsgSender:

```
template<typename Company>
class LoggingMsgSender: public MsgSender<Company> {
public:
    ...
    void sendClearMsg(const MsgInfo& info)
    {
        write "before sending" info to the log;

        sendClear(info);                    // if Company == CompanyZ,
                                            // this function doesn't exist!

        write "after sending" info to the log;
    }

    ...

};
```

As the comment notes, this code makes no sense when the base class is MsgSender<CompanyZ>, because that class offers no sendClear function. That's why C++ rejects the call: it recognizes that base class templates may be specialized and that such specializations may not offer the same interface as the general template. As a result, it generally refuses to look in templatized base classes for inherited names. In some sense, when we cross from Object-Oriented C++ to Template C++ (see Item 1), inheritance stops working.

To restart it, we have to somehow disable C++'s "don't look in templatized base classes" behavior. There are three ways to do this. First, you can preface calls to base class functions with "this->":

```
template<typename Company>
class LoggingMsgSender: public MsgSender<Company> {
public:
    ...
    void sendClearMsg(const MsgInfo& info)
    {
        write "before sending" info to the log;
        this->sendClear(info);              // okay, assumes that
                                            // sendClear will be inherited
        write "after sending" info to the log;
    }

    ...

};
```

Second, you can employ a using declaration, a solution that should strike you as familiar if you've read Item 33. That Item explains how using declarations bring hidden base class names into a derived class's scope. We can therefore write sendClearMsg like this:

```
template<typename Company>
class LoggingMsgSender: public MsgSender<Company> {
public:
    using MsgSender<Company>::sendClear;    // tell compilers to assume
    ...                                     // that sendClear is in the
                                            // base class
    void sendClearMsg(const MsgInfo& info)
    {
        ...
        sendClear(info);                    // okay, assumes that
        ...                                 // sendClear will be inherited
    }
    ...
};
```

(Although a using declaration will work both here and in Item 33, the problems being solved are different. Here, the situation isn't that base class names are hidden by derived class names, it's that compilers don't search base class scopes unless we tell them to.)

A final way to get your code to compile is to explicitly specify that the function being called is in the base class:

```
template<typename Company>
class LoggingMsgSender: public MsgSender<Company> {
public:
    ...
    void sendClearMsg(const MsgInfo& info)
    {
        ...
        MsgSender<Company>::sendClear(info);    // okay, assumes that
        ...                                     // sendClear will be
    }                                           // inherited
    ...
};
```

This is generally the least desirable way to solve the problem, because if the function being called is virtual, explicit qualification turns off the virtual binding behavior.

From a name visibility point of view, each of these approaches does the same thing: it promises compilers that any subsequent specializations of the base class template will support the interface offered by the general template. Such a promise is all compilers need when they parse a derived class template like LoggingMsgSender, but if the promise turns out to be unfounded, the truth will emerge during subsequent compilation. For example, if the source code later contains this,

```
LoggingMsgSender<CompanyZ> zMsgSender;
MsgInfo msgData;

...                                                 // put info in msgData
zMsgSender.sendClearMsg(msgData);                   // error! won't compile
```

the call to sendClearMsg won't compile, because at this point, compilers know that the base class is the template specialization Msg-Sender<CompanyZ>, and they know that class doesn't offer the sendClear function that sendClearMsg is trying to call.

Fundamentally, the issue is whether compilers will diagnose invalid references to base class members sooner (when derived class template definitions are parsed) or later (when those templates are instantiated with specific template arguments). C++'s policy is to prefer early diagnoses, and that's why it assumes it knows nothing about the contents of base classes when those classes are instantiated from templates.

Things to Remember

✦ In derived class templates, refer to names in base class templates via a "this->" prefix, via using declarations, or via an explicit base class qualification.

Item 44: Factor parameter-independent code out of templates.

Templates are a wonderful way to save time and avoid code replication. Instead of typing 20 similar classes, each with 15 member functions, you type one class template, and you let compilers instantiate the 20 specific classes and 300 functions you need. (Member functions of class templates are implicitly instantiated only when used, so you should get the full 300 member functions only if each is actually used.) Function templates are similarly appealing. Instead of writing many functions, you write one function template and let the compilers do the rest. Ain't technology grand?

Yes, well...sometimes. If you're not careful, using templates can lead to *code bloat*: binaries with replicated (or almost replicated) code, data, or both. The result can be source code that looks fit and trim, yet object code that's fat and flabby. Fat and flabby is rarely fashionable, so you need to know how to avoid such binary bombast.

Your primary tool has the imposing name *commonality and variability analysis*, but there's nothing imposing about the idea. Even if you've never written a template in your life, you do such analysis all the time.

When you're writing a function and you realize that some part of the function's implementation is essentially the same as another function's implementation, do you just replicate the code? Of course not. You factor the common code out of the two functions, put it into a third function, and have both of the other functions call the new one. That is, you analyze the two functions to find the parts that are common and those that vary, you move the common parts into a new function, and you keep the varying parts in the original functions. Similarly, if you're writing a class and you realize that some parts of the class are the same as parts of another class, you don't replicate the common parts. Instead, you move the common parts to a new class, then you use inheritance or composition (see Items 32, 38, and 39) to give the original classes access to the common features. The parts of the original classes that differ — the varying parts — remain in their original locations.

When writing templates, you do the same analysis, and you avoid replication in the same ways, but there's a twist. In non-template code, replication is explicit: you can *see* that there's duplication between two functions or two classes. In template code, replication is implicit: there's only one copy of the template source code, so you have to train yourself to sense the replication that may take place when a template is instantiated multiple times.

For example, suppose you'd like to write a template for fixed-size square matrices that, among other things, support matrix inversion.

```
template<typename T,              // template for n x n matrices of
         std::size_t n>           // objects of type T; see below for info
class SquareMatrix {              // on the size_t parameter
public:
   ...
   void invert();                 // invert the matrix in place
};
```

This template takes a type parameter, T, but it also takes a parameter of type size_t — a *non-type parameter*. Non-type parameters are less common than type parameters, but they're completely legal, and, as in this example, they can be quite natural.

Now consider this code:

```
SquareMatrix<double, 5> sm1;
...
sm1.invert();                     // call SquareMatrix<double, 5>::invert
SquareMatrix<double, 10> sm2;
...
sm2.invert();                     // call SquareMatrix<double, 10>::invert
```

Two copies of invert will be instantiated here. The functions won't be identical, because one will work on 5×5 matrices and one will work on 10×10 matrices, but other than the constants 5 and 10, the two functions will be the same. This is a classic way for template-induced code bloat to arise.

What would you do if you saw two functions that were character-for-character identical except for the use of 5 in one version and 10 in the other? Your instinct would be to create a version of the function that took a value as a parameter, then call the parameterized function with 5 or 10 instead of replicating the code. Your instinct serves you well! Here's a first pass at doing that for SquareMatrix:

```
template<typename T>                // size-independent base class for
class SquareMatrixBase {            // square matrices
protected:
  ...
  void invert(std::size_t matrixSize);   // invert matrix of the given size
  ...
};
template<typename T, std::size_t n>
class SquareMatrix: private SquareMatrixBase<T> {
private:
  using SquareMatrixBase<T>::invert;   // make base class version of invert
                                       // visible in this class; see Items 33
                                       // and 43
public:
  ...
  void invert() { invert(n); }        // make inline call to base class
};                                     // version of invert
```

As you can see, the parameterized version of invert is in a base class, SquareMatrixBase. Like SquareMatrix, SquareMatrixBase is a template, but unlike SquareMatrix, it's templatized only on the type of objects in the matrix, not on the size of the matrix. Hence, all matrices holding a given type of object will share a single SquareMatrixBase class. They will thus share a single copy of that class's version of invert. (Provided, of course, you refrain from declaring that function inline. If it's inlined, each instantiation of SquareMatrix::invert will get a copy of SquareMatrix-Base::invert's code (see Item 30), and you'll find yourself back in the land of object code replication.)

SquareMatrixBase::invert is intended only to be a way for derived classes to avoid code replication, so it's protected instead of being public. The additional cost of calling it should be zero, because derived classes' inverts call the base class version using inline functions. (The inline is implicit — see Item 30.) Notice also that the inheritance between SquareMatrix and SquareMatrixBase is private. This accurately reflects the fact that the reason for the base class is only to facilitate the derived classes' implementations, not to express a conceptual is-a relationship between SquareMatrix and SquareMatrixBase. (For information on private inheritance, see Item 39.)

So far, so good, but there's a sticky issue we haven't addressed yet. How does SquareMatrixBase::invert know what data to operate on? It knows the size of the matrix from its parameter, but how does it know where the data for a particular matrix is? Presumably only the derived class knows that. How does the derived class communicate that to the base class so that the base class can do the inversion?

One possibility would be to add another parameter to SquareMatrix-Base::invert, perhaps a pointer to the beginning of a chunk of memory with the matrix's data in it. That would work, but in all likelihood, invert is not the only function in SquareMatrix that can be written in a size-independent manner and moved into SquareMatrixBase. If there are several such functions, all will need a way to find the memory holding the values in the matrix. We could add an extra parameter to all of them, but we'd be telling SquareMatrixBase the same information repeatedly. That seems wrong.

An alternative is to have SquareMatrixBase store a pointer to the memory for the matrix values. And as long as it's storing that, it might as well store the matrix size, too. The resulting design looks like this:

```
template<typename T>
class SquareMatrixBase {
protected:
  SquareMatrixBase(std::size_t n, T *pMem)     // store matrix size and a
  : size(n), pData(pMem) {}                    // ptr to matrix values

  void setDataPtr(T *ptr) { pData = ptr; }     // reassign pData
  ...
private:
  std::size_t size;                            // size of matrix

  T *pData;                                    // pointer to matrix values
};
```

This lets derived classes decide how to allocate the memory. Some implementations might decide to store the matrix data right inside the SquareMatrix object:

```
template<typename T, std::size_t n>
class SquareMatrix: private SquareMatrixBase<T> {
public:
  SquareMatrix()                               // send matrix size and
  : SquareMatrixBase<T>(n, data) {}            // data ptr to base class
  ...
private:
  T data[n*n];
};
```

Objects of such types have no need for dynamic memory allocation, but the objects themselves could be very large. An alternative would be to put the data for each matrix on the heap:

```
template<typename T, std::size_t n>
class SquareMatrix: private SquareMatrixBase<T> {
public:
  SquareMatrix()                        // set base class data ptr to null,
    : SquareMatrixBase<T>(n, 0),        // allocate memory for matrix
      pData(new T[n*n])                 // values, save a ptr to the
  { this->setDataPtr(pData.get()); }    // memory, and give a copy of it
    ...                                 // to the base class

private:
  boost::scoped_array<T> pData;         // see Item 13 for info on
};                                      // boost::scoped_array
```

Regardless of where the data is stored, the key result from a bloat point of view is that now many — maybe all — of SquareMatrix's member functions can be simple inline calls to (non-inline) base class versions that are shared with all other matrices holding the same type of data, regardless of their size. At the same time, SquareMatrix objects of different sizes are distinct types, so even though, e.g., SquareMatrix<double, 5> and SquareMatrix<double, 10> objects use the same member functions in SquareMatrixBase<double>, there's no chance of passing a SquareMatrix<double, 5> object to a function expecting a SquareMatrix<double, 10>. Nice, no?

Nice, yes, but not free. The versions of invert with the matrix sizes hardwired into them are likely to generate better code than the shared version where the size is passed as a function parameter or is stored in the object. For example, in the size-specific versions, the sizes would be compile-time constants, hence eligible for such optimizations as constant propagation, including their being folded into the generated instructions as immediate operands. That can't be done in the size-independent version.

On the other hand, having only one version of invert for multiple matrix sizes decreases the size of the executable, and that could reduce the program's working set size and improve locality of reference in the instruction cache. Those things could make the program run faster, more than compensating for any lost optimizations in size-specific versions of invert. Which effect would dominate? The only way to know is to try it both ways and observe the behavior on your particular platform and on representative data sets.

Another efficiency consideration concerns the sizes of objects. If you're not careful, moving size-independent versions of functions up into a base class can increase the overall size of each object. For example, in the code I just showed, each SquareMatrix object has a pointer to its data in the SquareMatrixBase class, even though each derived class already has a way to get to the data. This increases the size of each SquareMatrix object by at least the size of a pointer. It's possible to modify the design so that these pointers are unnecessary, but, again, there are trade-offs. For example, having the base class store a protected pointer to the matrix data leads to the loss of encapsulation described in Item 22. It can also lead to resource management complications: if the base class stores a pointer to the matrix data, but that data may have been either dynamically allocated or physically stored inside the derived class object (as we saw), how will it be determined whether the pointer should be deleted? Such questions have answers, but the more sophisticated you try to be about them, the more complicated things become. At some point, a little code replication begins to look like a mercy.

This Item has discussed only bloat due to non-type template parameters, but type parameters can lead to bloat, too. For example, on many platforms, int and long have the same binary representation, so the member functions for, say, vector<int> and vector<long> would likely be identical — the very definition of bloat. Some linkers will merge identical function implementations, but some will not, and that means that some templates instantiated on both int and long could cause code bloat in some environments. Similarly, on most platforms, all pointer types have the same binary representation, so templates holding pointer types (e.g., list<int*>, list<const int*>, list<SquareMatrix<long, 3>*>, etc.) should often be able to use a single underlying implementation for each member function. Typically, this means implementing member functions that work with strongly typed pointers (i.e., T* pointers) by having them call functions that work with untyped pointers (i.e., void* pointers). Some implementations of the standard C++ library do this for templates like vector, deque, and list. If you're concerned about code bloat arising in your templates, you'll probably want to develop templates that do the same thing.

Things to Remember

+ Templates generate multiple classes and multiple functions, so any template code not dependent on a template parameter causes bloat.

+ Bloat due to non-type template parameters can often be eliminated by replacing template parameters with function parameters or class data members.

+ Bloat due to type parameters can be reduced by sharing implementations for instantiation types with identical binary representations.

Item 45: Use member function templates to accept "all compatible types."

Smart pointers are objects that act much like pointers but add functionality pointers don't provide. For example, Item 13 explains how the standard auto_ptr and tr1::shared_ptr can be used to automatically delete heap-based resources at the right time. Iterators into STL containers are almost always smart pointers; certainly you couldn't expect to move a built-in pointer from one node in a linked list to the next by using "++," yet that works for list::iterators.

One of the things that real pointers do well is support implicit conversions. Derived class pointers implicitly convert into base class pointers, pointers to non-const objects convert into pointers to const objects, etc. For example, consider some conversions that can occur in a three-level hierarchy:

```
class Top { ... };
class Middle: public Top { ... };
class Bottom: public Middle { ... };
Top *pt1 = new Middle;              // convert Middle* ⇒Top*
Top *pt2 = new Bottom;              // convert Bottom* ⇒Top*
const Top *pct2 = pt1;              // convert Top* ⇒const Top*
```

Emulating such conversions in user-defined smart pointer classes is tricky. We'd need the following code to compile:

```
template<typename T>
class SmartPtr {
public:                            // smart pointers are typically
  explicit SmartPtr(T *realPtr);   // initialized by built-in pointers
  ...
};
SmartPtr<Top> pt1 =                // convert SmartPtr<Middle> ⇒
  SmartPtr<Middle>(new Middle);    //   SmartPtr<Top>
SmartPtr<Top> pt2 =                // convert SmartPtr<Bottom> ⇒
  SmartPtr<Bottom>(new Bottom);    //   SmartPtr<Top>
SmartPtr<const Top> pct2 = pt1;    // convert SmartPtr<Top> ⇒
                                   //   SmartPtr<const Top>
```

There is no inherent relationship among different instantiations of the same template, so compilers view SmartPtr<Middle> and SmartPtr<Top> as completely different classes, no more closely related than, say, vector<float> and Widget. To get the conversions among SmartPtr classes that we want, we have to program them explicitly.

In the smart pointer sample code above, each statement creates a new smart pointer object, so for now we'll focus on how to write smart pointer constructors that behave the way we want. A key observation is that there is no way to write out all the constructors we need. In the hierarchy above, we can construct a SmartPtr<Top> from a SmartPtr<Middle> or a SmartPtr<Bottom>, but if the hierarchy is extended in the future, SmartPtr<Top> objects will have to be constructible from other smart pointer types. For example, if we later add

```
class BelowBottom: public Bottom { ... };
```

we'll need to support the creation of SmartPtr<Top> objects from SmartPtr<BelowBottom> objects, and we certainly won't want to have to modify the SmartPtr template to do it.

In principle, the number of constructors we need is unlimited. Since a template can be instantiated to generate an unlimited number of functions, it seems that we don't need a constructor *function* for SmartPtr, we need a constructor *template*. Such templates are examples of *member function templates* (often just known as *member templates*) — templates that generate member functions of a class:

```
template<typename T>
class SmartPtr {
public:
    template<typename U>                  // member template
    SmartPtr(const SmartPtr<U>& other);   // for a "generalized
    ...                                   // copy constructor"
};
```

This says that for every type T and every type U, a SmartPtr<T> can be created from a SmartPtr<U>, because SmartPtr<T> has a constructor that takes a SmartPtr<U> parameter. Constructors like this — ones that create one object from another object whose type is a different instantiation of the same template (e.g., create a SmartPtr<T> from a SmartPtr<U>) — are sometimes known as *generalized copy constructors*.

The generalized copy constructor above is not declared explicit. That's deliberate. Type conversions among built-in pointer types (e.g., from derived to base class pointers) are implicit and require no cast, so it's reasonable for smart pointers to emulate that behavior. Omitting explicit on the templatized constructor does just that.

As declared, the generalized copy constructor for SmartPtr offers more than we want. Yes, we want to be able to create a SmartPtr<Top> from a SmartPtr<Bottom>, but we don't want to be able to create a SmartPtr<Bottom> from a SmartPtr<Top>, as that's contrary to the meaning of public inheritance (see Item 32). We also don't want to be able to create a SmartPtr<int> from a SmartPtr<double>, because there is no corresponding implicit conversion from int* to double*. Somehow, we have to cull the herd of member functions that this member template will generate.

Assuming that SmartPtr follows the lead of auto_ptr and tr1::shared_ptr by offering a get member function that returns a copy of the built-in pointer held by the smart pointer object (see Item 15), we can use the implementation of the constructor template to restrict the conversions to those we want:

```
template<typename T>
class SmartPtr {
public:
  template<typename U>
  SmartPtr(const SmartPtr<U>& other)          // initialize this held ptr
    : heldPtr(other.get()) { ... }            // with other's held ptr

  T* get() const { return heldPtr; }
  ...
private:                                       // built-in pointer held
  T *heldPtr;                                  // by the SmartPtr
};
```

We use the member initialization list to initialize SmartPtr<T>'s data member of type T* with the pointer of type U* held by the SmartPtr<U>. This will compile only if there is an implicit conversion from a U* pointer to a T* pointer, and that's precisely what we want. The net effect is that SmartPtr<T> now has a generalized copy constructor that will compile only if passed a parameter of a compatible type.

The utility of member function templates isn't limited to constructors. Another common role for them is in support for assignment. For example, TR1's shared_ptr (again, see Item 13) supports construction from all compatible built-in pointers, tr1::shared_ptrs, auto_ptrs, and tr1::weak_ptrs (see Item 54), as well as assignment from all of those except tr1::weak_ptrs. Here's an excerpt from TR1's specification for tr1::shared_ptr, including its penchant for using class instead of typename when declaring template parameters. (As Item 42 explains, they mean exactly the same thing in this context.)

```
template<class T> class shared_ptr {
public:
  template<class Y>                           // construct from
    explicit shared_ptr(Y * p);               // any compatible
  template<class Y>                           // built-in pointer,
    shared_ptr(shared_ptr<Y> const& r);       // shared_ptr,
  template<class Y>                           // weak_ptr, or
    explicit shared_ptr(weak_ptr<Y> const& r); // auto_ptr
  template<class Y>
    explicit shared_ptr(auto_ptr<Y>& r);
```

```
      template<class Y>                              // assign from
        shared_ptr& operator=(shared_ptr<Y> const& r);   // any compatible
      template<class Y>                              // shared_ptr or
        shared_ptr& operator=(auto_ptr<Y>& r);       // auto_ptr
      ...
    };
```

All these constructors are explicit, except the generalized copy constructor. That means that implicit conversion from one type of shared_ptr to another is allowed, but *implicit* conversion from a built-in pointer or other smart pointer type is not permitted. (*Explicit* conversion — e.g., via a cast — is okay.) Also interesting is how the auto_ptrs passed to tr1::shared_ptr constructors and assignment operators aren't declared const, in contrast to how the tr1::shared_ptrs and tr1::weak_ptrs are passed. That's a consequence of the fact that auto_ptrs stand alone in being modified when they're copied (see Item 13).

Member function templates are wonderful things, but they don't alter the basic rules of the language. Item 5 explains that two of the four member functions that compilers may generate are the copy constructor and the copy assignment operator. tr1::shared_ptr declares a generalized copy constructor, and it's clear that when the types T and Y are the same, the generalized copy constructor could be instantiated to create the "normal" copy constructor. So will compilers generate a copy constructor for tr1::shared_ptr, or will they instantiate the generalized copy constructor template when one tr1::shared_ptr object is constructed from another tr1::shared_ptr object of the same type?

As I said, member templates don't change the rules of the language, and the rules state that if a copy constructor is needed and you don't declare one, one will be generated for you automatically. Declaring a generalized copy constructor (a member template) in a class doesn't keep compilers from generating their own copy constructor (a non-template), so if you want to control all aspects of copy construction, you must declare both a generalized copy constructor as well as the "normal" copy constructor. The same applies to assignment. Here's an excerpt from tr1::shared_ptr's definition that exemplifies this:

```
    template<class T> class shared_ptr {
    public:
      shared_ptr(shared_ptr const& r);                     // copy constructor
      template<class Y>                                    // generalized
        shared_ptr(shared_ptr<Y> const& r);                // copy constructor

      shared_ptr& operator=(shared_ptr const& r);          // copy assignment
      template<class Y>                                    // generalized
        shared_ptr& operator=(shared_ptr<Y> const& r);     // copy assignment
      ...
    };
```

Things to Remember

✦ Use member function templates to generate functions that accept all compatible types.

✦ If you declare member templates for generalized copy construction or generalized assignment, you'll still need to declare the normal copy constructor and copy assignment operator, too.

Item 46: Define non-member functions inside templates when type conversions are desired.

Item 24 explains why only non-member functions are eligible for implicit type conversions on all arguments, and it uses as an example the operator* function for a Rational class. I recommend you familiarize yourself with that example before continuing, because this Item extends the discussion with a seemingly innocuous modification to Item 24's example: it templatizes both Rational and operator*:

```
template<typename T>
class Rational {
public:
    Rational(const T& numerator = 0,      // see Item 20 for why params
             const T& denominator = 1);   // are now passed by reference

    const T numerator() const;            // see Item 28 for why return
    const T denominator() const;          // values are still passed by value,
    ...                                    // Item 3 for why they're const
};

template<typename T>
const Rational<T> operator*(const Rational<T>& lhs,
                            const Rational<T>& rhs)
{ ... }
```

As in Item 24, we want to support mixed-mode arithmetic, so we want the code below to compile. We expect that it will, because we're using the same code that works in Item 24. The only difference is that Rational and operator* are now templates:

```
Rational<int> oneHalf(1, 2);       // this example is from Item 24,
                                   // except Rational is now a template

Rational<int> result = oneHalf * 2;   // error! won't compile
```

The fact that this fails to compile suggests that there's something about the templatized Rational that's different from the non-template version, and indeed there is. In Item 24, compilers know what function we're trying to call (operator* taking two Rationals), but here, compilers do *not* know which function we want to call. Instead, they're trying to *figure out* what function to instantiate (i.e., create) from the template named operator*. They know that they're supposed to instantiate some function named operator* taking two parameters of type Rational<T>, but in order to do the instantiation, they have to figure out what T is. The problem is, they can't.

In attempting to deduce T, they look at the types of the arguments being passed in the call to operator*. In this case, those types are Rational<int> (the type of oneHalf) and int (the type of 2). Each parameter is considered separately.

The deduction using oneHalf is easy. operator*'s first parameter is declared to be of type Rational<T>, and the first argument passed to operator* (oneHalf) is of type Rational<int>, so T must be int. Unfortunately, the deduction for the other parameter is not so simple. operator*'s second parameter is declared to be of type Rational<T>, but the second argument passed to operator* (2) is of type int. How are compilers to figure out what T is in this case? You might expect them to use Rational<int>'s non-explicit constructor to convert 2 into a Rational<int>, thus allowing them to deduce that T is int, but they don't do that. They don't, because implicit type conversion functions are *never* considered during template argument deduction. Never. Such conversions are used during function calls, yes, but before you can call a function, you have to know which functions exist. In order to know that, you have to deduce parameter types for the relevant function templates (so that you can instantiate the appropriate functions). But implicit type conversion via constructor calls is not considered during template argument deduction. Item 24 involves no templates, so template argument deduction is not an issue. Now that we're in the template part of C++ (see Item 1), it's the primary issue.

We can relieve compilers of the challenge of template argument deduction by taking advantage of the fact that a friend declaration in a template class can refer to a specific function. That means the class Rational<T> can declare operator* for Rational<T> as a friend function. Class templates don't depend on template argument deduction (that process applies only to function templates), so T is always known at the time the class Rational<T> is instantiated. That makes it easy for the Rational<T> class to declare the appropriate operator* function as a friend:

```
template<typename T>
class Rational {
public:
    ...
```

```
friend                                      // declare operator*
   const Rational operator*(const Rational& lhs,   // function (see
                           const Rational& rhs);    // below for details)
};

template<typename T>                        // define operator*
const Rational<T> operator*(const Rational<T>& lhs,  // functions
                          const Rational<T>& rhs)
{ ... }
```

Now our mixed-mode calls to operator* will compile, because when the object oneHalf is declared to be of type Rational<int>, the class Rational<int> is instantiated, and as part of that process, the friend function operator* that takes Rational<int> parameters is automatically declared. As a declared *function* (not a function *template*), compilers can use implicit conversion functions (such as Rational's non-explicit constructor) when calling it, and that's how they make the mixed-mode call succeed.

Alas, "succeed" is a funny word in this context, because although the code will compile, it won't link. We'll deal with that in a moment, but first I want to remark on the syntax used to declare operator* inside Rational.

Inside a class template, the name of the template can be used as shorthand for the template and its parameters, so inside Rational<T>, we can just write Rational instead of Rational<T>. That saves us only a few characters in this example, but when there are multiple parameters or longer parameter names, it can both save typing and make the resulting code clearer. I bring this up, because operator* is declared taking and returning Rationals instead of Rational<T>s. It would have been just as valid to declare operator* like this:

```
template<typename T>
class Rational {
public:
   ...
friend
   const Rational<T> operator*(const Rational<T>& lhs,
                             const Rational<T>& rhs);
   ...
};
```

However, it's easier (and more common) to use the shorthand form.

Now back to the linking problem. The mixed-mode code compiles, because compilers know that we want to call a specific function (operator* taking a Rational<int> and a Rational<int>), but that function is only *declared* inside Rational, not *defined* there. Our intent is to have the operator* template outside the class provide that definition, but things don't work that way. If we declare a function ourselves (which is what we're doing inside the Rational template), we're also responsible for defining that function. In this case, we never provide a definition, and that's why linkers can't find one.

The simplest thing that could possibly work is to merge the body of operator* into its declaration:

```cpp
template<typename T>
class Rational {
public:
    ...
friend const Rational operator*(const Rational& lhs, const Rational& rhs)
{
   return Rational(lhs.numerator() * rhs.numerator(),        // same impl
                  lhs.denominator() * rhs.denominator());    // as in
}                                                            // Item 24
};
```

Indeed, this works as intended: mixed-mode calls to operator* now compile, link, and run. Hooray!

An interesting observation about this technique is that the use of friendship has nothing to do with a need to access non-public parts of the class. In order to make type conversions possible on all arguments, we need a non-member function (Item 24 still applies); and in order to have the proper function automatically instantiated, we need to declare the function inside the class. The only way to declare a non-member function inside a class is to make it a friend. So that's what we do. Unconventional? Yes. Effective? Without a doubt.

As Item 30 explains, functions defined inside a class are implicitly declared inline, and that includes friend functions like operator*. You can minimize the impact of such inline declarations by having operator* do nothing but call a helper function defined outside of the class. In the example in this Item, there's not much point in doing that, because operator* is already implemented as a one-line function, but for more complex function bodies, it may be desirable. It's worth taking a look at the "have the friend call a helper" approach.

The fact that Rational is a template means that the helper function will usually also be a template, so the code in the header file defining Rational will typically look something like this:

```cpp
template<typename T> class Rational;           // declare
                                               // Rational
                                               // template
```

```
template<typename T>                                       // declare
const Rational<T> doMultiply( const Rational<T>& lhs,      // helper
                             const Rational<T>& rhs);      // template

template<typename T>
class Rational {
public:

   ...

   friend
      const Rational<T> operator*(const Rational<T>& lhs,
                                 const Rational<T>& rhs)    // Have friend
      { return doMultiply(lhs, rhs); }                      // call helper

   ...

};
```

Many compilers essentially force you to put all template definitions in header files, so you may need to define doMultiply in your header as well. (As Item 30 explains, such templates need not be inline.) That could look like this:

```
template<typename T>                                       // define
const Rational<T> doMultiply(const Rational<T>& lhs,       // helper
                            const Rational<T>& rhs)        // template in
{                                                          // header file,
   return Rational<T>(lhs.numerator() * rhs.numerator(),   // if necessary
                     lhs.denominator() * rhs.denominator());
}
```

As a template, of course, doMultiply won't support mixed-mode multiplication, but it doesn't need to. It will only be called by operator*, and operator* *does* support mixed-mode operations! In essence, the *function* operator* supports whatever type conversions are necessary to ensure that two Rational objects are being multiplied, then it passes these two objects to an appropriate instantiation of the doMultiply *template* to do the actual multiplication. Synergy in action, no?

Things to Remember

✦ When writing a class template that offers functions related to the template that support implicit type conversions on all parameters, define those functions as friends inside the class template.

Item 47: Use traits classes for information about types.

The STL is primarily made up of templates for containers, iterators, and algorithms, but it also has a few utility templates. One of these is called advance. advance moves a specified iterator a specified distance:

```
template<typename IterT, typename DistT>       // move iter d units
void advance(IterT& iter, DistT d);            // forward; if d < 0,
                                               // move iter backward
```

Conceptually, advance just does iter += d, but advance can't be implemented that way, because only random access iterators support the += operation. Less powerful iterator types have to implement advance by iteratively applying ++ or -- d times.

Um, you don't remember your STL iterator categories? No problem, we'll do a mini-review. There are five categories of iterators, corresponding to the operations they support. *Input iterators* can move only forward, can move only one step at a time, can only read what they point to, and can read what they're pointing to only once. They're modeled on the read pointer into an input file; the C++ library's istream_iterators are representative of this category. *Output iterators* are analogous, but for output: they move only forward, move only one step at a time, can only write what they point to, and can write it only once. They're modeled on the write pointer into an output file; ostream_iterators epitomize this category. These are the two least powerful iterator categories. Because input and output iterators can move only forward and can read or write what they point to at most once, they are suitable only for one-pass algorithms.

A more powerful iterator category consists of *forward iterators*. Such iterators can do everything input and output iterators can do, plus they can read or write what they point to more than once. This makes them viable for multi-pass algorithms. The STL offers no singly linked list, but some libraries offer one (usually called slist), and iterators into such containers are forward iterators. Iterators into TR1's hashed containers (see Item 54) may also be in the forward category.

Bidirectional iterators add to forward iterators the ability to move backward as well as forward. Iterators for the STL's list are in this category, as are iterators for set, multiset, map, and multimap.

The most powerful iterator category is that of *random access iterators*. These kinds of iterators add to bidirectional iterators the ability to perform "iterator arithmetic," i.e., to jump forward or backward an arbitrary distance in constant time. Such arithmetic is analogous to pointer arithmetic, which is not surprising, because random access iterators are modeled on built-in pointers, and built-in pointers can act as random access iterators. Iterators for vector, deque, and string are random access iterators.

For each of the five iterator categories, C++ has a "tag struct" in the standard library that serves to identify it:

```
struct input_iterator_tag {};
struct output_iterator_tag {};
struct forward_iterator_tag: public input_iterator_tag {};
struct bidirectional_iterator_tag: public forward_iterator_tag {};
struct random_access_iterator_tag: public bidirectional_iterator_tag {};
```

The inheritance relationships among these structs are valid is-a relationships (see Item 32): it's true that all forward iterators are also input iterators, etc. We'll see the utility of this inheritance shortly.

But back to advance. Given the different iterator capabilities, one way to implement advance would be to use the lowest-common-denominator strategy of a loop that iteratively increments or decrements the iterator. However, that approach would take linear time. Random access iterators support constant-time iterator arithmetic, and we'd like to take advantage of that ability when it's present.

What we really want to do is implement advance essentially like this:

```
template<typename IterT, typename DistT>
void advance(IterT& iter, DistT d)
{
  if (iter is a random access iterator) {
     iter += d;                           // use iterator arithmetic
  }                                       // for random access iters
  else {
     if (d >= 0) { while (d--) ++iter; }  // use iterative calls to
     else { while (d++) --iter; }         // ++ or -- for other
  }                                       // iterator categories
}
```

This requires being able to determine whether iter is a random access iterator, which in turn requires knowing whether its type, IterT, is a random access iterator type. In other words, we need to get some information about a type. That's what *traits* let you do: they allow you to get information about a type during compilation.

Traits aren't a keyword or a predefined construct in C++; they're a technique and a convention followed by C++ programmers. One of the demands made on the technique is that it has to work as well for built-in types as it does for user-defined types. For example, if advance is called with a pointer (like a const char*) and an int, advance has to work, but that means that the traits technique must apply to built-in types like pointers.

The fact that traits must work with built-in types means that things like nesting information inside types won't do, because there's no way to nest information inside pointers. The traits information for a type, then, must be external to the type. The standard technique is to put it into a template and one or more specializations of that template. For iterators, the template in the standard library is named iterator_traits:

```
template<typename IterT>          // template for information about
struct iterator_traits;           // iterator types
```

As you can see, iterator_traits is a struct. By convention, traits are always implemented as structs. Another convention is that the structs used to implement traits are known as — I am not making this up — traits *classes*.

The way iterator_traits works is that for each type IterT, a typedef named iterator_category is declared in the struct iterator_traits<IterT>. This typedef identifies the iterator category of IterT.

iterator_traits implements this in two parts. First, it imposes the requirement that any user-defined iterator type must contain a nested typedef named iterator_category that identifies the appropriate tag struct. deque's iterators are random access, for example, so a class for deque iterators would look something like this:

```
template < ... >                          // template params elided
class deque {
public:
  class iterator {
  public:
    typedef random_access_iterator_tag iterator_category;
    ...
  };
  ...
};
```

list's iterators are bidirectional, however, so they'd do things this way:

```
template < ... >
class list {
public:
  class iterator {
  public:
    typedef bidirectional_iterator_tag iterator_category;
    ...
  };
  ...
};
```

iterator_traits just parrots back the iterator class's nested typedef:

```
// the iterator_category for type IterT is whatever IterT says it is;
// see Item 42 for info on the use of "typedef typename"
template<typename IterT>
struct iterator_traits {
  typedef typename IterT::iterator_category iterator_category;
  ...
};
```

This works well for user-defined types, but it doesn't work at all for iterators that are pointers, because there's no such thing as a pointer with a nested typedef. The second part of the iterator_traits implementation handles iterators that are pointers.

To support such iterators, iterator_traits offers a *partial template specialization* for pointer types. Pointers act as random access iterators, so that's the category iterator_traits specifies for them:

```
template<typename T>              // partial template specialization
struct iterator_traits<T*>        // for built-in pointer types
{
    typedef random_access_iterator_tag iterator_category;
    ...
};
```

At this point, you know how to design and implement a traits class:

- Identify some information about types you'd like to make available (e.g., for iterators, their iterator category).

- Choose a name to identify that information (e.g., iterator_category).

- Provide a template and set of specializations (e.g., iterator_traits) that contain the information for the types you want to support.

Given iterator_traits — actually std::iterator_traits, since it's part of C++'s standard library — we can refine our pseudocode for advance:

```
template<typename IterT, typename DistT>
void advance(IterT& iter, DistT d)
{
    if (typeid(typename std::iterator_traits<IterT>::iterator_category) ==
        typeid(std::random_access_iterator_tag))
        ...
}
```

Although this looks promising, it's not what we want. For one thing, it will lead to compilation problems, but we'll explore that in Item 48; right now, there's a more fundamental issue to consider. IterT's type is known during compilation, so iterator_traits<IterT>::iterator_category can also be determined during compilation. Yet the if statement is evaluated at runtime (unless your optimizer is crafty enough to get rid of it). Why do something at runtime that we can do during compilation? It wastes time (literally), and it bloats our executable.

What we really want is a conditional construct (i.e., an if...else statement) for types that is evaluated during compilation. As it happens, C++ already has a way to get that behavior. It's called overloading.

When you overload some function f, you specify different parameter types for the different overloads. When you call f, compilers pick the best overload, based on the arguments you're passing. Compilers essentially say, "If this overload is the best match for what's being passed, call this f; if this other overload is the best match, call it; if this third one is best, call it," etc. See? A compile-time conditional construct for types. To get advance to behave the way we want, all we have to do is create multiple versions of an overloaded function containing the "guts" of advance, declaring each to take a different type of iterator_category object. I use the name doAdvance for these functions:

```
template<typename IterT, typename DistT>        // use this impl for
void doAdvance(IterT& iter, DistT d,            // random access
               std::random_access_iterator_tag)  // iterators
{
    iter += d;
}

template<typename IterT, typename DistT>        // use this impl for
void doAdvance(IterT& iter, DistT d,            // bidirectional
               std::bidirectional_iterator_tag)  // iterators
{
    if (d >= 0) { while (d--) ++iter; }
    else { while (d++) --iter; }
}

template<typename IterT, typename DistT>        // use this impl for
void doAdvance(IterT& iter, DistT d,            // input iterators
               std::input_iterator_tag)
{
    if (d < 0 ) {
        throw std::out_of_range("Negative distance");   // see below
    }
    while (d--) ++iter;
}
```

Because forward_iterator_tag inherits from input_iterator_tag, the version of doAdvance for input_iterator_tag will also handle forward iterators. That's the motivation for inheritance among the various iterator_tag structs. (In fact, it's part of the motivation for *all* public inheritance: to be able to write code for base class types that also works for derived class types.)

The specification for advance allows both positive and negative distances for random access and bidirectional iterators, but behavior is undefined if you try to move a forward or input iterator a negative distance. The implementations I checked simply assumed that d was non-negative, thus entering a *very* long loop counting "down" to zero if a negative distance was passed in. In the code above, I've shown an exception being thrown instead. Both implementations are valid. That's the curse of undefined behavior: you *can't predict* what will happen.

Given the various overloads for doAdvance, all advance needs to do is call them, passing an extra object of the appropriate iterator category type so that the compiler will use overloading resolution to call the proper implementation:

```
template<typename IterT, typename DistT>
void advance(IterT& iter, DistT d)
{
  doAdvance(                                         // call the version
    iter, d,                                         // of doAdvance
    typename                                         // that is
      std::iterator_traits<IterT>::iterator_category()  // appropriate for
  );                                                 // iter's iterator
}                                                    // category
```

We can now summarize how to use a traits class:

- Create a set of overloaded "worker" functions or function templates (e.g., doAdvance) that differ in a traits parameter. Implement each function in accord with the traits information passed.

- Create a "master" function or function template (e.g., advance) that calls the workers, passing information provided by a traits class.

Traits are widely used in the standard library. There's iterator_traits, of course, which, in addition to iterator_category, offers four other pieces of information about iterators (the most useful of which is value_type — Item 42 shows an example of its use). There's also char_traits, which holds information about character types, and numeric_limits, which serves up information about numeric types, e.g., their minimum and maximum representable values, etc. (The name numeric_limits is a bit of a surprise, because the more common convention is for traits classes to end with "traits," but numeric_limits is what it's called, so numeric_limits is the name we use.)

TR1 (see Item 54) introduces a slew of new traits classes that give information about types, including is_fundamental<T> (whether T is a built-in type), is_array<T> (whether T is an array type), and is_base_of<T1, T2> (whether T1 is the same as or is a base class of T2). All told, TR1 adds over 50 traits classes to standard C++.

Things to Remember

- ✦ Traits classes make information about types available during compilation. They're implemented using templates and template specializations.

- ✦ In conjunction with overloading, traits classes make it possible to perform compile-time if...else tests on types.

Item 48: Be aware of template metaprogramming.

Template metaprogramming (TMP) is the process of writing template-based C++ programs that execute during compilation. Think about that for a minute: a template metaprogram is a program written in C++ that executes *inside the C++ compiler.* When a TMP program finishes running, its output — pieces of C++ source code instantiated from templates — is then compiled as usual.

If this doesn't strike you as just plain bizarre, you're not thinking about it hard enough.

C++ was not designed for template metaprogramming, but since TMP was discovered in the early 1990s, it has proven to be so useful, extensions are likely to be added to both the language and its standard library to make TMP easier. Yes, TMP was discovered, not invented. The features underlying TMP were introduced when templates were added to C++. All that was needed was for somebody to notice how they could be used in clever and unexpected ways.

TMP has two great strengths. First, it makes some things easy that would otherwise be hard or impossible. Second, because template metaprograms execute during C++ compilation, they can shift work from runtime to compile-time. One consequence is that some kinds of errors that are usually detected at runtime can be found during compilation. Another is that C++ programs making use of TMP can be more efficient in just about every way: smaller executables, shorter runtimes, lesser memory requirements. (However, a consequence of shifting work from runtime to compile-time is that compilation takes longer. Programs using TMP may take *much* longer to compile than their non-TMP counterparts.)

Consider the pseudocode for STL's advance introduced on page 228. (That's in Item 47. You may want to read that Item now, because in this Item, I'll assume you are familiar with the material in that one.) As on page 228, I've highlighted the pseudo part of the code:

```
template<typename IterT, typename DistT>
void advance(IterT& iter, DistT d)
{
   if (iter is a random access iterator) {
      iter += d;                              // use iterator arithmetic
   }                                          // for random access iters
   else {
      if (d >= 0) { while (d--) ++iter; }     // use iterative calls to
      else { while (d++) --iter; }            // ++ or -- for other
   }                                          // iterator categories
}
```

We can use typeid to make the pseudocode real. That yields a "normal" C++ approach to this problem — one that does all its work at runtime:

```
template<typename IterT, typename DistT>
void advance(IterT& iter, DistT d)
{
  if (typeid(typename std::iterator_traits<IterT>::iterator_category) ==
      typeid(std::random_access_iterator_tag)) {

    iter += d;                                    // use iterator arithmetic
  }                                               // for random access iters

  else {
    if (d >= 0) { while (d--) ++iter; }           // use iterative calls to
    else { while (d++) --iter; }                  // ++ or -- for other
  }                                               // iterator categories
}
```

Item 47 notes that this typeid-based approach is less efficient than the one using traits, because with this approach, (1) the type testing occurs at runtime instead of during compilation, and (2) the code to do the runtime type testing must be present in the executable. In fact, this example shows how TMP can be more efficient than a "normal" C++ program, because the traits approach *is* TMP. Remember, traits enable compile-time if...else computations on types.

I remarked earlier that some things are easier in TMP than in "normal" C++, and advance offers an example of that, too. Item 47 mentions that the typeid-based implementation of advance can lead to compilation problems, and here's an example where it does:

```
std::list<int>::iterator iter;

...

advance(iter, 10);                  // move iter 10 elements forward;
                                    // won't compile with above impl.
```

Consider the version of advance that will be generated for the above call. After substituting iter's and 10's types for the template parameters IterT and DistT, we get this:

```
void advance(std::list<int>::iterator& iter, int d)
{
  if (typeid(std::iterator_traits<std::list<int>::iterator>::iterator_category) ==
      typeid(std::random_access_iterator_tag)) {

    iter += d;                                        // error! won't compile
  }
  else {
    if (d >= 0) { while (d--) ++iter; }
    else { while (d++) --iter; }
  }
}
```

The problem is the highlighted line, the one using +=. In this case, we're trying to use += on a list<int>::iterator, but list<int>::iterator is a bidirectional iterator (see Item 47), so it doesn't support +=. Only random access iterators support +=. Now, we know we'll never try to execute the += line, because the typeid test will always fail for list<int>::iterators, but compilers are obliged to make sure that all source code is valid, even if it's not executed, and "iter += d" isn't valid when iter isn't a random access iterator. Contrast this with the traits-based TMP solution, where code for different types is split into separate functions, each of which uses only operations applicable to the types for which it is written.

TMP has been shown to be Turing-complete, which means that it is powerful enough to compute anything. Using TMP, you can declare variables, perform loops, write and call functions, etc. But such constructs look very different from their "normal" C++ counterparts. For example, Item 47 shows how if...else conditionals in TMP are expressed via templates and template specializations. But that's assembly-level TMP. Libraries for TMP (e.g., Boost's MPL — see Item 55) offer a higher-level syntax, though still not something you'd mistake for "normal" C++.

For another glimpse into how things work in TMP, let's look at loops. TMP has no real looping construct, so the effect of loops is accomplished via recursion. (If you're not comfortable with recursion, you'll need to address that before venturing into TMP. It's largely a functional language, and recursion is to functional languages as TV is to American pop culture: inseparable.) Even the recursion isn't the normal kind, however, because TMP loops don't involve recursive function calls, they involve recursive *template instantiations*.

The "hello world" program of TMP is computing a factorial during compilation. It's not a very exciting program, but then again, neither is "hello world," yet both are helpful as language introductions. TMP factorial computation demonstrates looping through recursive template instantiation. It also demonstrates one way in which variables are created and used in TMP. Look:

```
template<unsigned n>          // general case: the value of
struct Factorial {            // Factorial<n> is n times the value
                              // of Factorial<n-1>

   enum { value = n * Factorial<n-1>::value };

};

template<>                    // special case: the value of
struct Factorial<0> {         // Factorial<0> is 1
   enum { value = 1 };

};
```

Given this template metaprogram (really just the single template metafunction Factorial), you get the value of factorial(n) by referring to Factorial<n>::value.

The looping part of the code occurs where the template instantiation Factorial<n> references the template instantiation Factorial<n-1>. Like all good recursion, there's a special case that causes the recursion to terminate. Here, it's the template specialization Factorial<0>.

Each instantiation of the Factorial template is a struct, and each struct uses the enum hack (see Item 2) to declare a TMP variable named value. value is what holds the current value of the factorial computation. If TMP had a real looping construct, value would be updated each time around the loop. Since TMP uses recursive template instantiation in place of loops, each instantiation gets its own copy of value, and each copy has the proper value for its place in the "loop."

You could use Factorial like this:

```
int main()
{
  std::cout << Factorial<5>::value;          // prints 120
  std::cout << Factorial<10>::value;         // prints 3628800
}
```

If you think this is cooler than ice cream, you've got the makings of a template metaprogrammer. If the templates and specializations and recursive instantiations and enum hacks and the need to type things like Factorial<n-1>::value make your skin crawl, well, you're a pretty normal C++ programmer.

Of course, Factorial demonstrates the utility of TMP about as well as "hello world" demonstrates the utility of any conventional programming language. To grasp why TMP is worth knowing about, it's important to have a better understanding of what it can accomplish. Here are three examples:

- **Ensuring dimensional unit correctness**. In scientific and engineering applications, it's essential that dimensional units (e.g., mass, distance, time, etc.) be combined correctly. Assigning a variable representing mass to a variable representing velocity, for example, is an error, but dividing a distance variable by a time variable and assigning the result to a velocity variable is fine. Using TMP, it's possible to ensure (during compilation) that all dimensional unit combinations in a program are correct, no matter how complex the calculations. (This is an example of how TMP can be used for early error detection.) One interesting aspect of this use of TMP is that fractional dimensional exponents can be supported. This requires that such fractions be reduced *during compilation* so that compilers can confirm, for example, that the unit $time^{1/2}$ is the same as $time^{4/8}$.

- **Optimizing matrix operations**. Item 21 explains that some functions, including operator*, must return new objects, and Item 44 introduces the SquareMatrix class, so consider the following code:

```
typedef SquareMatrix<double, 10000> BigMatrix;
BigMatrix m1, m2, m3, m4, m5;              // create matrices and
...                                        // give them values
BigMatrix result = m1 * m2 * m3 * m4 * m5; // compute their product
```

  Calculating result in the "normal" way calls for the creation of four temporary matrices, one for the result of each call to operator*. Furthermore, the independent multiplications generate a sequence of four loops over the matrix elements. Using an advanced template technology related to TMP called *expression templates*, it's possible to eliminate the temporaries and merge the loops, all without changing the syntax of the client code above. The resulting software uses less memory and runs dramatically faster.

- **Generating custom design pattern implementations**. Design patterns like Strategy (see Item 35), Observer, Visitor, etc. can be implemented in many ways. Using a TMP-based technology called *policy-based design*, it's possible to create templates representing independent design choices ("policies") that can be combined in arbitrary ways to yield pattern implementations with custom behavior. For example, this technique has been used to allow a few templates implementing smart pointer behavioral policies to generate (during compilation) any of *hundreds* of different smart pointer types. Generalized beyond the domain of programming artifacts like design patterns and smart pointers, this technology is a basis for what's known as *generative programming*.

TMP is not for everybody. The syntax is unintuitive, and tool support is weak. (Debuggers for template metaprograms? Ha!) Being an "accidental" language that was only relatively recently discovered, TMP programming conventions are still somewhat experimental. Nevertheless, the efficiency improvements afforded by shifting work from runtime to compile-time can be impressive, and the ability to express behavior that is difficult or impossible to implement at runtime is attractive, too.

TMP support is on the rise. It's likely that the next version of C++ will provide explicit support for it, and TR1 already does (see Item 54). Books are beginning to come out on the subject, and TMP information on the web just keeps getting richer. TMP will probably never be mainstream, but for some programmers — especially library developers — it's almost certain to be a staple.

Things to Remember

+ Template metaprogramming can shift work from runtime to compile-time, thus enabling earlier error detection and higher runtime performance.

+ TMP can be used to generate custom code based on combinations of policy choices, and it can also be used to avoid generating code inappropriate for particular types.

Customizing
new **and** delete

In these days of computing environments boasting built-in support for garbage collection (e.g., Java and .NET), the manual C++ approach to memory management can look rather old-fashioned. Yet many developers working on demanding systems applications choose C++ *because* it lets them manage memory manually. Such developers study the memory usage characteristics of their software, and they tailor their allocation and deallocation routines to offer the best possible performance (in both time and space) for the systems they build.

Doing that requires an understanding of how C++'s memory management routines behave, and that's the focus of this chapter. The two primary players in the game are the allocation and deallocation routines (operator new and operator delete), with a supporting role played by the new-handler — the function called when operator new can't satisfy a request for memory.

Memory management in a multithreaded environment poses challenges not present in a single-threaded system, because the heap is a modifiable global resource, thus rife with opportunities for the race conditions that bedevil access to all such resources in threaded systems. Many Items in this chapter mention the use of modifiable static data, always something to put thread-aware programmers on high alert. Without proper synchronization, the use of lock-free algorithms, or careful design to prevent concurrent access, calls to memory routines can easily lead to corrupted heap management data structures. Rather than repeatedly remind you of this danger, I'll mention it here and assume that you keep it in mind for the rest of the chapter.

Something else to keep in mind is that operator new and operator delete apply only to allocations for single objects. Memory for arrays is allocated by operator new[] and deallocated by operator delete[]. (In both cases, note the "[]" part of the function names.) Unless indicated otherwise, everything I write about operator new and operator delete also applies to operator new[] and operator delete[].

Finally, note that heap memory for STL containers is managed by the containers' allocator objects, not by new and delete directly. That being the case, this chapter has nothing to say about STL allocators.

Item 49: Understand the behavior of the new-handler.

When operator new can't satisfy a memory allocation request, it throws an exception. Long ago, it returned a null pointer, and some older compilers still do that. You can still get the old behavior (sort of), but I'll defer that discussion until the end of this Item.

Before operator new throws an exception in response to an unsatisfiable request for memory, it calls a client-specifiable error-handling function called a *new-handler*. (This is not quite true. What operator new really does is a bit more complicated. Details are provided in Item 51.) To specify the out-of-memory-handling function, clients call set_new_handler, a standard library function declared in <new>:

```
namespace std {

    typedef void (*new_handler)();
    new_handler set_new_handler(new_handler p) throw();

}
```

As you can see, new_handler is a typedef for a pointer to a function that takes and returns nothing, and set_new_handler is a function that takes and returns a new_handler. (The "throw()" at the end of set_new_handler's declaration is an exception specification. It essentially says that this function won't throw any exceptions, though the truth is a bit more interesting. For details, see Item 29.)

set_new_handler's parameter is a pointer to the function operator new should call if it can't allocate the requested memory. The return value of set_new_handler is a pointer to the function in effect for that purpose before set_new_handler was called.

You use set_new_handler like this:

```
// function to call if operator new can't allocate enough memory
void outOfMem()
{
    std::cerr << "Unable to satisfy request for memory\n";
    std::abort();
}
```

```
int main()
{
  std::set_new_handler(outOfMem);
  int *pBigDataArray = new int[100000000L];
  ...
}
```

If operator new is unable to allocate space for 100,000,000 integers, outOfMem will be called, and the program will abort after issuing an error message. (By the way, consider what happens if memory must be dynamically allocated during the course of writing the error message to cerr....)

When operator new is unable to fulfill a memory request, it calls the new-handler function repeatedly until it *can* find enough memory. The code giving rise to these repeated calls is shown in Item 51, but this high-level description is enough to conclude that a well-designed new-handler function must do one of the following:

- **Make more memory available**. This may allow the next memory allocation attempt inside operator new to succeed. One way to implement this strategy is to allocate a large block of memory at program start-up, then release it for use in the program the first time the new-handler is invoked.

- **Install a different new-handler**. If the current new-handler can't make any more memory available, perhaps it knows of a different new-handler that can. If so, the current new-handler can install the other new-handler in its place (by calling set_new_handler). The next time operator new calls the new-handler function, it will get the one most recently installed. (A variation on this theme is for a new-handler to modify its *own* behavior, so the next time it's invoked, it does something different. One way to achieve this is to have the new-handler modify static, namespace-specific, or global data that affects the new-handler's behavior.)

- **Deinstall the new-handler**, i.e., pass the null pointer to set_new_handler. With no new-handler installed, operator new will throw an exception when memory allocation is unsuccessful.

- **Throw an exception** of type bad_alloc or some type derived from bad_alloc. Such exceptions will not be caught by operator new, so they will propagate to the site originating the request for memory.

- **Not return**, typically by calling abort or exit.

These choices give you considerable flexibility in implementing new-handler functions.

Sometimes you'd like to handle memory allocation failures in different ways, depending on the class of the object being allocated:

```
class X {
public:
    static void outOfMemory();
    ...
};

class Y {
public:
    static void outOfMemory();
    ...
};

X* p1 = new X;                  // if allocation is unsuccessful,
                                // call X::outOfMemory

Y* p2 = new Y;                  // if allocation is unsuccessful,
                                // call Y::outOfMemory
```

C++ has no support for class-specific new-handlers, but it doesn't need any. You can implement this behavior yourself. You just have each class provide its own versions of set_new_handler and operator new. The class's set_new_handler allows clients to specify the new-handler for the class (exactly like the standard set_new_handler allows clients to specify the global new-handler). The class's operator new ensures that the class-specific new-handler is used in place of the global new-handler when memory for class objects is allocated.

Suppose you want to handle memory allocation failures for the Widget class. You'll have to keep track of the function to call when operator new can't allocate enough memory for a Widget object, so you'll declare a static member of type new_handler to point to the new-handler function for the class. Widget will look something like this:

```
class Widget {
public:
    static std::new_handler set_new_handler(std::new_handler p) throw();
    static void* operator new(std::size_t size) throw(std::bad_alloc);

private:
    static std::new_handler currentHandler;
};
```

Static class members must be defined outside the class definition (unless they're const and integral — see Item 2), so:

```
std::new_handler Widget::currentHandler = 0;     // init to null in the class
                                                 // impl. file
```

The set_new_handler function in Widget will save whatever pointer is passed to it, and it will return whatever pointer had been saved prior to the call. This is what the standard version of set_new_handler does:

```
std::new_handler Widget::set_new_handler(std::new_handler p) throw()
{
  std::new_handler oldHandler = currentHandler;
  currentHandler = p;
  return oldHandler;
}
```

Finally, Widget's operator new will do the following:

1. Call the standard set_new_handler with Widget's error-handling function. This installs Widget's new-handler as the global new-handler.

2. Call the global operator new to perform the actual memory allocation. If allocation fails, the global operator new invokes Widget's new-handler, because that function was just installed as the global new-handler. If the global operator new is ultimately unable to allocate the memory, it throws a bad_alloc exception. In that case, Widget's operator new must restore the original global new-handler, then propagate the exception. To ensure that the original new-handler is always reinstated, Widget treats the global new-handler as a resource and follows the advice of Item 13 to use resource-managing objects to prevent resource leaks.

3. If the global operator new was able to allocate enough memory for a Widget object, Widget's operator new returns a pointer to the allocated memory. The destructor for the object managing the global new-handler automatically restores the global new-handler to what it was prior to the call to Widget's operator new.

Here's how you say all that in C++. We'll begin with the resource-handling class, which consists of nothing more than the fundamental RAII operations of acquiring a resource during construction and releasing it during destruction (see Item 13):

```
class NewHandlerHolder {
public:
  explicit NewHandlerHolder(std::new_handler nh)    // acquire current
  : handler(nh) {}                                  // new-handler

  ~NewHandlerHolder()                               // release it
  { std::set_new_handler(handler); }
private:
  std::new_handler handler;                         // remember it

  NewHandlerHolder(const NewHandlerHolder&);        // prevent copying
  NewHandlerHolder&                                 // (see Item 14)
    operator=(const NewHandlerHolder&);
};
```

This makes implementation of Widget's operator new quite simple:

```
void* Widget::operator new(std::size_t size) throw(std::bad_alloc)
{
    NewHandlerHolder                        // install Widget's
        h(std::set_new_handler(currentHandler));    // new-handler

    return ::operator new(size);            // allocate memory
                                            // or throw

}                                           // restore global
                                            // new-handler
```

Clients of Widget use its new-handling capabilities like this:

```
void outOfMem();                      // decl. of func. to call if mem. alloc.
                                      // for Widget objects fails

Widget::set_new_handler(outOfMem);   // set outOfMem as Widget's
                                      // new-handling function

Widget *pw1 = new Widget;            // if memory allocation
                                      // fails, call outOfMem

std::string *ps = new std::string;   // if memory allocation fails,
                                      // call the global new-handling
                                      // function (if there is one)

Widget::set_new_handler(0);          // set the Widget-specific
                                      // new-handling function to
                                      // nothing (i.e., null)

Widget *pw2 = new Widget;            // if mem. alloc. fails, throw an
                                      // exception immediately. (There is
                                      // no new- handling function for
                                      // class Widget.)
```

The code for implementing this scheme is the same regardless of the class, so a reasonable goal would be to reuse it in other places. An easy way to make that possible is to create a "mixin-style" base class, i.e., a base class that's designed to allow derived classes to inherit a single specific capability — in this case, the ability to set a class-specific new-handler. Then turn the base class into a template, so that you get a different copy of the class data for each inheriting class.

The base class part of this design lets derived classes inherit the set_new_handler and operator new functions they all need, while the template part of the design ensures that each inheriting class gets a different currentHandler data member. That may sound a bit complicated, but the code looks reassuringly familiar. In fact, the only real difference is that it's now available to any class that wants it:

```
template<typename T>                    // "mixin-style" base class for
class NewHandlerSupport {               // class-specific set_new_handler
public:                                 // support

  static std::new_handler set_new_handler(std::new_handler p) throw();
  static void* operator new(std::size_t size) throw(std::bad_alloc);

  ...                                   // other versions of op. new —
                                        // see Item 52
private:
  static std::new_handler currentHandler;
};

template<typename T>
std::new_handler
NewHandlerSupport<T>::set_new_handler(std::new_handler p) throw()
{
  std::new_handler oldHandler = currentHandler;
  currentHandler = p;
  return oldHandler;
}

template<typename T>
void* NewHandlerSupport<T>::operator new(std::size_t size)
  throw(std::bad_alloc)
{
  NewHandlerHolder h(std::set_new_handler(currentHandler));
  return ::operator new(size);
}

// this initializes each currentHandler to null
template<typename T>
std::new_handler NewHandlerSupport<T>::currentHandler = 0;
```

With this class template, adding set_new_handler support to Widget is easy: Widget just inherits from NewHandlerSupport<Widget>. (That may look peculiar, but I'll explain in more detail below exactly what's going on.)

```
class Widget: public NewHandlerSupport<Widget> {
  ...                          // as before, but without declarations for
};                             // set_new_handler or operator new
```

That's all Widget needs to do to offer a class-specific set_new_handler.

But maybe you're still fretting over Widget inheriting from NewHandler-Support<Widget>. If so, your fretting may intensify when you note that the NewHandlerSupport template never uses its type parameter T. It doesn't need to. All we need is a different copy of NewHandlerSupport — in particular, its static data member currentHandler — for each class that inherits from NewHandlerSupport. The template parameter T just distinguishes one inheriting class from another. The template mechanism itself automatically generates a copy of currentHandler for each T with which NewHandlerSupport is instantiated.

As for Widget inheriting from a templatized base class that takes Widget as a type parameter, don't feel bad if the notion makes you a little woozy. It initially has that effect on everybody. However, it turns out to be such a useful technique, it has a name, albeit one that reflects the fact that it looks natural to no one the first time they see it. It's called the *curiously recurring template pattern* (CRTP). Honest.

At one point, I published an article suggesting that a better name would be "Do It For Me," because when Widget inherits from NewHandlerSupport<Widget>, it's really saying, "I'm Widget, and I want to inherit from the NewHandlerSupport class for Widget." Nobody uses my proposed name (not even me), but thinking about CRTP as a way of saying "do it for me" may help you understand what the templatized inheritance is doing.

Templates like NewHandlerSupport make it easy to add a class-specific new-handler to any class that wants one. Mixin-style inheritance, however, invariably leads to the topic of multiple inheritance, and before starting down that path, you'll want to read Item 40.

Until 1993, C++ required that operator new return null when it was unable to allocate the requested memory. operator new is now specified to throw a bad_alloc exception, but a lot of C++ was written before compilers began supporting the revised specification. The C++ standardization committee didn't want to abandon the test-for-null code base, so they provided alternative forms of operator new that offer the traditional failure-yields-null behavior. These forms are called "nothrow" forms, in part because they employ nothrow objects (defined in the header <new>) at the point where new is used:

```
class Widget { ... };

Widget *pw1 = new Widget;               // throws bad_alloc if
                                        // allocation fails

if (pw1 == 0) ...                       // this test must fail


Widget *pw2 = new (std::nothrow) Widget;   // returns 0 if allocation for
                                           // the Widget fails

if (pw2 == 0) ...                       // this test may succeed
```

Nothrow new offers a less compelling guarantee about exceptions than is initially apparent. In the expression "new (std::nothrow) Widget," two things happen. First, the nothrow version of operator new is called to allocate enough memory for a Widget object. If that allocation fails, operator new returns the null pointer, just as advertised. If it succeeds, however, the Widget constructor is called, and at that point, all bets are off. The Widget constructor can do whatever it likes. It might itself new up some memory, and if it does, it's not constrained to use nothrow new. Although the operator new call in "new (std::nothrow) Widget" won't throw, then, the Widget constructor might. If it does, the exception will be propagated as usual. Conclusion? Using nothrow new guarantees only that operator new won't throw, not that an expression like "new (std::nothrow) Widget" will never yield an exception. In all likelihood, you will never have a need for nothrow new.

Regardless of whether you use "normal" (i.e., exception-throwing) new or its somewhat stunted nothrow cousin, it's important that you understand the behavior of the new-handler, because it's used with both forms.

Things to Remember

✦ set_new_handler allows you to specify a function to be called when memory allocation requests cannot be satisfied.

✦ Nothrow new is of limited utility, because it applies only to memory allocation; associated constructor calls may still throw exceptions.

Item 50: Understand when it makes sense to replace new **and** delete.

Let's return to fundamentals for a moment. Why would anybody want to replace the compiler-provided versions of operator new or operator delete in the first place? These are three of the most common reasons:

- **To detect usage errors.** Failure to delete memory conjured up by new leads to memory leaks. Using more than one delete on newed memory yields undefined behavior. If operator new keeps a list of allocated addresses and operator delete removes addresses from the list, it's easy to detect such usage errors. Similarly, a variety of programming mistakes can lead to data overruns (writing beyond the end of an allocated block) and underruns (writing prior to the beginning of an allocated block). Custom operator news can overal-locate blocks so there's room to put known byte patterns ("signa-tures") before and after the memory made available to clients. operator deletes can check to see if the signatures are still intact. If they're not, an overrun or underrun occurred sometime during the life of the allocated block, and operator delete can log that fact, along with the value of the offending pointer.

- **To improve efficiency.** The versions of operator new and operator delete that ship with compilers are designed for general-purpose use. They have to be acceptable for long-running programs (e.g., web servers), but they also have to be acceptable for programs that execute for less than a second. They have to handle series of requests for large blocks of memory, small blocks, and mixtures of the two. They have to accommodate allocation patterns ranging from the dynamic allocation of a few blocks that exist for the duration of the program to constant allocation and deallocation of a large number of short-lived objects. They have to worry about heap fragmentation, a process that, if unchecked, eventually leads to the inability to satisfy requests for large blocks of memory, even when ample free memory is distributed across many small blocks.

  Given the demands made on memory managers, it's no surprise that the operator news and operator deletes that ship with compilers take a middle-of-the-road strategy. They work reasonably well for everybody, but optimally for nobody. If you have a good understanding of your program's dynamic memory usage patterns, you can often find that custom versions of operator new and operator delete outperform the default ones. By "outperform," I mean they run faster — sometimes orders of magnitude faster — and they require less memory — up to 50% less. For some (though by no means all) applications, replacing the stock new and delete with custom versions is an easy way to pick up significant performance improvements.

- **To collect usage statistics.** Before heading down the path of writing custom news and deletes, it's prudent to gather information about how your software uses its dynamic memory. What is the distribution of allocated block sizes? What is the distribution of their lifetimes? Do they tend to be allocated and deallocated in FIFO ("first in, first out") order, LIFO ("last in, first out") order, or something closer to random order? Do the usage patterns change over time, e.g., does your software have different allocation/deallocation patterns in different stages of execution? What is the maximum amount of dynamically allocated memory in use at any one time (i.e., its "high water mark")? Custom versions of operator new and operator delete make it easy to collect this kind of information.

In concept, writing a custom operator new is pretty easy. For example, here's a quick first pass at a global operator new that facilitates the detection of under- and overruns. There are a lot of little things wrong with it, but we'll worry about those in a moment.

```
static const int signature = 0xDEADBEEF;
```

```
typedef unsigned char Byte;

// this code has several flaws — see below
void* operator new(std::size_t size) throw(std::bad_alloc)
{
    using namespace std;

    size_t realSize = size + 2 * sizeof(int);    // increase size of request so 2
                                                  // signatures will also fit inside

    void *pMem = malloc(realSize);                // call malloc to get the actual
    if (!pMem) throw bad_alloc();                 // memory

    // write signature into first and last parts of the memory
    *(static_cast<int*>(pMem)) = signature;
    *(reinterpret_cast<int*>(static_cast<Byte*>(pMem)+realSize-sizeof(int))) =
        signature;

    // return a pointer to the memory just past the first signature
    return static_cast<Byte*>(pMem) + sizeof(int);
}
```

Most of the shortcomings of this operator new have to do with its failure to adhere to the C++ conventions for functions of that name. For example, Item 51 explains that all operator news should contain a loop calling a new-handling function, but this one doesn't. However, Item 51 is devoted to such conventions, so I'll ignore them here. I want to focus on a more subtle issue now: *alignment*.

Many computer architectures require that data of particular types be placed in memory at particular kinds of addresses. For example, an architecture might require that pointers occur at addresses that are a multiple of four (i.e., be *four-byte aligned*) or that doubles must occur at addresses that are a multiple of eight (i.e., be *eight-byte aligned*). Failure to follow such constraints could lead to hardware exceptions at runtime. Other architectures are more forgiving, though they may offer better performance if alignment preferences are satisfied. For example, doubles may be aligned on any byte boundary on the Intel x86 architecture, but access to them is a lot faster if they are eight-byte aligned.

Alignment is relevant here, because C++ requires that all operator news return pointers that are suitably aligned for *any* data type. malloc labors under the same requirement, so having operator new return a pointer it gets from malloc is safe. However, in operator new above, we're not returning a pointer we got from malloc, we're returning a pointer we got from malloc *offset by the size of an int*. There is no guarantee that this is safe! If the client called operator new to get enough memory for a double (or, if we were writing operator new[], an array of doubles) and we were running on a machine where ints were four bytes in size but doubles were required to be eight-byte aligned, we'd probably return a pointer with improper alignment. That might cause the program to crash. Or it might just cause it to run more slowly. Either way, it's probably not what we had in mind.

Details like alignment are the kinds of things that distinguish professional-quality memory managers from ones thrown together by programmers distracted by the need to get on to other tasks. Writing a custom memory manager that almost works is pretty easy. Writing one that works *well* is a lot harder. As a general rule, I suggest you not attempt it unless you have to.

In many cases, you don't have to. Some compilers have switches that enable debugging and logging functionality in their memory management functions. A quick glance through your compilers' documentation may eliminate your need to consider writing new and delete. On many platforms, commercial products can replace the memory management functions that ship with compilers. To avail yourself of their enhanced functionality and (presumably) improved performance, all you need do is relink. (Well, you also have to buy them.)

Another option is open source memory managers. They're available for many platforms, so you can download and try those. One such open source allocator is the Pool library from Boost (see Item 55). The Pool library offers allocators tuned for one of the most common situations in which custom memory management is helpful: allocation of a large number of small objects. Many C++ books, including earlier editions of this one, show the code for a high-performance small-object allocator, but they usually omit such pesky details as portability and alignment considerations, thread safety, etc. Real libraries tend to have code that's a lot more robust. Even if you decide to write your own news and deletes, looking at open source versions is likely to give you insights into the easy-to-overlook details that separate almost working from really working. (Given that alignment is one such detail, it's worth noting that TR1 (see Item 54) includes support for discovering type-specific alignment requirements.)

The topic of this Item is knowing when it can make sense to replace the default versions of new and delete, either globally or on a per-class basis. We're now in a position to summarize when in more detail than we did before.

- **To detect usage errors** (as above).

- **To collect statistics about the use of dynamically allocated memory** (also as above).

- **To increase the speed of allocation and deallocation.** General-purpose allocators are often (though not always) a lot slower than custom versions, especially if the custom versions are designed for objects of a particular type. Class-specific allocators are an example application of fixed-size allocators such as those offered by Boost's Pool library. If your application is single-threaded, but your compilers' default memory management routines are thread-safe, you may be able to win measurable speed improvements by writing thread-unsafe allocators. Of course, before jumping to the conclusion that operator new and operator delete are worth speeding up, be sure to profile your program to confirm that these functions are truly a bottleneck.

- **To reduce the space overhead of default memory management.** General-purpose memory managers are often (though not always) not just slower than custom versions, they often use more memory, too. That's because they often incur some overhead for each allocated block. Allocators tuned for small objects (such as those in Boost's Pool library) essentially eliminate such overhead.

- **To compensate for suboptimal alignment in the default allocator.** As I mentioned earlier, it's fastest to access doubles on the x86 architecture when they are eight-byte aligned. Alas, the operator news that ship with some compilers don't guarantee eight-byte alignment for dynamic allocations of doubles. In such cases, replacing the default operator new with one that guarantees eight-byte alignment could yield big increases in program performance.

- **To cluster related objects near one another.** If you know that particular data structures are generally used together and you'd like to minimize the frequency of page faults when working on the data, it can make sense to create a separate heap for the data structures so they are clustered together on as few pages as possible. Placement versions of new and delete (see Item 52) can make it possible to achieve such clustering.

- **To obtain unconventional behavior.** Sometimes you want operators new and delete to do something that the compiler-provided versions don't offer. For example, you might want to allocate and deallocate blocks in shared memory, but have only a C API through which to manage that memory. Writing custom versions of new and delete (probably placement versions — again, see Item 52) would allow you to drape the C API in C++ clothing. As another example, you might write a custom operator delete that overwrites deallocated memory with zeros in order to increase the security of application data.

Things to Remember

✦ There are many valid reasons for writing custom versions of new and delete, including improving performance, debugging heap usage errors, and collecting heap usage information.

Item 51: Adhere to convention when writing new and delete.

Item 50 explains when you might want to write your own versions of operator new and operator delete, but it doesn't explain the conventions you must follow when you do it. The rules aren't hard to follow, but some of them are unintuitive, so it's important to know what they are.

We'll begin with operator new. Implementing a conformant operator new requires having the right return value, calling the new-handling function when insufficient memory is available (see Item 49), and being prepared to cope with requests for no memory. You'll also want to avoid inadvertently hiding the "normal" form of new, though that's more a class interface issue than an implementation requirement; it's addressed in Item 52.

The return value part of operator new is easy. If you can supply the requested memory, you return a pointer to it. If you can't, you follow the rule described in Item 49 and throw an exception of type bad_alloc.

It's not quite that simple, however, because operator new actually tries to allocate memory more than once, calling the new-handling function after each failure. The assumption here is that the new-handling function might be able to do something to free up some memory. Only when the pointer to the new-handling function is null does operator new throw an exception.

Curiously, C++ requires that operator new return a legitimate pointer even when zero bytes are requested. (Requiring this odd-sounding behavior simplifies things elsewhere in the language.) That being the case, pseudocode for a non-member operator new looks like this:

```
void* operator new(std::size_t size) throw(std::bad_alloc)
{                                           // your operator new might
  using namespace std;                      // take additional params

  if (size == 0) {                          // handle 0-byte requests
    size = 1;                               // by treating them as
  }                                         // 1-byte requests

  while (true) {
    attempt to allocate size bytes;
```

```
        if (the allocation was successful)
            return (a pointer to the memory);

        // allocation was unsuccessful; find out what the
        // current new-handling function is (see below)
        new_handler globalHandler = set_new_handler(0);
        set_new_handler(globalHandler);

        if (globalHandler) (*globalHandler)();
        else throw std::bad_alloc();
    }
}
```

The trick of treating requests for zero bytes as if they were really requests for one byte looks slimy, but it's simple, it's legal, it works, and how often do you expect to be asked for zero bytes, anyway?

You may also look askance at the place in the pseudocode where the new-handling function pointer is set to null, then promptly reset to what it was originally. Unfortunately, there is no way to get at the new-handling function pointer directly, so you have to call set_new_handler to find out what it is. Crude, yes, but also effective, at least for single-threaded code. In a multithreaded environment, you'll probably need some kind of lock to safely manipulate the (global) data structures behind the new-handling function.

Item 49 remarks that operator new contains an infinite loop, and the code above shows that loop explicitly; "while (true)" is about as infinite as it gets. The only way out of the loop is for memory to be successfully allocated or for the new-handling function to do one of the things described in Item 49: make more memory available, install a different new-handler, deinstall the new-handler, throw an exception of or derived from bad_alloc, or fail to return. It should now be clear why the new-handler must do one of those things. If it doesn't, the loop inside operator new will never terminate.

Many people don't realize that operator new member functions are inherited by derived classes. That can lead to some interesting complications. In the pseudocode for operator new above, notice that the function tries to allocate size bytes (unless size is zero). That makes perfect sense, because that's the argument that was passed to the function. However, as Item 50 explains, one of the most common reasons for writing a custom memory manager is to optimize allocation for objects of a *specific* class, not for a class or any of its derived classes. That is, given an operator new for a class X, the behavior of that function is typically tuned for objects of size sizeof(X) — nothing larger and nothing smaller. Because of inheritance, however, it is possible that the operator new in a base class will be called to allocate memory for an object of a derived class:

```
class Base {
public:
   static void* operator new(std::size_t size) throw(std::bad_alloc);
   ...
};

class Derived: public Base          // Derived doesn't declare
{ ... };                            // operator new

Derived *p = new Derived;           // calls Base::operator new!
```

If Base's class-specific operator new wasn't designed to cope with this — and chances are that it wasn't — the best way for it to handle the situation is to slough off calls requesting the "wrong" amount of memory to the standard operator new, like this:

```
void* Base::operator new(std::size_t size) throw(std::bad_alloc)
{
   if (size != sizeof(Base))        // if size is "wrong,"
      return ::operator new(size);  // have standard operator
                                    // new handle the request

   ...                              // otherwise handle
                                    // the request here
}
```

"Hold on!" I hear you cry, "You forgot to check for the pathological-but-nevertheless-possible case where size is zero!" Actually, I didn't, and please stop using hyphens when you cry out. The test is still there, it's just been incorporated into the test of size against sizeof(Base). C++ works in some mysterious ways, and one of those ways is to decree that all freestanding objects have non-zero size (see Item 39). By definition, sizeof(Base) can never be zero, so if size is zero, the request will be forwarded to ::operator new, and it will become that function's responsibility to treat the request in a reasonable fashion.

If you'd like to control memory allocation for arrays on a per-class basis, you need to implement operator new's array-specific cousin, operator new[]. (This function is usually called "array new," because it's hard to figure out how to pronounce "operator new[]".) If you decide to write operator new[], remember that all you're doing is allocating a chunk of raw memory — you can't do anything to the as-yet-nonexistent objects in the array. In fact, you can't even figure out how many objects will be in the array. First, you don't know how big each object is. After all, a base class's operator new[] might, through inheritance, be called to allocate memory for an array of derived class objects, and derived class objects are usually bigger than base class objects.

Hence, you can't assume inside Base::operator new[] that the size of each object going into the array is sizeof(Base), and that means you can't assume that the number of objects in the array is (*bytes requested*)/sizeof(Base). Second, the size_t parameter passed to operator new[] may be for more memory than will be filled with objects, because, as Item 16 explains, dynamically allocated arrays may include extra space to store the number of array elements.

So much for the conventions you need to follow when writing operator new. For operator delete, things are simpler. About all you need to remember is that C++ guarantees it's always safe to delete the null pointer, so you need to honor that guarantee. Here's pseudocode for a non-member operator delete:

```
void operator delete(void *rawMemory) throw()
{
  if (rawMemory == 0) return;        // do nothing if the null
                                     // pointer is being deleted

  deallocate the memory pointed to by rawMemory;
}
```

The member version of this function is simple, too, except you've got to be sure to check the size of what's being deleted. Assuming your class-specific operator new forwards requests of the "wrong" size to ::operator new, you've got to forward "wrongly sized" deletion requests to ::operator delete:

```
class Base {                         // same as before, but now
public:                              // operator delete is declared

  static void* operator new(std::size_t size) throw(std::bad_alloc);
  static void operator delete(void *rawMemory, std::size_t size) throw();
  ...
};
void Base::operator delete(void *rawMemory, std::size_t size) throw()
{
  if (rawMemory == 0) return;        // check for null pointer

  if (size != sizeof(Base)) {        // if size is "wrong,"
    ::operator delete(rawMemory);    // have standard operator
    return;                          // delete handle the request
  }

  deallocate the memory pointed to by rawMemory;

  return;
}
```

Interestingly, the size_t value C++ passes to operator delete may be incorrect if the object being deleted was derived from a base class lacking a virtual destructor. This is reason enough for making sure your base classes have virtual destructors, but Item 7 describes a second, arguably better reason. For now, simply note that if you omit virtual destructors in base classes, operator delete functions may not work correctly.

Things to Remember

✦ operator new should contain an infinite loop trying to allocate memory, should call the new-handler if it can't satisfy a memory request, and should handle requests for zero bytes. Class-specific versions should handle requests for larger blocks than expected.

✦ operator delete should do nothing if passed a pointer that is null. Class-specific versions should handle blocks that are larger than expected.

Item 52: Write placement delete if you write placement new.

Placement new and placement delete aren't the most commonly encountered beasts in the C++ menagerie, so don't worry if you're not familiar with them. Instead, recall from Items 16 and 17 that when you write a new expression such as this,

    Widget *pw = new Widget;

two functions are called: one to operator new to allocate memory, a second to Widget's default constructor.

Suppose that the first call succeeds, but the second call results in an exception being thrown. In that case, the memory allocation performed in step 1 must be undone. Otherwise we'll have a memory leak. Client code can't deallocate the memory, because if the Widget constructor throws an exception, pw is never assigned. There'd be no way for clients to get at the pointer to the memory that should be deallocated. The responsibility for undoing step 1 must therefore fall on the C++ runtime system.

The runtime system is happy to call the operator delete that corresponds to the version of operator new it called in step 1, but it can do that only if it knows which operator delete — there may be many — is the proper one to call. This isn't an issue if you're dealing with the versions of new and delete that have the normal signatures, because the normal operator new,

    void* operator new(std::size_t) throw(std::bad_alloc);

corresponds to the normal operator delete:

```
void operator delete(void *rawMemory) throw();        // normal signature
                                                      // at global scope
void operator delete(void *rawMemory,                 // typical normal
                   std::size_t size) throw();          // signature at class
                                                      // scope
```

When you're using only the normal forms of new and delete, then, the runtime system has no trouble finding the delete that knows how to undo what new did. The which-delete-goes-with-this-new issue does arise, however, when you start declaring non-normal forms of operator new — forms that take additional parameters.

For example, suppose you write a class-specific operator new that requires specification of an ostream to which allocation information should be logged, and you also write a normal class-specific operator delete:

```
class Widget {
public:
   ...
   static void* operator new(std::size_t size,        // non-normal
                          std::ostream& logStream)      // form of new
         throw(std::bad_alloc);
   static void operator delete(void *pMemory,          // normal class-
                          std::size_t size) throw();     // specific form
                                                      // of delete
   ...
};
```

This design is problematic, but before we see why, we need to make a brief terminological detour.

When an operator new function takes extra parameters (other than the mandatory size_t argument), that function is known as a *placement* version of new. The operator new above is thus a placement version. A particularly useful placement new is the one that takes a pointer specifying where an object should be constructed. That operator new looks like this:

```
void* operator new(std::size_t, void *pMemory) throw();     // "placement
                                                      // new"
```

This version of new is part of C++'s standard library, and you have access to it whenever you #include <new>. Among other things, this new is used inside vector to create objects in the vector's unused capacity. It's also the *original* placement new. In fact, that's how this function is known: as *placement new*. Which means that the term "placement new" is overloaded. Most of the time when people talk about placement new, they're talking about this specific function, the operator new taking a single extra argument of type void*. Less commonly, they're talking about any version of operator new that takes extra arguments. Context generally clears up any ambiguity, but it's important to understand that the general term "placement new" means any version of new taking extra arguments, because the phrase "placement delete" (which we'll encounter in a moment) derives directly from it.

But let's get back to the declaration of the Widget class, the one whose design I said was problematic. The difficulty is that this class will give rise to subtle memory leaks. Consider this client code, which logs allocation information to cerr when dynamically creating a Widget:

```
Widget *pw = new (std::cerr) Widget;    // call operator new, passing cerr as
                                        // the ostream; this leaks memory
                                        // if the Widget constructor throws
```

Once again, if memory allocation succeeds and the Widget constructor throws an exception, the runtime system is responsible for undoing the allocation that operator new performed. However, the runtime system can't really understand how the called version of operator new works, so it can't undo the allocation itself. Instead, the runtime system looks for a version of operator delete that takes *the same number and types of extra arguments* as operator new, and, if it finds it, that's the one it calls. In this case, operator new takes an extra argument of type ostream&, so the corresponding operator delete would have this signature:

```
void operator delete(void*, std::ostream&) throw();
```

By analogy with placement versions of new, versions of operator delete that take extra parameters are known as *placement deletes*. In this case, Widget declares no placement version of operator delete, so the runtime system doesn't know how to undo what the call to placement new does. As a result, it does nothing. In this example, *no operator delete is called* if the Widget constructor throws an exception!

The rule is simple: if an operator new with extra parameters isn't matched by an operator delete with the same extra parameters, no operator delete will be called if a memory allocation by the new needs to be undone. To eliminate the memory leak in the code above, Widget needs to declare a placement delete that corresponds to the logging placement new:

```
class Widget {
public:
  ...
```

```
    static void* operator new(std::size_t size, std::ostream& logStream)
        throw(std::bad_alloc);
    static void operator delete(void *pMemory) throw();

    static void operator delete(void *pMemory, std::ostream& logStream)
        throw();

    ...
};
```

With this change, if an exception is thrown from the Widget constructor in this statement,

```
    Widget *pw = new (std::cerr) Widget;     // as before, but no leak this time
```

the corresponding placement delete is automatically invoked, and that
allows Widget to ensure that no memory is leaked.

However, consider what happens if no exception is thrown (which will
usually be the case) and we get to a delete in client code:

```
    delete pw;                              // invokes the normal
                                           // operator delete
```

As the comment indicates, this calls the normal operator delete, not
the placement version. Placement delete is called *only* if an exception
arises from a constructor call that's coupled to a call to a placement
new. Applying delete to a pointer (such as pw above) never yields a call
to a placement version of delete. *Never.*

This means that to forestall all memory leaks associated with placement versions of new, you must provide both the normal operator
delete (for when no exception is thrown during construction) and a
placement version that takes the same extra arguments as operator
new does (for when one is). Do that, and you'll never lose sleep over
subtle memory leaks again. Well, at least not *these* subtle memory
leaks.

Incidentally, because member function names hide functions with the
same names in outer scopes (see Item 33), you need to be careful to
avoid having class-specific news hide other news (including the normal versions) that your clients expect. For example, if you have a base
class that declares only a placement version of operator new, clients
will find that the normal form of new is unavailable to them:

```
    class Base {
    public:
      ...
      static void* operator new(std::size_t size,            // this new hides
                               std::ostream& logStream)      // the normal
        throw(std::bad_alloc);                               // global forms
      ...
    };
```

```
Base *pb = new Base;                    // error! the normal form of
                                        // operator new is hidden

Base *pb = new (std::cerr) Base;        // fine, calls Base's
                                        // placement new
```

Similarly, operator news in derived classes hide both global and inherited versions of operator new:

```
class Derived: public Base {            // inherits from Base above
public:
    ...
    static void* operator new(std::size_t size)   // redeclares the normal
        throw(std::bad_alloc);                     // form of new

    ...
};
Derived *pd = new (std::clog) Derived;  // error! Base's placement
                                        // new is hidden

Derived *pd = new Derived;              // fine, calls Derived's
                                        // operator new
```

Item 33 discusses this kind of name hiding in considerable detail, but for purposes of writing memory allocation functions, what you need to remember is that by default, C++ offers the following forms of operator new at global scope:

```
void* operator new(std::size_t) throw(std::bad_alloc);   // normal new

void* operator new(std::size_t, void*) throw();          // placement new

void* operator new(std::size_t,                          // nothrow new —
            const std::nothrow_t&) throw();              // see Item 49
```

If you declare any operator news in a class, you'll hide all these standard forms. Unless you mean to prevent class clients from using these forms, be sure to make them available in addition to any custom operator new forms you create. For each operator new you make available, of course, be sure to offer the corresponding operator delete, too. If you want these functions to behave in the usual way, just have your class-specific versions call the global versions.

An easy way to do this is to create a base class containing all the normal forms of new and delete:

```
class StandardNewDeleteForms {
public:
    // normal new/delete
    static void* operator new(std::size_t size) throw(std::bad_alloc)
    { return ::operator new(size); }

    static void operator delete(void *pMemory) throw()
    { ::operator delete(pMemory); }
```

```
// placement new/delete
static void* operator new(std::size_t size, void *ptr) throw()
{ return ::operator new(size, ptr); }

static void operator delete(void *pMemory, void *ptr) throw()
{ return ::operator delete(pMemory, ptr); }

// nothrow new/delete
static void* operator new(std::size_t size, const std::nothrow_t& nt) throw()
{ return ::operator new(size, nt); }

static void operator delete(void *pMemory, const std::nothrow_t&) throw()
{ ::operator delete(pMemory); }
};
```

Clients who want to augment the standard forms with custom forms can then just use inheritance and using declarations (see Item 33) to get the standard forms:

```
class Widget: public StandardNewDeleteForms {      // inherit std forms
public:
  using StandardNewDeleteForms::operator new;      // make those
  using StandardNewDeleteForms::operator delete;   // forms visible

  static void* operator new(std::size_t size,      // add a custom
                    std::ostream& logStream)       // placement new
       throw(std::bad_alloc);

  static void operator delete(void *pMemory,       // add the corres-
                    std::ostream& logStream)       // ponding place-
       throw();                                    // ment delete
  ...
};
```

Things to Remember

✦ When you write a placement version of operator new, be sure to write the corresponding placement version of operator delete. If you don't, your program may experience subtle, intermittent memory leaks.

✦ When you declare placement versions of new and delete, be sure not to unintentionally hide the normal versions of those functions.

9 Miscellany

Welcome to the catch-all "Miscellany" chapter. There are only three Items here, but don't let their diminutive number or unglamorous setting fool you. They're important.

The first Item emphasizes that compiler warnings are not to be trifled with, at least not if you want your software to behave properly. The second offers an overview of the contents of the standard C++ library, including the significant new functionality being introduced in TR1. Finally, the last Item provides an overview of Boost, arguably the most important general-purpose C++-related web site. Trying to write effective C++ software without the information in these Items is, at best, an uphill battle.

Item 53: Pay attention to compiler warnings.

Many programmers routinely ignore compiler warnings. After all, if the problem were serious, it would be an error, right? This thinking may be relatively harmless in other languages, but in C++, it's a good bet compiler writers have a better grasp of what's going on than you do. For example, here's an error everybody makes at one time or another:

```
class B {
public:
  virtual void f() const;
};

class D: public B {
public:
  virtual void f();
};
```

The idea is for D::f to redefine the virtual function B::f, but there's a mistake: in B, f is a const member function, but in D it's not declared const. One compiler I know says this about that:

    warning: D::f() hides virtual B::f()

Too many inexperienced programmers respond to this message by saying to themselves, "Of *course* D::f hides B::f — that's what it's *supposed* to do!" Wrong. This compiler is trying to tell you that the f declared in B has not been redeclared in D; instead, it's been hidden entirely (see Item 33 for a description of why this is so). Ignoring this compiler warning will almost certainly lead to erroneous program behavior, followed by a lot of debugging to discover something this compiler detected in the first place.

After you gain experience with the warning messages from a particular compiler, you'll learn to understand what the different messages mean (which is often very different from what they *seem* to mean, alas). Once you have that experience, you may choose to ignore a whole range of warnings, though it's generally considered better practice to write code that compiles warning-free, even at the highest warning level. Regardless, it's important to make sure that before you dismiss a warning, you understand exactly what it's trying to tell you.

As long as we're on the topic of warnings, recall that warnings are inherently implementation-dependent, so it's not a good idea to get sloppy in your programming, relying on compilers to spot your mistakes for you. The function-hiding code above, for instance, goes through a different (but widely used) compiler with nary a squawk.

Things to Remember

✦ Take compiler warnings seriously, and strive to compile warning-free at the maximum warning level supported by your compilers.

✦ Don't become dependent on compiler warnings, because different compilers warn about different things. Porting to a new compiler may eliminate warning messages you've come to rely on.

Item 54: Familiarize yourself with the standard library, including TR1.

The standard for C++ — the document defining the language and its library — was ratified in 1998. In 2003, a minor "bug-fix" update was issued. The standardization committee continues its work, however, and a "Version 2.0" C++ standard is expected in 2009 (though all substantive work is likely to be completed by the end of 2007). Until recently, the expected year for the next version of C++ was undecided, and that explains why people usually refer to the next version of C++ as "C++0x" — the year 200x version of C++.

C++0x will probably include some interesting new language features, but most new C++ functionality will come in the form of additions to the standard library. We already know what some of the new library functionality will be, because it's been specified in a document known as TR1 ("Technical Report 1" from the C++ Library Working Group). The standardization committee reserves the right to modify TR1 functionality before it's officially enshrined in C++0x, but significant changes are unlikely. For all intents and purposes, TR1 heralds the beginning of a new release of C++ — what we might call standard C++ 1.1. You can't be an effective C++ programmer without being familiar with TR1 functionality, because that functionality is a boon to virtually every kind of library and application.

Before surveying what's in TR1, it's worth reviewing the major parts of the standard C++ library specified by C++98:

- **The Standard Template Library (STL)**, including containers (vector, string, map, etc.); iterators; algorithms (find, sort, transform, etc.); function objects (less, greater, etc.); and various container and function object adapters (stack, priority_queue, mem_fun, not1, etc.).

- **Iostreams**, including support for user-defined buffering, internationalized IO, and the predefined objects cin, cout, cerr, and clog.

- **Support for internationalization**, including the ability to have multiple active locales. Types like wchar_t (usually 16 bits/char) and wstring (strings of wchar_ts) facilitate working with Unicode.

- **Support for numeric processing**, including templates for complex numbers (complex) and arrays of pure values (valarray).

- **An exception hierarchy**, including the base class exception, its derived classes logic_error and runtime_error, and various classes that inherit from those.

- **C89's standard library**. Everything in the 1989 C standard library is also in C++.

If any of the above is unfamiliar to you, I suggest you schedule some quality time with your favorite C++ reference to rectify the situation.

TR1 specifies 14 new components (i.e., pieces of library functionality). All are in the std namespace, more precisely, in the nested namespace tr1. The full name of the TR1 component shared_ptr (see below) is thus std::tr1::shared_ptr. In this book, I customarily omit the std:: when discussing components of the standard library, but I always prefix TR1 components with tr1::.

This book shows examples of the following TR1 components:

- The **smart pointers** tr1::shared_ptr and tr1::weak_ptr. tr1::shared_ptrs act like built-in pointers, but they keep track of how many tr1::shared_ptrs point to an object. This is known as *reference counting*. When the last such pointer is destroyed (i.e., when the reference count for an object becomes zero), the object is automatically deleted. This works well in preventing resource leaks in acyclic data structures, but if two or more objects contain tr1::shared_ptrs such that a cycle is formed, the cycle may keep each object's reference count above zero, even when all external pointers to the cycle have been destroyed (i.e., when the group of objects as a whole is unreachable). That's where tr1::weak_ptrs come in. tr1::weak_ptrs are designed to act as cycle-inducing pointers in otherwise acyclic tr1::shared_ptr-based data structures. tr1::weak_ptrs don't participate in reference counting. When the last tr1::shared_ptr to an object is destroyed, the object is deleted, even if tr1::weak_ptrs continue to point there. Such tr1::weak_ptrs are automatically marked as invalid, however.

  tr1::shared_ptr may be the most widely useful component in TR1. I use it many times in this book, including in Item 13, where I explain why it's so important. (The book contains no uses of tr1::weak_ptr, sorry.)

- **tr1::function**, which makes it possible to represent any *callable entity* (i.e., any function or function object) whose signature is consistent with a target signature. If we wanted to make it possible to register callback functions that take an int and return a string, we could do this:

```
void registerCallback(std::string func(int));      // param type is a function
                                                    // taking an int and
                                                    // returning a string
```

The parameter name func is optional, so registerCallback could be declared this way, instead:

```
void registerCallback(std::string (int));          // same as above; param
                                                    // name is omitted
```

Note here that "std::string (int)" is a function signature.

tr1::function makes it possible to make registerCallback much more flexible, accepting as its argument any callable entity that takes an int or *anything an int can be converted into* and that returns a string or *anything convertible to a string*. tr1::function takes as a template parameter its target function signature:

```
void registerCallback(std::tr1::function<std::string (int)> func);
                                         // the param "func" will
                                         // take any callable entity
                                         // with a sig consistent
                                         // with "std::string (int)"
```

This kind of flexibility is astonishingly useful, something I do my best to demonstrate in Item 35.

- **tr1::bind**, which does everything the STL binders bind1st and bind2nd do, plus much more. Unlike the pre-TR1 binders, tr1::bind works with both const and non-const member functions. Unlike the pre-TR1 binders, tr1::bind works with by-reference parameters. Unlike the pre-TR1 binders, tr1::bind handles function pointers without help, so there's no need to mess with ptr_fun, mem_fun, or mem_fun_ref before calling tr1::bind. Simply put, tr1::bind is a second-generation binding facility that is significantly better than its predecessor. I show an example of its use in Item 35.

I divide the remaining TR1 components into two sets. The first group offers fairly discrete standalone functionality:

- **Hash tables** used to implement sets, multisets, maps, and multimaps. Each new container has an interface modeled on that of its pre-TR1 counterpart. The most surprising thing about TR1's hash tables are their names: tr1::unordered_set, tr1::unordered_multiset, tr1::unordered_map, and tr1::unordered_multimap. These names emphasize that, unlike the contents of a set, multiset, map, or multimap, the elements in a TR1 hash-based container are not in any predictable order.

- **Regular expressions**, including the ability to do regular expression-based search and replace operations on strings, to iterate through strings from match to match, etc.

- **Tuples**, a nifty generalization of the pair template that's already in the standard library. Whereas pair objects can hold only two objects, however, tr1::tuple objects can hold an arbitrary number. Expat Python and Eiffel programmers, rejoice! A little piece of your former homeland is now part of C++.

- **tr1::array**, essentially an "STLified" array, i.e., an array supporting member functions like begin and end. The size of a tr1::array is fixed during compilation; the object uses no dynamic memory.

- **tr1::mem_fn**, a syntactically uniform way of adapting member function pointers. Just as tr1::bind subsumes and extends the capabilities of C++98's bind1st and bind2nd, tr1::mem_fn subsumes and extends the capabilities of C++98's mem_fun and mem_fun_ref.

- **tr1::reference_wrapper**, a facility to make references act a bit more like objects. Among other things, this makes it possible to create containers that act as if they hold references. (In reality, containers can hold only objects or pointers.)

- **Random number generation** facilities that are vastly superior to the rand function that C++ inherited from C's standard library.

- **Mathematical special functions**, including Laguerre polynomials, Bessel functions, complete elliptic integrals, and many more.

- **C99 compatibility extensions**, a collection of functions and templates designed to bring many new C99 library features to C++.

The second set of TR1 components consists of support technology for more sophisticated template programming techniques, including template metaprogramming (see Item 48):

- **Type traits**, a set of traits classes (see Item 47) to provide compile-time information about types. Given a type T, TR1's type traits can reveal whether T is a built-in type, offers a virtual destructor, is an empty class (see Item 39), is implicitly convertible to some other type U, and much more. TR1's type traits can also reveal the proper alignment for a type, a crucial piece of information for programmers writing custom memory allocation functions (see Item 50).

- **tr1::result_of**, a template to deduce the return types of function calls. When writing templates, it's often important to be able to refer to the type of object returned from a call to a function (template), but the return type can depend on the function's parameter types in complex ways. tr1::result_of makes referring to function return types easy. tr1::result_of is used in several places in TR1 itself.

Although the capabilities of some pieces of TR1 (notably tr1::bind and tr1::mem_fn) subsume those of some pre-TR1 components, TR1 is a pure addition to the standard library. No TR1 component replaces an existing component, so legacy code written with pre-TR1 constructs continues to be valid.

TR1 itself is just a document.† To take advantage of the functionality it specifies, you need access to code that implements it. Eventually, that code will come bundled with compilers, but as I write this in 2005, there is a good chance that if you look for TR1 components in your standard library implementations, at least some will be missing. Fortunately, there is someplace else to look: 10 of the 14 components in TR1 are based on libraries freely available from Boost (see Item 55), so that's an excellent resource for TR1-like functionality. I say "TR1-like," because, though much TR1 functionality is based on Boost libraries, there are places where Boost functionality is currently not an exact match for the TR1 specification. It's possible that by the time you read this, Boost not only will have TR1-conformant implementations for the TR1 components that evolved from Boost libraries, it will also offer implementations of the four TR1 components that were not based on Boost work.

If you'd like to use Boost's TR1-like libraries as a stopgap until compilers ship with their own TR1 implementations, you may want to avail yourself of a namespace trick. All Boost components are in the namespace boost, but TR1 components are supposed to be in std::tr1. You can tell your compilers to treat references to std::tr1 the same as references to boost. This is how:

```
namespace std {
    namespace tr1 = ::boost;        // namespace std::tr1 is an alias
}                                   // for namespace boost
```

Technically, this puts you in the realm of undefined behavior, because, as Item 25 explains, you're not allowed to add anything to the std namespace. In practice, you're unlikely to run into any trouble. When your compilers provide their own TR1 implementations, all you'll need to do is eliminate the above namespace alias; code referring to std::tr1 will continue to be valid.

Probably the most important part of TR1 not based on Boost libraries is hash tables, but hash tables have been available for many years from several sources under the names hash_set, hash_multiset, hash_map, and hash_multimap. There is a good chance that the libraries shipping with your compilers already contain these templates. If not, fire up your favorite search engine and search for these names (as well as their TR1 appellations), because you're sure to find several sources for them, both commercial and freeware.

---

† As I write this in early 2005, the document has not been finalized, and its URL is subject to change. I therefore suggest you consult the *Effective C++ TR1 Information Page*, http://aristeia.com/EC3E/TR1_info.html. That URL will remain stable.

Things to Remember

✦ The primary standard C++ library functionality consists of the STL, iostreams, and locales. The C89 standard library is also included.

✦ TR1 adds support for smart pointers (e.g., tr1::shared_ptr), generalized function pointers (tr1::function), hash-based containers, regular expressions, and 10 other components.

✦ TR1 itself is only a specification. To take advantage of TR1, you need an implementation. One source for implementations of TR1 components is Boost.

Item 55: Familiarize yourself with Boost.

Searching for a collection of high-quality, open source, platform- and compiler-independent libraries? Look to Boost. Interested in joining a community of ambitious, talented C++ developers working on state-of-the-art library design and implementation? Look to Boost. Want a glimpse of what C++ might look like in the future? Look to Boost.

Boost is both a community of C++ developers and a collection of freely downloadable C++ libraries. Its web site is http://boost.org. You should bookmark it now.

There are many C++ organizations and web sites, of course, but Boost has two things going for it that no other organization can match. First, it has a uniquely close and influential relationship with the C++ standardization committee. Boost was founded by committee members, and there continues to be strong overlap between the Boost and committee memberships. In addition, Boost has always had as one of its goals to act as a testing ground for capabilities that could be added to Standard C++. One result of this relationship is that of the 14 new libraries introduced into C++ by TR1 (see Item 54), more than two-thirds are based on work done at Boost.

The second special characteristic of Boost is its process for accepting libraries. It's based on public peer review. If you'd like to contribute a library to Boost, you start by posting to the Boost developers mailing list to gauge interest in the library and initiate the process of preliminary examination of your work. Thus begins a cycle that the web site summarizes as "Discuss, refine, resubmit. Repeat until satisfied."

Eventually, you decide that your library is ready for formal submission. A review manager confirms that your library meets Boost's minimal requirements. For example, it must compile under at least two compilers (to demonstrate nominal portability), and you have to attest that the library can be made available under an acceptable license (e.g., the library must allow free commercial and non-commercial use). Then your submission is made available to the Boost community for official review. During the review period, volunteers go over your library materials (e.g., source code, design documents, user documentation, etc.) and consider questions such as these:

- How good are the design and implementation?

- Is the code portable across compilers and operating systems?

- Is the library likely to be of use to its target audience, i.e., people working in the domain the library addresses?

- Is the documentation clear, complete, and accurate?

These comments are posted to a Boost mailing list, so reviewers and others can see and respond to one another's remarks. At the end of the review period, the review manager decides whether your library is accepted, conditionally accepted, or rejected.

Peer reviews do a good job of keeping poorly written libraries out of Boost, but they also help educate library authors in the considerations that go into the design, implementation, and documentation of industrial-strength cross-platform libraries. Many libraries require more than one official review before being declared worthy of acceptance.

Boost contains dozens of libraries, and more are added on a continuing basis. From time to time, some libraries are also removed, typically because their functionality has been superseded by a newer library that offers greater functionality or a better design (e.g., one that is more flexible or more efficient).

The libraries vary widely in size and scope. At one extreme are libraries that conceptually require only a few lines of code (but are typically much longer after support for error handling and portability is added). One such library is **Conversion**, which provides safer or more convenient cast operators. Its numeric_cast function, for example, throws an exception if converting a numeric value from one type to another leads to overflow or underflow or a similar problem, and lexical_cast makes it possible to cast any type supporting operator<< into a string — very useful for diagnostics, logging, etc. At the other extreme are libraries offering such extensive capabilities, entire books have been written about them. These include the **Boost Graph Library** (for programming with arbitrary graph structures) and the **Boost MPL Library** ("metaprogramming library").

Boost's bevy of libraries addresses a cornucopia of topics, grouped into over a dozen general categories. Those categories include:

- **String and text processing**, including libraries for type-safe printf-like formatting, regular expressions (the basis for similar functionality in TR1 — see Item 54), and tokenizing and parsing.

- **Containers**, including libraries for fixed-size arrays with an STL-like interface (see Item 54), variable-sized bitsets, and multidimensional arrays.

- **Function objects and higher-order programming**, including several libraries that were used as the basis for functionality in TR1. One interesting library is the Lambda library, which makes it so easy to create function objects on the fly, you're unlikely to realize that's what you're doing:

  ```
  using namespace boost::lambda;            // make boost::lambda
                                            // functionality visible

  std::vector<int> v;

  ...

  std::for_each(v.begin(), v.end(),         // for each element x in
          std::cout << _1 * 2 + 10 << "\n");  // v, print x*2+10;
                                            // "_1" is the Lambda
                                            // library's placeholder
                                            // for the current element
  ```

- **Generic programming**, including an extensive set of traits classes. (See Item 47 for information on traits.)

- **Template metaprogramming** (TMP — see Item 48), including a library for compile-time assertions, as well as the Boost MPL Library. Among the nifty things in MPL is support for STL-like data structures of compile-time entities like *types*, e.g.,

  ```
  // create a list-like compile-time container of three types (float,
  // double, and long double) and call the container "floats"
  typedef boost::mpl::list<float, double, long double> floats;

  // create a new compile-time list of types consisting of the types in
  // "floats" plus "int" inserted at the front; call the new container "types"
  typedef boost::mpl::push_front<floats, int>::type types;
  ```

  Such containers of types (often known as *typelists*, though they can also be based on an mpl::vector as well as an mpl::list) open the door to a wide range of powerful and important TMP applications.

- **Math and numerics**, including libraries for rational numbers; octonions and quaternions; greatest common divisor and least common multiple computations; and random numbers (yet another library that influenced related functionality in TR1).

- **Correctness and testing**, including libraries for formalizing implicit template interfaces (see Item 41) and for facilitating test-first programming.

- **Data structures**, including libraries for type-safe unions (i.e., storing variant "any" types) and the tuple library that led to the corresponding TR1 functionality.

- **Inter-language support**, including a library to allow seamless interoperability between C++ and Python.

- **Memory**, including the Pool library for high-performance fixed-size allocators (see Item 50); and a variety of smart pointers (see Item 13), including (but not limited to) the smart pointers in TR1. One such non-TR1 smart pointer is scoped_array, an auto_ptr-like smart pointer for dynamically allocated arrays; Item 44 shows an example use.

- **Miscellaneous**, including libraries for CRC checking, date and time manipulations, and traversing file systems.

Remember, that's just a sampling of the libraries you'll find at Boost. It's not an exhaustive list.

Boost offers libraries that do many things, but it doesn't cover the entire programming landscape. For example, there is no library for GUI development, nor is there one for communicating with databases. At least there's not now — not as I write this. By the time you read it, however, there might be. The only way to know for sure is to check. I suggest you do it right now: http://boost.org. Even if you don't find exactly what you're looking for, you're certain to find something interesting there.

Things to Remember

- ✦ Boost is a community and web site for the development of free, open source, peer-reviewed C++ libraries. Boost plays an influential role in C++ standardization.

- ✦ Boost offers implementations of many TR1 components, but it also offers many other libraries, too.

 **Beyond *Effective C++***

Effective C++ covers what I consider to be the most important general guidelines for practicing C++ programmers, but if you're interested in more ways to improve your effectiveness, I encourage you to examine my other C++ books, *More Effective C++* and *Effective STL*.

More Effective C++ covers additional programming guidelines and includes extensive treatments of topics such as efficiency and programming with exceptions. It also describes important C++ programming techniques like smart pointers, reference counting, and proxy objects.

Effective STL is a guideline-oriented book like *Effective C++*, but it focuses exclusively on making effective use of the Standard Template Library.

Tables of contents for both books are summarized below.

Contents of *More Effective C++*

Basics

Item 1: Distinguish between pointers and references
Item 2: Prefer C++-style casts
Item 3: Never treat arrays polymorphically
Item 4: Avoid gratuitous default constructors

Operators

Item 5: Be wary of user-defined conversion functions
Item 6: Distinguish between prefix and postfix forms of increment and decrement operators
Item 7: Never overload &&, ||, or ,
Item 8: Understand the different meanings of new and delete

Exceptions

Item 9:   Use destructors to prevent resource leaks
Item 10: Prevent resource leaks in constructors
Item 11: Prevent exceptions from leaving destructors
Item 12: Understand how throwing an exception differs from passing a parameter or calling a virtual function
Item 13: Catch exceptions by reference
Item 14: Use exception specifications judiciously
Item 15: Understand the costs of exception handling

Efficiency

Item 16: Remember the 80-20 rule
Item 17: Consider using lazy evaluation
Item 18: Amortize the cost of expected computations
Item 19: Understand the origin of temporary objects
Item 20: Facilitate the return value optimization
Item 21: Overload to avoid implicit type conversions
Item 22: Consider using *op=* instead of stand-alone *op*
Item 23: Consider alternative libraries
Item 24: Understand the costs of virtual functions, multiple inheritance, virtual base classes, and RTTI

Techniques

Item 25: Virtualizing constructors and non-member functions
Item 26: Limiting the number of objects of a class
Item 27: Requiring or prohibiting heap-based objects
Item 28: Smart pointers
Item 29: Reference counting
Item 30: Proxy classes
Item 31: Making functions virtual with respect to more than one object

Miscellany

Item 32: Program in the future tense
Item 33: Make non-leaf classes abstract
Item 34: Understand how to combine C++ and C in the same program
Item 35: Familiarize yourself with the language standard

Contents of *Effective STL*

Chapter 1: Containers

Item 1:   Choose your containers with care.

Item 2:   Beware the illusion of container-independent code.

Item 3:   Make copying cheap and correct for objects in containers.

Item 4:   Call empty instead of checking size() against zero.

Item 5:   Prefer range member functions to their single-element counterparts.

Item 6:   Be alert for C++'s most vexing parse.

Item 7:   When using containers of newed pointers, remember to delete the pointers before the container is destroyed.

Item 8:   Never create containers of auto_ptrs.

Item 9:   Choose carefully among erasing options.

Item 10: Be aware of allocator conventions and restrictions.

Item 11: Understand the legitimate uses of custom allocators.

Item 12: Have realistic expectations about the thread safety of STL containers.

Chapter 2: vector and string

Item 13: Prefer vector and string to dynamically allocated arrays.

Item 14: Use reserve to avoid unnecessary reallocations.

Item 15: Be aware of variations in string implementations.

Item 16: Know how to pass vector and string data to legacy APIs.

Item 17: Use "the swap trick" to trim excess capacity.

Item 18: Avoid using vector<bool>.

Chapter 3: Associative Containers

Item 19: Understand the difference between equality and equivalence.

Item 20: Specify comparison types for associative containers of pointers.

Item 21: Always have comparison functions return false for equal values.

Item 22: Avoid in-place key modification in set and multiset.

Item 23: Consider replacing associative containers with sorted vectors.

Item 24: Choose carefully between map::operator[] and map::insert when efficiency is important.

Item 25: Familiarize yourself with the nonstandard hashed containers.

Chapter 4: Iterators

Item 26: Prefer iterator to const_iterator, reverse_iterator, and const_reverse_iterator.

Item 27: Use distance and advance to convert a container's const_iterators to iterators.

Item 28: Understand how to use a reverse_iterator's base iterator.

Item 29: Consider istreambuf_iterators for character-by-character input.

Chapter 5: Algorithms

Item 30: Make sure destination ranges are big enough.

Item 31: Know your sorting options.

Item 32: Follow remove-like algorithms by erase if you really want to remove something.

Item 33: Be wary of remove-like algorithms on containers of pointers.

Item 34: Note which algorithms expect sorted ranges.

Item 35: Implement simple case-insensitive string comparisons via mismatch or lexicographical_compare.

Item 36: Understand the proper implementation of copy_if.

Item 37: Use accumulate or for_each to summarize ranges.

Chapter 6: Functors, Functor Classes, Functions, etc.

Item 38: Design functor classes for pass-by-value.

Item 39: Make predicates pure functions.

Item 40: Make functor classes adaptable.

Item 41: Understand the reasons for ptr_fun, mem_fun, and mem_fun_ref.

Item 42: Make sure less<T> means operator<.

Chapter 7: Programming with the STL

Item 43: Prefer algorithm calls to hand-written loops.

Item 44: Prefer member functions to algorithms with the same names.

Item 45: Distinguish among count, find, binary_search, lower_bound, upper_bound, and equal_range.

Item 46: Consider function objects instead of functions as algorithm parameters.

Item 47: Avoid producing write-only code.

Item 48: Always #include the proper headers.

Item 49: Learn to decipher STL-related compiler diagnostics.

Item 50: Familiarize yourself with STL-related web sites.

Item Mappings Between Second and Third Editions

This third edition of *Effective C++* differs from the second edition in many ways, most significantly in that it includes lots of new information. However, most of the second edition's content remains in the third edition, albeit often in a modified form and location. In the tables on the pages that follow, I show where information in second edition Items may be found in the third edition and vice versa.

The tables show a mapping of *information*, not text. For example, the ideas in Item 39 of the second edition ("Avoid casts down the inheritance hierarchy") are now found in Item 27 of the current edition ("Minimize casting"), even though the third edition text and examples for that Item are entirely new. A more extreme example involves the second edition's Item 18 ("Strive for class interfaces that are complete and minimal"). One of the primary conclusions of that Item was that prospective member functions that need no special access to the non-public parts of the class should generally be non-members. In the third edition, that same result is reached via different (stronger) reasoning, so Item 18 in the second edition maps to Item 23 in the third edition ("Prefer non-member non-friend functions to member functions"), even though about the only thing the two Items have in common is their conclusion.

Second Edition to Third Edition

2nd Ed.	3rd Ed.	2nd Ed.	3rd Ed.	2nd Ed.	3rd Ed.
1	2	18	23	35	32
2	—	19	24	36	34
3	—	20	22	37	36
4	—	21	3	38	37
5	16	22	20	39	27
6	13	23	21	40	38
7	49	24	—	41	41
8	51	25	—	42	39, 44
9	52	26	—	43	40
10	50	27	6	44	—
11	14	28	—	45	5
12	4	29	28	46	18
13	4	30	28	47	4
14	7	31	21	48	53
15	10	32	26	49	54
16	12	33	30	50	—
17	11	34	31		

Third Edition to Second Edition

3rd Ed.	2nd Ed.	3rd Ed.	2nd Ed.	3rd Ed.	2nd Ed.
1	—	20	22	39	42
2	1	21	23, 31	40	43
3	21	22	20	41	41
4	12, 13, 47	23	18	42	—
5	45	24	19	43	—
6	27	25	—	44	42
7	14	26	32	45	—
8	—	27	39	46	—
9	—	28	29, 30	47	—
10	15	29	—	48	—
11	17	30	33	49	7
12	16	31	34	50	10
13	6	32	35	51	8
14	11	33	9	52	9
15	—	34	36	53	48
16	5	35	—	54	49
17	—	36	37	55	—
18	46	37	38		
19	pp. 77–79	38	40		

Index

Operators are listed under *operator*. That is, operator<< is listed under operator<<, not under <<, etc.

Example classes, structs, and class or struct templates are indexed under *example classes/templates*. Example function and function templates are indexed under *example functions/templates*.

Before A

.NET 7, 81, 135, 145, 194
  see also C#
=, in initialization vs. assignment 6
1066 150
2nd edition of this book
  compared to 3rd edition xv–xvi, 277–279
  see also inside back cover
3rd edition of this book
  compared to 2nd edition xv–xvi, 277–279
  see also inside back cover
80-20 rule 139, 168

A

Abrahams, David xvii, xviii, xix
abstract classes 43
accessibility
  control over data members' 95
  name, multiple inheritance and 193
accessing names, in templatized
  bases 207–212
addresses
  inline functions 136
  objects 118
aggregation, see composition
Alexandrescu, Andrei xix
aliasing 54
alignment 249–250
allocators, in the STL 240

alternatives to virtual functions 169–177
ambiguity
  multiple inheritance and 192
  nested dependent names and types 205
Arbiter, Petronius vii
argument-dependent lookup 110
arithmetic, mixed-mode 103, 222–226
array layout, vs. object layout 73
array new 254–255
array, invalid index and 7
ASPECT_RATIO 13
assignment
  see also operator=
  chaining assignments 52
  copy-and-swap and 56
  generalized 220
  to self, operator= and 53–57
  vs. initialization 6, 27–29, 114
assignment operator, copy 5
auto_ptr, see std::auto_ptr
automatically generated functions 34–37
  copy constructor and copy assignment
    operator 221
  disallowing 37–39
avoiding code duplication 50, 60

B

Bai, Yun xix
Barry, Dave, allusion to 229
Bartolucci, Guido xix

base classes
  copying 59
  duplication of data in 193
  lookup in, this-> and 210
  names hidden in derived classes 263
  polymorphic 44
  polymorphic, destructors and 40–44
  templatized 207–212
  virtual 193
basic guarantee, the 128
Battle of Hastings 150
Berck, Benjamin xix
bidirectional iterators 227
bidirectional_iterator_tag 228
binary upgradeability, inlining and 138
binding
  dynamic, see dynamic binding
  static, see static binding
birds and penguins 151–153
bitwise const member functions 21–22
books
  C++ Programming Language, The xvii
  C++ Templates xviii
  Design Patterns xvii
  Effective STL 273, 275–276
  Exceptional C++ xvii
  Exceptional C++ Style xvii, xviii
  More Effective C++ 273, 273–274
  More Exceptional C++ xvii
  Satyricon vii
  *Some Must Watch While Some Must
      Sleep* 150
Boost 10, 269–272
  containers 271
  Conversion library 270
  correctness and testing support 272
  data structures 272
  function objects and higher-order pro-
      gramming utilities 271
  functionality not provided 272
  generic programming support 271
  Graph library 270
  inter-language support 272
  Lambda library 271
  math and numerics utilities 271
  memory management utilities 272
  MPL library 270, 271
  noncopyable base class 39
  Pool library 250, 251
  scoped_array 65, 216, 272
  shared_array 65
  shared_ptr implementation, costs 83
  smart pointers 65, 272
    web page xvii
  string and text utilities 271
  template metaprogramming
      support 271
  TR1 and 9–10, 268, 269
  typelist support 271
  web site 10, 269, 272
boost, as synonym for std::tr1 268
Bosch, Derek xviii
breakpoints, and inlining 139
Buffy the Vampire Slayer xx
bugs, reporting xvi
built-in types 26–27
  efficiency and passing 89
  incompatibilities with 80

C

C standard library and C++ standard
      library 264
C# 43, 76, 97, 100, 116, 118, 190
  see also .NET
C++ Programming Language, The xvii
C++ standard library 263–269
  <iosfwd> and 144
  array replacements and 75
  C standard library and 264
  C89 standard library and 264
  header organization of 101
  list template 186
  logic_error and 113
  set template 185
  vector template 75
C++ Templates xviii
C++, as language federation 11–13
C++0x 264
C++-style casts 117
C, as sublanguage of C++ 12
C99 standard library, TR1 and 267
caching
  const and 22
  mutable and 22
Cai, Steve xix
calling swap 110
calls to base classes, casting and 119
Cargill, Tom xviii
Carrara, Enrico xix
Carroll, Glenn xviii
casting 116–123
  see also const_cast, static_cast,
      dynamic_cast, and reinterpret_cast
  base class calls and 119
  constness away 24–25
  encapsulation and 123
  grep and 117
  syntactic forms 116–117
  type systems and 116
  undefined behavior and 119
chaining assignments 52

Chang, Brandon xix
Clamage, Steve xviii
class definitions
    artificial client dependencies,
        eliminating 143
    class declarations vs. 143
    object sizes and 141
class design, see type design
class names, explicitly specifying 162
class, vs. typename 203
classes
    see also class definitions, interfaces
    abstract 43, 162
    base
        see also base classes
        duplication of data in 193
        polymorphic 44
        templatized 207–212
        virtual 193
    defining 4
    derived
        see also inheritance
        virtual base initialization of 194
    Handle 144–145
    Interface 145–147
    meaning of no virtual functions 41
    RAII, see RAII
    specification, see interfaces
    traits 226–232
client 7
clustering objects 251
code
    bloat 24, 135, 230
        avoiding, in templates 212–217
    copy assignment operator 60
    duplication, see duplication
    exception-safe 127–134
    factoring out of templates 212–217
    incorrect, efficiency and 90
    reuse 195
    sharing, see duplication, avoiding
Cohen, Jake xix
Comeau, Greg xviii
    URL for his C/C++ FAQ xviii
common features and inheritance 164
commonality and variability analysis 212
compatibility, vptrs and 42
compatible types, accepting 218–222
compilation dependencies 140–148
    minimizing 140–148, 190
    pointers, references, and objects
        and 143
compiler warnings 262–263
    calls to virtuals and 50
    inlining and 136
    partial copies and 58

compiler-generated functions 34–37
    disallowing 37–39
    functions compilers may generate 221
compilers
    parsing nested dependent names 204
    programs executing within, see tem-
        plate metaprogramming
    register usage and 89
    reordering operations 76
    typename and 207
    when errors are diagnosed 212
compile-time polymorphism 201
composition 184–186
    meanings of 184
    replacing private inheritance with 189
    synonyms for 184
    vs. private inheritance 188
conceptual constness, see const, logical
consistency with the built-in types 19, 86
const 13, 17–26
    bitwise 21–22
    caching and 22
    casting away 24–25
    function declarations and 18
    logical 22–23
    member functions 19–25
        duplication and 23–25
    members, initialization of 29
    overloading on 19–20
    pass by reference and 86–90
    passing std::auto_ptr and 220
    pointers 17
    return value 18
    uses 17
    vs. #define 13–14
const_cast 25, 117
    see also casting
const_iterator, vs. iterators 18
constants, see const
constraints on interfaces, from
        inheritance 85
constructors 84
    copy 5
    default 4
    empty, illusion of 137
    explicit 5, 85, 104
    implicitly generated 34
    inlining and 137–138
    operator new and 137
    possible implementation in derived
        classes 138
    relationship to new 73
    static functions and 52
    virtual 146, 147
    virtual functions and 48–52
    with vs. without arguments 114
containers, in Boost 271

containment, see composition
continue, delete and 62
control over data members'
    accessibility 95
convenience functions 100
Conversion library, in Boost 270
conversions, type, see type conversions
copies, partial 58
copy assignment operator 5
    code in copy constructor and 60
    derived classes and 60
copy constructors
    default definition 35
    derived classes and 60
    generalized 219
    how used 5
    implicitly generated 34
    pass-by-value and 6
copy-and-swap 131
    assignment and 56
    exception-safe code and 132
copying
    base class parts 59
    behavior, resource management
        and 66–69
    functions, the 57
    objects 57–60
correctness
    designing interfaces for 78–83
    testing and, Boost support 272
corresponding forms of new and
    delete 73–75
corrupt data structures, exception-safe
    code and 127
cows, coming home 139
crimes against English 39, 204
cross-DLL problem 82
CRTP 246
C-style casts 116
ctor 8
curiously recurring template pattern 246

D

dangling handles 126
Dashtinezhad, Sasan xix
data members
    adding, copying functions and 58
    control over accessibility 95
    protected 97
    static, initialization of 242
    why private 94–98
data structures
    exception-safe code and 127
    in Boost 272
Davis, Tony xviii

deadly MI diamond 193
debuggers
    #define and 13
    inline functions and 139
declarations 3
    inline functions 135
    replacing definitions 143
    static const integral members 14
default constructors 4
    construction with arguments vs. 114
    implicitly generated 34
default implementations
    for virtual functions, danger of 163–167
    of copy constructor 35
    of operator= 35
default initialization, unintended 59
default parameters 180–183
    impact if changed 183
    static binding of 182
#define
    debuggers and 13
    disadvantages of 13, 16
    vs. const 13–14
    vs. inline functions 16–17
definitions 4
    classes 4
    deliberate omission of 38
    functions 4
    implicitly generated functions 35
    objects 4
    pure virtual functions 162, 166–167
    replacing with declarations 143
    static class members 242
    static const integral members 14
    templates 4
    variable, postponing 113–116
delete
    see also operator delete
    forms of 73–75
    operator delete and 73
    relationship to destructors 73
    usage problem scenarios 62
delete [], std::auto_ptr and tr1::shared_ptr
    and 65
deleters
    std::auto_ptr and 68
    tr1::shared_ptr and 68, 81–83
Delphi 97
Dement, William 150
dependencies, compilation 140–148
dependent names 204
dereferencing a null pointer, undefined
    behavior of 6
derived classes
    copy assignment operators and 60
    copy constructors and 60
    hiding names in base classes 263

implementing constructors in 138
virtual base initialization and 194
design
  contradiction in 179
  of interfaces 78–83
  of types 78–86
Design Patterns xvii
design patterns
  curiously recurring template
      (CRTP) 246
  encapsulation and 173
  generating from templates 237
  Singleton 31
  Strategy 171–177
  Template Method 170
  TMP and 237
destructors 84
  exceptions and 44–48
  inlining and 137–138
  pure virtual 43
  relationship to delete 73
  resource managing objects and 63
  static functions and 52
  virtual
    operator delete and 255
    polymorphic base classes and 40–44
  virtual functions and 48–52
Dewhurst, Steve xvii
dimensional unit correctness, TMP
    and 236
DLLs, delete and 82
dtor 8
Dulimov, Peter xix
duplication
  avoiding 23–25, 29, 50, 60, 164, 183, 212–
      217
  base class data and 193
  init function and 60
dynamic binding
  definition of 181
  of virtual functions 179
dynamic type, definition of 181
dynamic_cast 50, 117, 120–123
  see also casting
  efficiency of 120

E

early binding 180
easy to use correctly and hard to use
    incorrectly 78–83
EBO, see empty base optimization
Effective C++, compared to *More Effective
    C++* and *Effective STL* 273
Effective STL 273, 275–276
  compared to *Effective C++* 273

contents of 275–276
efficiency
  assignment vs. construction and
      destruction 94
  default parameter binding 182
  dynamic_cast 120
  Handle classes 147
  incorrect code and 90, 94
  init. with vs. without args 114
  Interface classes 147
  macros vs. inline functions 16
  member init. vs. assignment 28
  minimizing compilation
      dependencies 147
  operator new/operator delete and 248
  pass-by-reference and 87
  pass-by-value and 86–87
  passing built-in types and 89
  runtime vs. compile-time tests 230
  template metaprogramming and 233
  template vs. function parameters 216
  unused objects 113
  virtual functions 168
Eiffel 100
embedding, see composition
empty base optimization (EBO) 190–191
encapsulation 95, 99
  casts and 123
  design patterns and 173
  handles and 124
  measuring 99
  protected members and 97
  RAII classes and 72
enum hack 15–16, 236
errata list, for this book xvi
errors
  detected during linking 39, 44
  runtime 152
evaluation order, of parameters 76
example classes/templates
  A 4
  ABEntry 27
  AccessLevels 95
  Address 184
  Airplane 164, 165, 166
  Airport 164
  AtomicClock 40
  AWOV 43
  B 4, 178, 262
  Base 54, 118, 137, 157, 158, 159, 160, 254,
      255, 259
  BelowBottom 219
  bidirectional_iterator_tag 228
  Bird 151, 152, 153
  Bitmap 54
  BorrowableItem 192
  Bottom 218
  BuyTransaction 49, 51

C 5
Circle 181
CompanyA 208
CompanyB 208
CompanyZ 209
CostEstimate 15
CPerson 198
CTextBlock 21, 22, 23
Customer 57, 58
D 178, 262
DatabaseID 197
Date 58, 79
Day 79
DBConn 45, 47
DBConnection 45
deque 229
deque::iterator 229
Derived 54, 118, 137, 157, 158, 159, 160,
    206, 254, 260
Directory 31
ElectronicGadget 192
Ellipse 161
Empty 34, 190
EvilBadGuy 172, 174
EyeCandyCharacter 175
Factorial 235
Factorial<0> 235
File 193, 194
FileSystem 30
FlyingBird 152
Font 71
forward_iterator_tag 228
GameCharacter 169, 170, 172, 173, 176
GameLevel 174
GamePlayer 14, 15
GraphNode 4
GUIObject 126
HealthCalcFunc 176
HealthCalculator 174
HoldsAnInt 190, 191
HomeForSale 37, 38, 39
input_iterator_tag 228
input_iterator_tag<Iter*> 230
InputFile 193, 194
Investment 61, 70
IOFile 193, 194
IPerson 195, 197
iterator_traits 229
    see also std::iterator_traits
list 229
list::iterator 229
Lock 66, 67, 68
LoggingMsgSender 208, 210, 211
Middle 218
ModelA 164, 165, 167
ModelB 164, 165, 167
ModelC 164, 166, 167
Month 79, 80
MP3Player 192

MsgInfo 208
MsgSender 208
MsgSender<CompanyZ> 209
NamedObject 35, 36
NewHandlerHolder 243
NewHandlerSupport 245
output_iterator_tag 228
OutputFile 193, 194
Penguin 151, 152, 153
Person 86, 135, 140, 141, 142, 145, 146,
    150, 184, 187
PersonInfo 195, 197
PhoneNumber 27, 184
PMImpl 131
Point 26, 41, 123
PrettyMenu 127, 130, 131
PriorityCustomer 58
random_access_iterator_tag 228
Rational 90, 102, 103, 105, 222, 223, 224,
    225, 226
RealPerson 147
Rectangle 124, 125, 154, 161, 181, 183
RectData 124
SellTransaction 49
Set 185
Shape 161, 162, 163, 167, 180, 182, 183
SmartPtr 218, 219, 220
SpecialString 42
SpecialWindow 119, 120, 121, 122
SpeedDataCollection 96
Square 154
SquareMatrix 213, 214, 215, 216
SquareMatrixBase 214, 215
StandardNewDeleteForms 260
Student 86, 150, 187
TextBlock 20, 23, 24
TimeKeeper 40, 41
Timer 188
Top 218
Transaction 48, 50, 51
Uncopyable 39
WaterClock 40
WebBrowser 98, 100, 101
Widget 4, 5, 44, 52, 53, 54, 56, 107, 108,
    109, 118, 189, 199, 201, 242, 245, 246,
    257, 258, 261
Widget::WidgetTimer 189
WidgetImpl 106, 108
Window 88, 119, 121, 122
WindowWithScrollBars 88
WristWatch 40
X 242
Y 242
Year 79
example functions/templates
ABEntry::ABEntry 27, 28
AccessLevels::getReadOnly 95
AccessLevels::getReadWrite 95
AccessLevels::setReadOnly 95

AccessLevels::setWriteOnly 95
advance 228, 230, 232, 233, 234
Airplane::defaultFly 165
Airplane::fly 164, 165, 166, 167
askUserForDatabaseID 195
AWOV::AWOV 43
B::mf 178
Base::operator delete 255
Base::operator new 254
Bird::fly 151
BorrowableItem::checkOut 192
boundingBox 126
BuyTransaction::BuyTransaction 51
BuyTransaction::createLogString 51
calcHealth 174
callWithMax 16
changeFontSize 71
Circle::draw 181
clearAppointments 143, 144
clearBrowser 98
CPerson::birthDate 198
CPerson::CPerson 198
CPerson::name 198
CPerson::valueDelimClose 198
CPerson::valueDelimOpen 198
createInvestment 62, 70, 81, 82, 83
CTextBlock::length 22, 23
CTextBlock::operator[] 21
Customer::Customer 58
Customer::operator= 58
D::mf 178
Date::Date 79
Day::Day 79
daysHeld 69
DBConn::~DBConn 45, 46, 47
DBConn::close 47
defaultHealthCalc 172, 173
Derived::Derived 138, 206
Derived::mf1 160
Derived::mf4 157
Directory::Directory 31, 32
doAdvance 231
doMultiply 226
doProcessing 200, 202
doSomething 5, 44, 54, 110
doSomeWork 118
eat 151, 187
ElectronicGadget::checkOut 192
Empty::~Empty 34
Empty::Empty 34
Empty::operator= 34
encryptPassword 114, 115
error 152
EvilBadGuy::EvilBadGuy 172
f 62, 63, 64
FlyingBird::fly 152
Font::~Font 71
Font::Font 71
Font::get 71

Font::operator FontHandle 71
GameCharacter::doHealthValue 170
GameCharacter::GameCharacter 172, 174,
   176
GameCharacter::healthValue 169, 170,
   172, 174, 176
GameLevel::health 174
getFont 70
hasAcceptableQuality 6
HealthCalcFunc::calc 176
HealthCalculator::operator() 174
lock 66
Lock::~Lock 66
Lock::Lock 66, 68
logCall 57
LoggingMsgSender::sendClear 208, 210,
   211
loseHealthQuickly 172
loseHealthSlowly 172
main 141, 142, 236, 241
makeBigger 154
makePerson 195
max 135
ModelA::fly 165, 167
ModelB::fly 165, 167
ModelC::fly 166, 167
Month::Dec 80
Month::Feb 80
Month::Jan 80
Month::Month 79, 80
MsgSender::sendClear 208
MsgSender::sendSecret 208
MsgSender<CompanyZ>::sendSecret 209
NewHandlerHolder::~NewHandlerHolder 243
NewHandlerHolder::NewHandlerHolder 243
NewHandlerSupport::operator new 245
NewHandlerSupport::set_new_handler 245
numDigits 4
operator delete 255
operator new 249, 252
operator* 91, 92, 94, 105, 222, 224, 225,
   226
operator== 93
outOfMem 240
Penguin::fly 152
Person::age 135
Person::create 146, 147
Person::name 145
Person::Person 145
PersonInfo::theName 196
PersonInfo::valueDelimClose 196
PersonInfo::valueDelimOpen 196
PrettyMenu::changeBackground 127, 128,
   130, 131
print 20
print2nd 204, 205
printNameAndDisplay 88, 89
priority 75
PriorityCustomer::operator= 59

PriorityCustomer::PriorityCustomer 59
processWidget 75
RealPerson::~RealPerson 147
RealPerson::RealPerson 147
Rectangle::doDraw 183
Rectangle::draw 181, 183
Rectangle::lowerRight 124, 125
Rectangle::upperLeft 124, 125
releaseFont 70
Set::insert 186
Set::member 186
Set::remove 186
Set::size 186
Shape::doDraw 183
Shape::draw 161, 162, 180, 182, 183
Shape::error 161, 163
Shape::objectID 161, 167
SmartPtr::get 220
SmartPtr::SmartPtr 220
someFunc 132, 156
SpecialWindow::blink 122
SpecialWindow::onResize 119, 120
SquareMatrix::invert 214
SquareMatrix::setDataPtr 215
SquareMatrix::SquareMatrix 215, 216
StandardNewDeleteForms::operator
    delete 260, 261
StandardNewDeleteForms::operator
    new 260, 261
std::swap 109
std::swap<Widget> 107, 108
study 151, 187
swap 106, 109
tempDir 32
TextBlock::operator[] 20, 23, 24
tfs 32
Timer::onTick 188
Transaction::init 50
Transaction::Transaction 49, 50, 51
Uncopyable::operator= 39
Uncopyable::Uncopyable 39
unlock 66
validateStudent 87
Widget::onTick 189
Widget::operator new 244
Widget::operator+= 53
Widget::operator= 53, 54, 55, 56, 107
Widget::set_new_handler 243
Widget::swap 108
Window::blink 122
Window::onResize 119
workWithIterator 206, 207
Year::Year 79
exception specifications 85
Exceptional C++ xvii
Exceptional C++ Style xvii, xviii
exceptions 113
    delete and 62

destructors and 44–48
member swap and 112
standard hierarchy for 264
swallowing 46
unused objects and 114
exception-safe code 127–134
copy-and-swap and 132
legacy code and 133
pimpl idiom and 131
side effects and 132
exception-safety guarantees 128–129
explicit calls to base class functions 211
explicit constructors 5, 85, 104
generalized copy construction and 219
explicit inline request 135
explicit specification, of class names 162
explicit type conversions vs. implicit 70–
    72
expression templates 237
expressions, implicit interfaces and 201

F

factoring code, out of templates 212–217
factory function 40, 62, 69, 81, 146, 195
Fallenstedt, Martin xix
federation, of languages, C++ as 11–13
Feher, Attila F. xix
final classes, in Java 43
final methods, in Java 190
fixed-size static buffers, problems of 196
forms of new and delete 73–75
FORTRAN 42
forward iterators 227
forward_iterator_tag 228
forwarding functions 144, 160
French, Donald xx
friend functions 38, 85, 105, 135, 173, 223–
    225
    vs. member functions 98–102
friendship
    in real life 105
    without needing special access
        rights 225
Fruchterman, Thomas xix
FUDGE_FACTOR 15
Fuller, John xx
function declarations, const in 18
function objects
    definition of 6
    higher-order programming utilities
        and, in Boost 271
functions
    convenience 100
    copying 57

defining 4
deliberately not defining 38
factory, see factory function
forwarding 144, 160
implicitly generated 34–37, 221
    disallowing 37–39
inline, declaring 135
member
    templatized 218–222
    vs. non-member 104–105
non-member
    templates and 222–226
    type conversions and 102–105, 222–226
non-member non-friend, vs
    member 98–102
non-virtual, meaning 168
return values, modifying 21
signatures, explicit interfaces and 201
static
    ctors and dtors and 52
virtual, see virtual functions
function-style casts 116

G

Gamma, Erich xvii
Geller, Alan xix
generalized assignment 220
generalized copy constructors 219
generative programming 237
generic programming support, in
    Boost 271
get, smart pointers and 70
goddess, see Urbano, Nancy L.
goto, delete and 62
Graph library, in Boost 270
grep, casts and 117
guarantees, exception safety 128–129
Gutnik, Gene xix

H

Handle classes 144–145
handles 125
    dangling 126
    encapsulation and 124
    operator[] and 126
    returning 123–126
has-a relationship 184
hash tables, in TR1 266
Hastings, Battle of 150
Haugland, Solveig xx
head scratching, avoiding 95
header files, see headers

headers
    for declarations vs. for definitions 144
    inline functions and 135
    namespaces and 100
    of C++ standard library 101
    templates and 136
    usage, in this book 3
hello world, template metaprogramming
    and 235
Helm, Richard xvii
Henney, Kevlin xix
Hicks, Cory xix
hiding names, see name hiding
higher-order programming and function
    object utilities, in Boost 271
highlighting, in this book 5

I

identity test 55
if...else for types 230
#ifdef 17
#ifndef 17
implementation-dependent behavior,
    warnings and 263
implementations
    decoupling from interfaces 165
    default, danger of 163–167
    inheritance of 161–169
    of derived class constructors and
        destructors 137
    of Interface classes 147
    references 89
    std::max 135
    std::swap 106
implicit inline request 135
implicit interfaces 199–203
implicit type conversions vs. explicit 70–72
implicitly generated functions 34–37, 221
    disallowing 37–39
#include directives 17
    compilation dependencies and 140
incompatibilities, with built-in types 80
incorrect code and efficiency 90
infinite loop, in operator new 253
inheritance
    accidental 165–166
    combining with templates 243–245
    common features and 164
    intuition and 151–155
    mathematics and 155
    mixin-style 244
    name hiding and 156–161
    of implementation 161–169
    of interface 161–169

of interface vs. implementation 161–169
operator new and 253–254
penguins and birds and 151–153
private 187–192
protected 151
public 150–155
rectangles and squares and 153–155
redefining non-virtual functions
          and 178–180
scopes and 156
sharing features and 164
inheritance, multiple 192–198
ambiguity and 192
combining public and private 197
deadly diamond 193
inheritance, private 214
combining with public 197
eliminating 189
for redefining virtual functions 197
meaning 187
vs. composition 188
inheritance, public
combining with private 197
is-a relationship and 150–155
meaning of 150
name hiding and 159
virtual inheritance and 194
inheritance, virtual 194
init function 60
initialization 4, 26–27
assignment vs. 6
built-in types 26–27
const members 29
const static members 14
default, unintended 59
in-class, of static const integral
          members 14
local static objects 31
non-local static objects 30
objects 26–33
reference members 29
static members 242
virtual base classes and 194
vs. assignment 27–29, 114
with vs. without arguments 114
initialization order
class members 29
importance of 31
non-local statics 29–33
inline functions
see also inlining
address of 136
as request to compiler 135
debuggers and 139
declaring 135
headers and 135
optimizing compilers and 134
recursion and 136
vs. #define 16–17

vs. macros, efficiency and 16
inlining 134–139
constructors/destructors and 137–138
dynamic linking and 139
Handle classes and 148
inheritance and 137–138
Interface classes and 148
library design and 138
recompiling and 139
relinking and 139
suggested strategy for 139
templates and 136
time of 135
virtual functions and 136
input iterators 227
input_iterator_tag 228
input_iterator_tag<lter*> 230
insomnia 150
instructions, reordering by compilers 76
integral types 14
Interface classes 145–147
interfaces
decoupling from implementations 165
definition of 7
design considerations 78–86
explicit, signatures and 201
implicit 199–203
          expressions and 201
inheritance of 161–169
new types and 79–80
separating from implementations 140
template parameters and 199–203
undeclared 85
inter-language support, in Boost 272
internationalization, library support
          for 264
invalid array index, undefined behavior
          and 7
invariants
NVI and 171
over specialization 168
<iosfwd> 144
is-a relationship 150–155
is-implemented-in-terms-of 184–186, 187
istream_iterators 227
iterator categories 227–228
iterator_category 229
iterators as handles 125
iterators, vs. const_iterators 18

J

Jagdhar, Emily xix
Janert, Philipp xix
Java 7, 43, 76, 81, 100, 116, 118, 142, 145,
          190, 194

Johnson, Ralph xvii
Johnson, Tim xviii, xix
Josuttis, Nicolai M. xviii

K

Kaelbling, Mike xviii
Kakulapati, Gunavardhan xix
Kalenkovich, Eugene xix
Kennedy, Glenn xix
Kernighan, Brian xviii, xix
Kimura, Junichi xviii
Kirman, Jak xviii
Kirmse, Andrew xix
Knox, Timothy xviii, xix
Koenig lookup 110
Kourounis, Drosos xix
Kreuzer, Gerhard xix

L

Laeuchli, Jesse xix
Lambda library, in Boost 271
Langer, Angelika xix
languages, other, compatibility with 42
Lanzetta, Michael xix
late binding 180
layering, see composition
layouts, objects vs. arrays 73
Lea, Doug xviii
leaks, exception-safe code and 127
Leary-Coutu, Chanda xx
Lee, Sam xix
legacy code, exception-safety and 133
Lejter, Moises xviii, xx
lemur, ring-tailed 196
Lewandowski, Scott xviii
lhs, as parameter name 8
Li, Greg xix
link-time errors 39, 44
link-time inlining 135
list 186
local static objects
    definition of 30
    initialization of 31
locales 264
locks, RAII and 66–68
logic_error class 113
logically const member functions 22–23

M

mailing list for Scott Meyers xvi

maintenance
    common base classes and 164
    delete and 62
managing resources, see resource man-
        agement
Manis, Vincent xix
Marin, Alex xix
math and numerics utilities, in Boost 271
mathematical functions, in TR1 267
mathematics, inheritance and 155
matrix operations, optimizing 237
Matthews, Leon xix
max, std, implementation of 135
Meadowbrooke, Chrysta xix
meaning
    of classes without virtual functions 41
    of composition 184
    of non-virtual functions 168
    of pass-by-value 6
    of private inheritance 187
    of public inheritance 150
    of pure virtual functions 162
    of references 91
    of simple virtual functions 163
measuring encapsulation 99
Meehan, Jim xix
member data, see data members
member function templates 218–222
member functions
    bitwise const 21–22
    common design errors 168–169
    const 19–25
    duplication and 23–25
    encapsulation and 99
    implicitly generated 34–37, 221
        disallowing 37–39
    logically const 22–23
    private 38
    protected 166
    vs. non-member functions 104–105
    vs. non-member non-friends 98–102
member initialization
    for const static integral members 14
    lists 28–29
        vs. assignment 28–29
    order 29
memory allocation
    arrays and 254–255
    error handling for 240–246
memory leaks, new expressions and 256
memory management
    functions, replacing 247–252
    multithreading and 239, 253
    utilities, in Boost 272
metaprogramming, see template metapro-
        gramming

Meyers, Scott
    mailing list for xvi
    web site for xvi
mf, as identifier 9
Michaels, Laura xviii
Mickelsen, Denise xx
minimizing compilation
        dependencies 140–148, 190
Mittal, Nishant xix
mixed-mode arithmetic 103, 104, 222–226
mixin-style inheritance 244
modeling is-implemented-in-terms-
        of 184–186
modifying function return values 21
Monty Python, allusion to 91
Moore, Vanessa xx
More Effective C++ 273, 273–274
    compared to *Effective C++* 273
    contents of 273–274
More Exceptional C++ xvii
Moroff, Hal xix
MPL library, in Boost 270, 271
multiparadigm programming language,
        C++ as 11
multiple inheritance, see inheritance
multithreading
    memory management routines
        and 239, 253
    non-const static objects and 32
    treatment in this book 9
mutable 22–23
mutexes, RAII and 66–68

N

Nagler, Eric xix
Nahil, Julie xx
name hiding
    inheritance and 156–161
    operators new/delete and 259–261
    using declarations and 159
name lookup
    this-> and 210
    using declarations and 211
name shadowing, see name hiding
names
    accessing in templatized bases 207–212
    available in both C and C++ 3
    dependent 204
    hidden by derived classes 263
    nested, dependent 204
    non-dependent 204
namespaces 110
    headers and 100
    namespace pollution in a class 166
Nancy, see Urbano, Nancy L.

Nauroth, Chris xix
nested dependent names 204
nested dependent type names, typename
        and 205
new
    see also operator new
    expressions, memory leaks and 256
    forms of 73–75
    operator new and 73
    relationship to constructors 73
    smart pointers and 75–77
new types, interface design and 79–80
new-handler 240–247
    definition of 240
    deinstalling 241
    identifying 253
new-handling functions, behavior of 241
new-style casts 117
noncopyable base class, in Boost 39
non-dependent names 204
non-local static objects, initialization
        of 30
non-member functions
    member functions vs. 104–105
    templates and 222–226
    type conversions and 102–105, 222–226
non-member non-friend functions 98–102
non-type parameters 213
non-virtual
    functions 178–180
        static binding of 178
    interface idiom, see NVI
nothrow guarantee, the 129
nothrow new 246
null pointer
    deleting 255
    dereferencing 6
    set_new_handler and 241
NVI 170–171, 183

O

object-oriented C++, as sublanguage of
        C++ 12
object-oriented principles, encapsulation
        and 99
objects
    alignment of 249–250
    clustering 251
    compilation dependencies and 143
    copying all parts 57–60
    defining 4
    definitions, postponing 113–116
    handles to internals of 123–126
    initialization, with vs. without
        arguments 114
    layout vs. array layout 73

multiple addresses for 118
partial copies of 58
placing in shared memory 251
resource management and 61–66
returning, vs. references 90–94
size, pass-by-value and 89
sizes, determining 141
vs. variables 3
Oldham, Jeffrey D. xix
old-style casts 117
operations, reordering by compilers 76
operator delete 84
see also delete
behavior of 255
efficiency of 248
name hiding and 259–261
non-member, pseudocode for 255
placement 256–261
replacing 247–252
standard forms of 260
virtual destructors and 255
operator delete[] 84, 255
operator new 84
see also new
arrays and 254–255
bad_alloc and 246, 252
behavior of 252–255
efficiency of 248
infinite loop within 253
inheritance and 253–254
member, and "wrongly sized"
    requests 254
name hiding and 259–261
new-handling functions and 241
non-member, pseudocode for 252
out-of-memory conditions and 240–241,
    252–253
placement 256–261
replacing 247–252
returning 0 and 246
standard forms of 260
std::bad_alloc and 246, 252
operator new[] 84, 254–255
operator() (function call operator) 6
operator=
const members and 36–37
default implementation 35
implicit generation 34
reference members and 36–37
return value of 52–53
self-assignment and 53–57
when not implicitly generated 36–37
operator[] 126
overloading on const 19–20
return type of 21
optimization
by compilers 94

during compilation 134
    inline functions and 134
order
    initialization of non-local statics 29–33
    member initialization 29
ostream_iterators 227
other languages, compatibility with 42
output iterators 227
output_iterator_tag 228
overloading
    as if...else for types 230
    on const 19–20
    std::swap 109
overrides of virtuals, preventing 189
ownership transfer 68

P

Pal, Balog xix
parameters
    see also pass-by-value, pass-by-refer-
        ence, passing small objects
    default 180–183
    evaluation order 76
    non-type, for templates 213
    type conversions and, see type conver-
        sions
Pareto Principle, see 80-20 rule
parsing problems, nested dependent
    names and 204
partial copies 58
partial specialization
    function templates 109
    std::swap 108
parts, of objects, copying all 57–60
pass-by-reference, efficiency and 87
pass-by-reference-to-const, vs pass-by-
    value 86–90
pass-by-value
    copy constructor and 6
    efficiency of 86–87
    meaning of 6
    object size and 89
    vs. pass-by-reference-to-const 86–90
patterns
    see design patterns
Pedersen, Roger E. xix
penguins and birds 151–153
performance, see efficiency
Persephone ix, xx, 36
pessimization 93
physical constness, see const, bitwise
pimpl idiom
    definition of 106
    exception-safe code and 131

placement delete, see operator delete
placement new, see operator new
Plato 87
pointer arithmetic and undefined
    behavior 119
pointers
    see also smart pointers
    as handles 125
    bitwise const member functions and 21
    compilation dependencies and 143
    const 17
        in headers 14
    null, dereferencing 6
    template parameters and 217
    to single vs. multiple objects, and
        delete 73
polymorphic base classes, destructors
    and 40–44
polymorphism 199–201
    compile-time 201
    runtime 200
Pool library, in Boost 250, 251
postponing variable definitions 113–116
Prasertsith, Chuti xx
preconditions, NVI and 171
pregnancy, exception-safe code and 133
private data members, why 94–98
private inheritance, see inheritance
private member functions 38
private virtual functions 171
properties 97
protected
    data members 97
    inheritance, see inheritance
    member functions 166
    members, encapsulation of 97
public inheritance, see inheritance
pun, really bad 152
pure virtual destructors
    defining 43
    implementing 43
pure virtual functions 43
    defining 162, 166–167
    meaning 162

R

Rabbani, Danny xix
Rabinowitz, Marty xx
RAII 63, 70, 243
    classes 72
    copying behavior and 66–69
    encapsulation and 72
    mutexes and 66–68
random access iterators 227

random number generation, in TR1 267
random_access_iterator_tag 228
RCSP, see smart pointers
reading uninitialized values 26
rectangles and squares 153–155
recursive functions, inlining and 136
redefining inherited non-virtual
    functions 178–180
Reed, Kathy xx
Reeves, Jack xix
references
    as handles 125
    compilation dependencies and 143
    functions returning 31
    implementation 89
    meaning 91
    members, initialization of 29
    returning 90–94
    to static object, as function return
        value 92–94
register usage, objects and 89
regular expressions, in TR1 266
reinterpret_cast 117, 249
    see also casting
relationships
    has-a 184
    is-a 150–155
    is-implemented-in-terms-of 184–186,
        187
reordering operations, by compilers 76
replacing definitions with
    declarations 143
replacing new/delete 247–252
replication, see duplication
reporting, bugs in this book xvi
Resource Acquisition Is Initialization, see
    RAII
resource leaks, exception-safe code
    and 127
resource management
    see also RAII
    copying behavior and 66–69
    objects and 61–66
    raw resource access and 69–73
resources, managing objects and 69–73
return by reference 90–94
return types
    const 18
    objects vs. references 90–94
    of operator[] 21
return value of operator= 52–53
returning handles 123–126
reuse, see code reuse
revenge, compilers taking 58
rhs, as parameter name 8

Roze, Mike xix
rule of 80-20 139, 168
runtime
    errors 152
    inlining 135
    polymorphism 200

S

Saks, Dan xviii
Santos, Eugene, Jr. xviii
Satch 36
Satyricon vii
Scherpelz, Jeff xix
Schirripa, Steve xix
Schober, Hendrik xviii, xix
Schroeder, Sandra xx
scoped_array 65, 216, 272
scopes, inheritance and 156
sealed classes, in C# 43
sealed methods, in C# 190
second edition, see 2nd edition
self-assignment, operator= and 53–57
set 185
set_new_handler
    class-specific, implementing 243–245
    using 240–246
set_unexpected function 129
shadowing, names, see name shadowing
Shakespeare, William 156
shared memory, placing objects in 251
shared_array 65
shared_ptr implementation in Boost,
    costs 83
sharing code, see duplication, avoiding
sharing common features 164
Shewchuk, John xviii
side effects, exception safety and 132
signatures
    definition of 3
    explicit interfaces and 201
simple virtual functions, meaning of 163
Singh, Siddhartha xix
Singleton pattern 31
size_t 3
sizeof 253, 254
    empty classes and 190
    freestanding classes and 254
sizes
    of freestanding classes 254
    of objects 141
sleeping pills 150
slist 227
Smallberg, David xviii, xix

Smalltalk 142
smart pointers 63, 64, 70, 81, 121, 146, 237
    see also std::auto_ptr and tr1::shared_ptr
    get and 70
    in Boost 65, 272
        web page for xvii
    in TR1 265
    newed objects and 75–77
    type conversions and 218–220
Socrates 87
*Some Must Watch While Some Must
    Sleep* 150
Somers, Jeff xix
specialization
    invariants over 168
    partial, of std::swap 108
    total, of std::swap 107, 108
specification, see interfaces
squares and rectangles 153–155
standard exception hierarchy 264
standard forms of operator new/delete 260
standard library, see C++ standard
    library, C standard library
standard template library, see STL
Stasko, John xviii
statements using new, smart pointers
    and 75–77
static
    binding
        of default parameters 182
        of non-virtual functions 178
    objects, returning references to 92–94
    type, definition of 180
static functions, ctors and dtors and 52
static members
    const member functions and 21
    definition 242
    initialization 242
static objects
    definition of 30
    multithreading and 32
static_cast 25, 82, 117, 119, 249
    see also casting
std namespace, specializing templates
    in 107
std::auto_ptr 63–65, 70
    conversion to tr1::shared_ptr and 220
    delete [] and 65
    pass by const and 220
std::auto_ptr, deleter support and 68
std::char_traits 232
std::iterator_traits, pointers and 230
std::list 186
std::max, implementation of 135
std::numeric_limits 232

std::set 185
std::size_t 3
std::swap
    see also swap
    implementation of 106
    overloading 109
    partial specialization of 108
    total specialization of 107, 108
std::tr1, see TR1
stepping through functions, inlining
        and 139
STL
    allocators 240
    as sublanguage of C++ 12
    containers, swap and 108
    definition of 6
    iterator categories in 227–228
Strategy pattern 171–177
string and text utilities, in Boost 271
strong guarantee, the 128
Stroustrup, Bjarne xvii, xviii
Stroustrup, Nicholas xix
Sutter, Herb xvii, xviii, xix
swallowing exceptions 46
swap 106–112
    see also std::swap
    calling 110
    exceptions and 112
    STL containers and 108
    when to write 111
symbols, available in both C and C++ 3

T

template C++, as sublanguage of C++ 12
template metaprogramming 233–238
    efficiency and 233
    hello world in 235
    pattern implementations and 237
    support in Boost 271
    support in TR1 267
Template Method pattern 170
templates
    code bloat, avoiding in 212–217
    combining with inheritance 243–245
    defining 4
    errors, when detected 212
    expression 237
    headers and 136
    in std, specializing 107
    inlining and 136
    instantiation of 222
    member functions 218–222
    names in base classes and 207–212
    non-type parameters 213
    parameters, omitting 224

    pointer type parameters and 217
    shorthand for 224
    specializations 229, 235
        partial 109, 230
        total 107, 209
    type conversions and 222–226
    type deduction for 223
temporary objects, eliminated by
        compilers 94
terminology, used in this book 3–8
testing and correctness, Boost support
        for 272
text and string utilities, in Boost 271
third edition, see 3rd edition
this->, to force base class lookup 210
threading, see multithreading
Tilly, Barbara xviii
TMP, see template metaprogramming
Tondo, Clovis xviii
Topic, Michael xix
total class template specialization 209
total specialization of std::swap 107, 108
total template specializations 107
TR1 9, 264–267
    array component 267
    bind component 266
    Boost and 9–10, 268, 269
    boost as synonym for std::tr1 268
    C99 compatibility component 267
    function component 265
    hash tables component 266
    math functions component 267
    mem_fn component 267
    random numbers component 267
    reference_wrapper component 267
    regular expression component 266
    result_of component 267
    smart pointers component 265
    support for TMP 267
    tuples component 266
    type traits component 267
    URL for information on 268
tr1::array 267
tr1::bind 175, 266
tr1::function 173–175, 265
tr1::mem_fn 267
tr1::reference_wrapper 267
tr1::result_of 267
tr1::shared_ptr 53, 64–65, 70, 75–77
    construction from other smart pointers
        and 220
    cross-DLL problem and 82
    delete [] and 65
    deleter support in 68, 81–83
    member template ctors in 220–221
tr1::tuple 266

tr1::unordered_map 43, 266
tr1::unordered_multimap 266
tr1::unordered_multiset 266
tr1::unordered_set 266
tr1::weak_ptr 265
traits classes 226–232
transfer, ownership 68
translation unit, definition of 30
Trux, Antoine xviii
Tsao, Mike xix
tuples, in TR1 266
type conversions 85, 104
    explicit ctors and 5
    implicit 104
    implicit vs. explicit 70–72
    non-member functions and 102–105,
        222–226
    private inheritance and 187
    smart pointers and 218–220
    templates and 222–226
type deduction, for templates 223
type design 78–86
type traits, in TR1 267
typedef, typename and 206–207
typedefs, new/delete and 75
typeid 50, 230, 234, 235
typelists 271
typename 203–207
    compiler variations and 207
    typedef and 206–207
    vs. class 203
types
    built-in, initialization 26–27
    compatible, accepting all 218–222
    if...else for 230
    integral, definition of 14
    traits classes and 226–232

U

undeclared interface 85
undefined behavior
    advance and 231
    array deletion and 73
    casting + pointer arithmetic and 119
    definition of 6
    destroyed objects and 91
    exceptions and 45
    initialization order and 30
    invalid array index and 7
    multiple deletes and 63, 247
    null pointers and 6
    object deletion and 41, 43, 74
    uninitialized values and 26
undefined values of members before con-
        struction and after destruction 50

unexpected function 129
uninitialized
    data members, virtual functions and 49
    values, reading 26
unnecessary objects, avoiding 115
unused objects
    cost of 113
    exceptions and 114
Urbano, Nancy L. vii, xviii, xx
    see also goddess
URLs
    Boost 10, 269, 272
    Boost smart pointers xvii
    Effective C++ errata list xvi
    Effective C++ TR1 Info. Page 268
    Greg Comeau's C/C++ FAQ xviii
    Scott Meyers' mailing list xvi
    Scott Meyers' web site xvi
    this book's errata list xvi
usage statistics, memory management
        and 248
using declarations
    name hiding and 159
    name lookup and 211

V

valarray 264
value, pass by, see pass-by-value
Van Wyk, Chris xviii, xix
Vandevoorde, David xviii
variable, vs. object 3
variables definitions, postponing 113–116
vector template 75
Viciana, Paco xix
virtual base classes 193
virtual constructors 146, 147
virtual destructors
    operator delete and 255
    polymorphic base classes and 40–44
virtual functions
    alternatives to 169–177
    ctors/dtors and 48–52
    default implementations and 163–167
    default parameters and 180–183
    dynamic binding of 179
    efficiency and 168
    explict base class qualification and 211
    implementation 42
    inlining and 136
    language interoperability and 42
    meaning of none in class 41
    preventing overrides 189
    private 171
    pure, see pure virtual functions
    simple, meaning of 163

uninitialized data members and 49
virtual inheritance, see inheritance
virtual table 42
virtual table pointer 42
Vlissides, John xvii
vptr 42
vtbl 42

W

Wait, John xx
warnings, from compiler 262–263
   calls to virtuals and 50
   inlining and 136
   partial copies and 58
web sites, see URLs
Widget class, as used in this book 8
Wiegers, Karl xix
Wilson, Matthew xix
Wizard of Oz, allusion to 154

X

XP, allusion to 225
XYZ Airlines 163

Z

Zabluda, Oleg xviii
Zolman, Leor xviii, xix

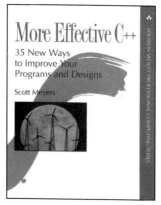

Register
Your Book

at www.awprofessional.com/register

You may be eligible to receive:

- Advance notice of forthcoming editions of the book
- Related book recommendations
- Chapter excerpts and supplements of forthcoming titles
- Information about special contests and promotions throughout the year
- Notices and reminders about author appearances, tradeshows, and online chats with special guests

Contact us

If you are interested in writing a book or reviewing manuscripts prior to publication, please write to us at:

Editorial Department
Addison-Wesley Professional
75 Arlington Street, Suite 300
Boston, MA 02116 USA
Email: AWPro@aw.com

Addison-Wesley

Visit us on the Web: http://www.awprofessional.com

THIS BOOK IS SAFARI ENABLED

INCLUDES FREE 45-DAY ACCESS TO THE ONLINE EDITION

The Safari® Enabled icon on the cover of your favorite technology book means the book is available through Safari Bookshelf. When you buy this book, you get free access to the online edition for 45 days.

Safari Bookshelf is an electronic reference library that lets you easily search thousands of technical books, find code samples, download chapters, and access technical information whenever and wherever you need it.

TO GAIN 45-DAY SAFARI ENABLED ACCESS TO THIS BOOK:

- Go to **http://www.awprofessional.com/safarienabled**

- Complete the brief registration form

- Enter the coupon code found in the front of this book on the "Copyright" page

If you have difficulty registering on Safari Bookshelf or accessing the online edition, please e-mail customer-service@safaribooksonline.com.